In this thought-provoking study, Ali Mirsepassi explores the concept of modernity, exposing the Eurocentric prejudices and hostility to non-Western culture that have characterized its development. Focussing on the Iranian experience of modernity, he charts its political and intellectual history and develops a new interpretation of Islamic Fundamentalism through the detailed analysis of the ideas of key Islamic intellectuals. The author argues that the Iranian Revolution was not a simple clash between modernity and tradition but an attempt to accommodate modernity within a sense of authentic Islamic identity, culture and historical experience. He concludes by assessing the future of secularism and democracy in the Middle East in general, and in Iran in particular. A significant contribution to the literature on modernity, social change and Islamic Studies, this book will be essential reading for scholars and students of social theory and change, Middle Eastern Studies, Cultural Studies and many related areas.

Ali Mirsepassi is professor of Sociology and Near Eastern Studies and dean for Multicultural Education at Hampshire College, Amherst. He has published extensively in journals such as *Contemporary Sociology*, *Radical History* and *Social Text*.

Intellectual Discourse and the
Politics of Modernization

Cambridge Cultural Social Studies

Series editors: JEFFREY C. ALEXANDER, *Department of Sociology,*
University of California, Los Angeles, and STEVEN SEIDMAN, *Department*
of Sociology, University at Albany, State University of New York.

Titles in the series

Intellectual Discourse and the Politics of Modernization

Negotiating Modernity in Iran

Ali Mirsepassi

CAMBRIDGE
UNIVERSITY PRESS

PUBLISHED BY THE PRESS SYNDICATE OF THE UNIVERSITY OF CAMBRIDGE
The Pitt Building, Trumpington Street, Cambridge, United Kingdom

CAMBRIDGE UNIVERSITY PRESS
The Edinburgh Building, Cambridge CB2 2RU, UK http://www.cup.cam.ac.uk
40 West 20th Street, New York NY 10011-4211, USA http://www.cup.org
10 Stamford Road, Oakleigh, Melbourne 3166, Australia
Ruiz de Alarcón 13, 28014 Madrid, Spain

First published 2000

Printed in the United Kingdom at the University Press, Cambridge

Typeface Plantin MT 10/13 pt   *System* QuarkXPress™   [SE]

A catalogue record for this book is available from the British Library

Library of Congress Cataloguing in Publication data

Mirsepassi, Ali.
  Intellectual discourses and the politics of modernization: negotiating
modernity in Iran / Ali Mirsepassi.
    p. cm. (Cambridge cultural social studies)
  Includes bibliographical references.
  ISBN 0 521 65000 3 (hb)
    1. Iran–Politics and government–20th century. 2. Politics and culture–Iran.
  3. Islam and politics–Iran. 4. Islam and secularism–Iran. I. Title. II. Series.
  DS316.6.M57 2000
  955.05–dc21   99-049057

ISBN 0 521 65000 3 hardback
ISBN 0 521 65997 3 paperback

To the memory of my father

Contents

Acknowledgments

As soon as I completed my Ph.D. dissertation in 1985, I knew I had to begin writing a different book. My dissertation project was an attempt to come up with a "new" and more complex structural approach in understanding the Iranian Revolution. Soon after I completed that project, I realized it is not enough to acknowledge that culture matters or that ideas can change society. Ideas, ideologies, and cultural imageries produce social realities, which deserve the attention of scholars and merit the focus of their analysis. This book is the result of my desire to go beyond a merely structural explanation of social and cultural analysis and to take ideas, discourses, and cultural imagination seriously.

The concept and organization of this book reflect my intellectual concerns and interests. However, the project is truly the result of a collective effort. Many of the my students and colleagues have contributed to the writing of this book in many different ways. I would like to thank them and express my deep appreciation for their work and support of this project. Hampshire College supported me while I was working on this book – I would like to thank the President's Office, the Dean of Faculty Office, and the School of Social Sciences for their intellectual and financial support without which I could not have completed this project.

Early in this project, I enjoyed a great deal of intellectual support from my longtime friends, Mohamad Razavi, Mehrzad Boroujerdi, Abdi Kalantari, Mehrdad Mashayekhi, and Val Moghadam. They helped me in articulating the idea of this book in a more focussed and meaningful way. Mohamad Razavi and I conducted the interviews, in chapter 7, while I was in Iran. I would like to thank him for his help and his rare intellectual insight. I have also benefited a great deal from my friendship with Ervand Abrahamian. The ideas and high academic standards he has set forth have greatly influenced this book.

Throughout the process, my colleagues in the School of Social Science at Hampshire College read parts of the manuscript and helped me by their comments and criticism. I also benefited tremendously from engaging in conversations with them and by being part of their intellectual community. I would like to thank Margaret Cerullo, Fred Weaver, Carol Bengelsdorf, Frank Holmquist, Fran White, and Aaron Berman for their friendship and collegial support. My friends and colleagues at the Great Barrington Theory Group read two chapters of this book and my discussion with them and their comments helped me elucidate many important theoretical issues. I would like to express my thanks to them.

Two of my former students at Hampshire College, Tadd Fernee and Dylan Ruediger, have helped me a great deal in preparing this manuscript. Tadd, in particular, worked with me for several months and helped me tremendously in putting some of my ideas on paper. He wrote and rewrote parts of the manuscript and helped me clarify many of the ideas articulated in this book. I would like to thank him for all the time he spent working in my office in the Fall of 1996. I would especially like to give him credit for his work on chapters 4 and 5. Dylan and Tadd are two of the most thoughtful students I have ever had. Dylan and I worked together on the Introduction and his editorial and intellectual help enhanced this section of the book. Dylan's meticulous editing and critical suggestions were greatly appreciated. Val Moghadam and I wrote an earlier version of chapter 6, which at the time was published in *Radical History*. I would like to express my thanks to Val for her permission to include this chapter in the book.

Steven Seidman, the Series co-editor of Cambridge Cultural Social Studies, read several different versions of this manuscript and his comments and criticism helped me a great deal in improving the final version of the manuscript. I would like to express my appreciation for his generous support of me and his intellectual contribution to this book. I also received very important critical comments from the Cambridge University Press reviewers. I would like to thank them for taking this project seriously and giving me their thoughtful suggestions. Joanne Hill, the copy-editor at Cambridge University Press, did the most thorough and rigorous editing one can imagine. I would like to thank her for bringing clarity, consistency, and better organization to this book.

Finally, my sincerest appreciation to Arshid, Sahar, and Shadi, who offered me love and support while I was working long hours, often at weekends, to complete this project. In addition, I would like to thank my mother for her love and support from a long distance. This book is also dedicated to Arshid, Sahar, Shadi, and my mother.

Introduction: modernity and "culture"

Many here [in the West] and some in Iran are waiting for and hoping for the moment when secularization will at last come back to the fore and reveal the good, old type of revolution we have always known. I wonder how far they will be taken along this strange, unique road, in which they seek, against the stubbornness of their destiny, against everything they have been for centuries, "something quite different."

Michel Foucault[1]

Identifying a tension

Michel Foucault welcomed the Iranian Revolution and its "Islamic spirit" as an intellectually exciting revolt against the rigidity of modern-secular imagination. He sarcastically asked, "What is it about what happened in Iran that a whole lot of people, on the left and on the right, find somewhat irritating?"[2] Answering this question requires a serious exploration into the genealogy of the Western narrative of modernity and its dichotomizing representation of non-Western cultures and societies. Is modernity a totalizing (dominating and exclusionary) ideology primarily, and inescapably, grounded in European cultural and moral experience, and therefore incapable of understanding other cultures as anything other than as its inferior "other"? Or, is modernity a mode of social and cultural experience of the present that is open to all forms of contemporary experiences and possibilities?[3] The dilemma here is how to reconcile the tension between modernity's promise of openness and inclusive qualities (the Enlightenment moral promise and the modernist radical vision) and the blatant Eurocentric narrative of modernization that forecloses the possibility of real "local" experiences and of their contribution in the realization of modernity.[4] This study lays out a story of Iranian modernity, intending to explore this troubled, and troubling, situation.

This critical and complex question is at the heart of social theories of both modernity and postmodernity.[5] The liberal tradition of modernity (Montesquieu, Hegel, Weber, Durkheim, Orientalism) privileges Western cultural and moral dispositions, defining modernity in terms of

1

Western cultural and historical experiences. The liberal vision of modernity, as we will see in the next chapter, considers Western culture an essential part of modernization, viewing non-Western cultures and traditions as fundamentally hostile to modernity and incompatible with modernization.[6] A more radical vision of modernity (as articulated by Marx, Habermas, Giddens, Berman) envisions modernization as a practical and empirical experience that liberates societies from their oppressive "material" conditions.[7] While the radical vision of modernity shares many important intellectual assumptions of liberal enlightenment (as we shall see shortly), its emphasis on modernity as a material condition leaves some room for the possibility of a more "locally" imagined interpretation of modernization.[8] Marshall Berman, a contemporary radical modernist, lays out an interpretation of modernity grounded in the everyday life experiences of the present:

> There is a mode of vital experience – experience of space and time, of the self and others, of life's possibilities and perils – that is shared by men and women all over the world today. I will call this "modernity." Modern environments and experience cut across all boundaries of geography and ethnicity, of class and nationality, of religion and ideology: in this sense, modernity can be said to unite all mankind. But it is a paradoxical unity, a unity of disunity: it pours us all into a maelstrom of perpetual disintegration and renewal, of struggle and contradiction, of ambiguity and anguish.[9]

Berman goes on to suggest that the various experiences of modernity only become meaningful in the reflexive experience of their context (what Berman calls modernity of the street) and therefore, that the culture of modernity is not and should not be necessarily based on Western experience or cultural beliefs. For Berman, a blueprint of modernity is unnecessary: modernity is part of the experience of everyday life, of a life in which "all that is solid melts into air." This experience, Berman contends, is "spread all over the world," and cannot be understood as an essentially Western experience.[10] Indeed, Berman explicitly argues that people in the "Third World" experience this shared world culture:

> If this culture [modernity] were really exclusively Western, and hence as irrelevant to the Third World as most of its governments say, would these governments need to expend as much energy repressing it as they do? What they are projecting onto aliens, and prohibiting as "Western decadence," is in fact their own people's energies and desires and critical spirit.[11]

For Berman, the continuing demands of the world market system, namely the injunction to "develop or disintegrate," compel Third World nations to enter into the dynamics of modernization and modernity. Thus, modernity is not exhausted, but rather "just beginning to come into its own."[12] The encounter with modernity will presumably engender a "drive for free development" in the Third World, a drive that Berman includes among the most important characteristics of modern peoples.[13] Berman's model of modernity is this shared experience of continual disintegration: "To be modern . . . is to experience personal and social life as a maelstrom, to find one's world and oneself in perpetual disintegration . . ."[14] This perpetual disintegration, however, is not a source of despair; indeed, Berman's effort is to recuperate the human potential of this ambiguity and anguish as a source of affirmation and strength.[15] Modernization, then, is understood as a world-historical process resulting in the entire world crossing the threshold of this shared experience. After crossing this point, all that remains is an affirmation of the potential of modernity. This should not be misconstrued as an entirely utopian projection. Berman is well aware that modernization can be exploitative, but he deems the continual chaos of modernity as a perfect forum for the process of a potentially unlimited self-development.[16] As he puts it, "the process of modernization, even as it exploits and torments us, brings our energies and imaginations to life, drives us to grasp and confront the world that modernization makes, and to strive to make it our own."[17]

Jurgen Habermas's theory of modernity also attempts a rejuvenation of modernity. For Habermas, the "crisis of modernity" is not indicative of the final collapse of the Enlightenment project, but instead reveals the deficiencies of what has heretofore been a one-sided and inadequate modernity. Thus, modernity is an "incomplete" project, and the question of modernization becomes central to completing modernity.[18] Habermas argues that our contemporary experience of modernity has been unduly dominated by a single type of rationality, specifically by purposive or instrumental rationality.[19] The discontents of modernity, then, are not rooted in rationalization or modernization as such, but "in the failure to develop and institutionalize all the different dimensions of reason in a balanced way."[20] This (re)opening of modernity to different means of rationalizing the life world has led John Tomilson to suggest that Habermas's vision denies an inevitable path of modernization, that ". . . the sort of modernity that the West has developed and passed on to the 'developing world' is not the only possible historical route out of the chains of tradition."[21] However, Habermas makes this opening while retaining a commitment to the Enlightenment project of universal modernity. His modernization of modernity would re-route towards a model of communicative action, and a more open rationality of ideal speech acts. Thus, modernization becomes an intellectual/rational project working towards an ideal speech situation.

Anthony Giddens shares with Habermas the view that modernity as an institutional design is in fact a "Western project." He points out that the two unique institutions of modernity, the nation-state and capitalism, are Western in origin. However, he believes that the globalization of modernity across the world introduces new forms of world interdependence, in which, once again, there are no "others."

Is modernity peculiarly Western from the standpoint of its globalizing tendencies? No, it cannot be, since we are speaking here of emergent forms of world interdependence and planetary consciousness. The ways in which these issues are approached and coped with, however, will inevitably involve conceptions and strategies derived from non-Western settings. For neither the radicalizing of modernity nor the globalizing of social life are processes which are in any sense complete. Many kinds of cultural responses to such institutions are possible given the world cultural diversity as a whole.[22]

Berman's populist theory of the modern experience, Habermas's hope for a complete modernization, and Giddens's reflexive modernity may offer more inclusive approaches to modernity. Yet what do their theories of modernization offer the "Third World"? This is not the time to attempt a full critique of these theorists, but we must explore what – for my purposes at least – is the most glaring weakness in their respective schemata. This weakness is a historical one. Modernity as both an intellectual and a political project has a long history of differentiating, excluding and dominating the non-Western parts of the world. What kind of understanding about the relationship between modernity, Eurocentrism and modernization does this history suggest?

Initially, colonialism can no longer be considered a minor period in the history of modernity. This argument goes far beyond the fairly familiar analysis of the economic importance of the colonies in the development of capitalism and the material basis of modernity by noting the importance of colonialism to the cultural, literary and scientific culture of modernity. Edward Said, among others, has painstakingly charted the importance of the colonies in the self-definition of Europe and in the constitution of modernity, showing in great detail the importance of colonialism in the development of the "modern" realist novel.[23] For Said, modernity needs to be re-theorized in light of an increased awareness that:

In the same period as the construction of divided colonial capitals, a similar operation was being made on a global scale, in the form of a cultural and historical "break" dividing the modern West, as the place of order, reason, and power, from the outside world it was in the process of colonizing and seeking to control.[24]

At the very least, the radical modernists can be accused of ignoring the colonial terrain of modernity and universalism. A major aim of this study is to theorize carefully the relations between the legacy of imperialism, modernity and modernization.

The failure to adequately theorize colonialism leaves radical visions of modernization perilously close to, and open to appropriation by, the Eurocentrism of mainstream theories of modernity and modernization. Habermas, who has acknowledged his "eurocentrically limited view," is instructive in this regard.[25] His notion of an ideal communicative rationality is undermined by his insistence that if the Third World acts passively in modernization, its "lifeworld," transformed by the pressures of universalism and individualization, will be rationalized, its "traditional nuclei" shrunk to "abstract elements."[26] Here at least, Habermas's prescriptions ring eerily with the discourse of development that has monopolized the discussion of modernization since roughly the end of World War II. This is not to argue that radical visions of modernity should be considered as in every respect "the same" as the ideologues of development, but to suggest that modernization is not just a structural or material transformation, but a practice grounded in discursive assumptions (most glaringly of the economic, cultural and institutional superiority of the West). Recent attempts at revitalizing modernity from the Left share with liberal and conservative modernists an inadequate reading of these assumptions, leaving them on disturbingly similar ground as the dominant narrative of modernization, to which we now turn.

Problems in the discourse of development

Early modern Europe defined its own modernity in opposition to the colonial "primitive" living in the "state of nature." A tangled web of discourse, in diverse genres including philosophy, literature and theology – similar to the discourse of Orientalism, but with the Americas as a primary referent – represented colonial others as inferior and in need of "civilizing" from Europe.[27] Colonialism was represented, as in John Locke's *Second Treatise* for example, as beneficial to the colonized "primitive" who will gain the benefits of civilization and Christianity.[28] Operative from the literal beginnings of European colonialism, the opposition between savage and civil forms an important link in the genealogy of the modern/traditional opposition of the nineteenth and twentieth centuries, and also to theories of modernization circulating since the 1950s.

Modernization theory rose to the fore in the wake of multiple successful movements for national independence in the Third World. Retooling both the savage–civil and modern–traditional binaries so integral to colonialism, this new discourse deployed a distinction between the liberal, modern, and economically "developed" nations and the (recently decolonized) "undeveloped," or "underdeveloped" nations. The project of modernization becomes one of "development," or "catching up" with, and homogenizing into, the economically, politically and culturally modern West. A major support to these projects is a group of theories presenting modernization as a rational and universal social project, superior to any other societal model in history.

This is the "scientific discourse" of social theory which, despite the turbulent and energetic clashes marking contemporary sociological debate, still holds tight reins on the voices whose narratives define modernity. "Scientific" theorists ground their tacit theoretical assumptions about the nature of reality on a materialist epistemology. The central truth claim of this epistemology is considered a scientific claim: our knowledge can only come from an "objective" reality that may be identified independently of subjective and cultural norms. Culture, within this discourse, does not have an independent existence: instead, the root source of human consciousness is in "empirical" and "actual" experience. Within our daily life experiences ultimately the "productive" economic activities are the most meaningful aspects of life. Thus, economics are at the root of culture and politics, and economic transformations are critical to development. In this regard, Marxism does not really differ from liberal or conservative modernization theory in its views of knowledge. They differ only in their conception of the ends to be achieved: for modernization theory, the goal is to bring the Third World into the orbit of the capitalist economy, while for Marxism the goal is to do the same thing so that both the First and Third Worlds can attain the universalist utopia of socialism. The materialist epistemology is not merely one theoretical construct among many which happen to be espoused by Marxist and other scholars of Third World development. For modernization theory "native" cultures represent false (illusionary) consciousness functioning to impede successful development, while for Marxism they are a mask which prevents class awareness; for both they are a self-delusional fantasy.

The impact of developmentalist discourse can be measured in its embodiment in colonial and post-colonial states. The offensive simplicity of modernity's categories and prescriptions, applied with a gruesome and dogmatic determination, could scarcely be enacted except through the sheer coercive might of a centralized authoritarian state apparatus. A coercive, powerful, we may say almost transcendental force is required to bridge the chasm between the intention, the imaginary, and existing reality in any and every "traditional" society which fell prey to the modernizing designs of colonialism. The massive and brutal overhaul of society and tradition, the tyrannical and almost childish lust for the raising of a completely "new world" upon the decimated remains of the "old," the broadest and shallowest conceptions of "human progress": such "ideals" could only be achieved with the aid of a modern state in all its darker and more sinister dimensions.

It is little wonder, then, that these "universalizing" and "civilizing" states emerged as the most brutal and repressive regimes in power today. Colonial states were set up with absolute power in order to control every aspect of society. With political independence, these state machines were passed on to the modernized elite frequently drawn from a particular ethnic set. In societies where the arbitrary national borders drawn up by colonialism contained a diversity of ethnic groups, these dynamics inherently instigated – indeed established – inter-ethnic struggle as the inevitable pattern of politics.[29] There is no reason to stare in surprise or wonder from the pluralistic shores of the West at the blatant elitism and brutality of post-colonial states constructed or influenced by colonial and imperial powers on the basis of ideals of modernization.

However, in recent decades a community of scholars has suggested new approaches towards understanding the epistemological underpinnings of the "development" discourse. These critics, Edward Said, Arturo Escobar and Timothy Mitchell, to name a few, charge the discourse of "development" with excessive Eurocentrism, questioning its continued relevance to the study of non-Western societies.[30] They understand "development" as part of a strategy to preserve Western hegemony, rationalize relationships of exploitation, ignore external determinants of "underdevelopment," and further imbricate an image of the non-West forever in need of guidance by the "developed" world. Their criticisms see "development" discourse as representing non-Western cultures as the First World's "other," and call for this discourse to be subjected to a critique within the power/knowledge frame of analysis. As Escobar notes in his recent book *Encountering Development*:

Once Third World communities became the target of new and increasingly detailed interventions, their economies, societies, and cultures were appropriated as objects of knowledge by modern development disciplines and subdisciplines that, in turn, made them into new targets of power and intervention. The productivity of development thus must be seen in terms of this efficient apparatus that systematically links knowledge and power as it deploys each one of its strategies and inventions. The depiction of the Third World as "underdeveloped" has been an essential and constitutive element of the globalization of capital in the post-World War II period; perhaps more importantly, a cultural discourse began that not only placed the Third World in a position of inferiority but that, more clearly and efficiently than ever, subjected it to the "scientific," normalizing action of Western cultural-political technologies . . .[31]

In developmentalist discourse, the "Third World" (itself a developmentalist term) is treated as lacking some of the most essential institutional and cultural characteristics of Western modernity, and as lacking the cultural and ethical imagination to achieve modernity by itself. The "discourse of development" is a specific historical construct based on a colonial imaginary that evolved in conjunction with the Western theorization of desire for dominating the Oriental "other." Somewhat generally stated, the various critiques of development argue that constructing the "Third World" as the First World's "other" is both harmful and misleading for several reasons. (1) It defines the "Third World" as a singular, essentialized entity not in terms of its own existing qualities, but in terms of "First World" qualities which it lacks. In this depiction, the First World is the ideal model while the non-Western world's existence can be summed up in terms of what it *is not* in relation to this ideal. The cultures of the "Third World" are constructed as the "local," existing in opposition to the universalist ideals of Western modernity. This implies an underlying teleological historical scheme of progress; a universally linear struggle for the attainment of an ideal based on a metaphysic of development. In addition, it frames the West as having an unchanging cultural essence, and "East" and "West" as disconnected, static, and ontologically separate "things," each an unfolding of its own timeless essence. An endless logic of reductionist binaries springs from these obscure and essentialized categories. (2) It defines contemporary conditions in the Third World in terms of abstracted conditions of European historical experience; the Third World is seen as *embodying* aspects of Europe's past (feudalism, etc.). The application of theories based on stages from Europe's past rests on the assumption that contemporary Third World conditions correspond to these stages, but without examining those conditions in their specificity and detail to see if there is any truth to this general comparison. (3) It makes the assumption that only one essential path to modernity exists in the world, and Europe has experienced this path in advance of the non-Western world. Taking into consideration the tacit assumptions and attitudes which compose this prevailing model of development and the original historical conditions under which its main concepts were conceived, a case can be made that the model is fundamentally informed by the residual narratives that defined modernity throughout the era of colonial domination in the "Third World." The deconstruction of these development models unmasks their "scientific/universal" pretensions and reveals an underlying cultural-conceptual content which is decidedly Eurocentric and geared toward continued Western domination.

Such new critical studies are usually challenged and even ridiculed for a supposedly excessive emphasis on culture and subjectivism, for lacking analytical rigor, and for extending a discourse concerning the whims of Western intellectuals (postmodernism) to an inappropriate Third World setting. A frequent charge raised by Marxist and mainstream scholars against the new literature is that it is "culturalist" and "subjectivist," and thereby almost totally ignores material and structural realities. For those who take a Marxist or political economy approach, the post-structuralist emphasis on power/knowledge relations is perceived as placing excessive priority on secondary factors (i.e., culture), while the more fundamental and determinate structures are disregarded. At the harmonious intersection between liberal and Marxist development theories, then, we locate the core conception of modernization theory as it stands in opposition to the "cultural" approach. It is in the shared belief that they are engaged in a scientific effort and that their theories, concepts, and categories are objective, culturally neutral, and universally applicable to all societies. Based on these observations, we can see how it is that culture cannot be the first issue on the developmentalist agenda for this reason: culture, values, morality, and religion, represent only particularisms, aspects of the superstructure, masking the underlying empirical truth to be found in economic structures. If all other modes of knowledge – as every cultural system in some sense claims to be – are masks and the materialist epistemology provides the *only* objective truth, then developmentalism would naturally have difficulty appreciating a central role for culture in any social movement, theory, or practice. It is ironic, however, that the dismissal of this new literature is occurring simultaneously with a confession by abundant social scientists, many of whom have produced volumes of writings about the "Third World," that something is seriously and fundamentally wrong with the development discourse.

We may say, for all those "scientists" who sternly and impatiently refer everybody to "reality" every time the issue of culture or subjectivity (or power) is mentioned in sociological debate: *the Iranian Revolution was the reality.* Contrary to every scientific and obliviously optimistic forecast of Iran's steady arrival into the calm waters of modernity and secularism – "everything is going according to plan . . ." – reality intervened in the form of a revolution and completely shattered the ill informed and arrogant presumptions/predictions/world views nurtured by authorities in the West until the very eve of the revolution. Yet however ill informed their views might have been with regard to the actual reality taking place inside Iran, they were all too well founded upon the entire discourse of modernity and development in its abstract and trans-historical form. We may say, with regard to that paradigm: *every expectation was defied.*

More interesting still is the response on the part of these "scientific" scholars. Rather than reconsidering their system of interpretation (which is almost sacrosanct and no mere analytical tool) in light of its newly revealed limits and grossly mistaken calculations, there was instead a dramatic reversion to the very rudiments of the system's logic deep in the outdated colonial imagination. They begin blaming the "reality": "these people are so backward and fettered by their traditions that even modernity cannot save them!" All the veils of enlightenment and tolerance were cast aside, and the "scientists" threw up their hands in a frank concession that all humanist virtues were a purely "Western" quality, while the "other" must be left to fend for itself amidst the blood-curdling savagery of its own cultural-traditional inheritance. The irony of this discursive turn is that the revolution in Iran was fought most emphatically for modernity and all of its promises as a social ideal, but also against the perverted modernity imposed under the Shah which betrayed every humanistic principle modernity is supposed to represent. And yet the Iranian experience of modernity under the Shah was no mere deviation or corrupted moment in an otherwise flawless and morally pure design; the discrepancy between ideal and reality under the Shah – and dictators like him – is a revelation of the interlocked "other" face of modernity, the unspoken one whose brutal intrusions have decimated all corners of the world. It is this "other" face of modernity, in its systematic and historically interrelated unity with the much touted modern face of Western freedom, that we intend to lay bare in this study. For silent though it may be – and silence is simply that which is unspoken – we may count its enforced silence among the systematic strategies for perpetuating egregious forms of injustice upon the world, under the concealing gaze of one, dominant tradition of conceptualizing modernity. In the act of articulating it, of flushing it from the darkness of its systematic disguises and cover-ups, we thereby hope to hasten its exposure, rectification, and demise.

Recovering the local: the Iranian Revolution

The history of the encounter of Iran with modernity is relatively long and quite extensive. Since the 1850s, Iran has invested its intellectual, cultural, economic and political resources, and desires in the hopes of transforming itself into a modern nation-state. Political elites and intellectuals representing variations of the modern project, including liberal and nationalist ideas, radical discourses, and Islamic reformist movements, have worked through mass movements, intellectual trends, political parties and other institutional and imaginative formations to shape their country in the image of European modernity. Yet this longing for modernization has been ambivalent from the start. Modernity and the West have been viewed both as an undesirable "other" and, if Iran is to have a viable future, as an inescapable fate. At the same time, Islam has been viewed as the authentic cultural identity of Iran, the imagined traditional community of the disappearing past. The Islamic discourse of authenticity embodies both aspiration for change and the Iranian encounter with modernity. Therefore, it offers an excellent case study of a modernizing society torn between a desire to achieve material advancement and trepidation over losing its unique national, moral, and cultural identity.

It is with the imposition of Eurocentrist "universalism" by the West that the emphasis on the "local" has become important in non-Western struggles for modernization. Narratives of modernity, by constructing an ontologically differentiated universe between "West" and "East" or "modernity" and "tradition," set the stage for the clashes which are proliferating in the contest between champions of "authenticity" and defenders of "universalism." It is in the ingrained, universalistic precepts of modernity to do violence to local cultures – and for this reason, local cultures become natural and effective axes for politicization in any society coming to terms with the universal-modernist scheme. Nineteenth-century colonial efforts at modernization are indicative of the self-definition of modernity through an abjection of the "traditional" other. Society is divided into two parts: an elite class, drawn into the cultural orbit of the West through political and economic ties, and the mass of people. The former constitutes the "modernized" and "Westernized" while the latter constitutes the "traditional" and "backward," with this binary corresponding invariably to the divisions between rich and poor, ruler and ruled. This scheme inherently linked "tradition" with failure and pointed out a *single road* to prosperity and power. The explicit delegitimizing of local culture by an outside invader, who in turn insisted upon the singular universality of their own culture and practices, is especially relevant for our purpose because such a division led to the complete loss of the Shah's state power and the ruling class's legitimacy in pre-revolutionary Iran.[32]

All forms of resistance to the dominant political forms of modernity have in one way or another turned to the "authenticity" of the local, because only a critical attitude toward the dominant narrative of modernity can effectively resist domination by the imperial West. It would be misleading to conceive this local resistance, based on notions of cultural authenticity, as isolated and spontaneous demonstrations of identity based on the obstinacy of roots. We should interpret "local" politics based on local "identities" in the "Third World" as the invention of resistance against Western power, but not for this reason as anti-modern. A more precise account of this dynamic in Iran is given in chapters 2 and 3.

The broader theoretical question here is whether modernity is a totalizing ideology and inherently hostile to "local" social and cultural experiences (as Weber would have it) or whether there is any possibility for different paths to modernity. The history of modernity embodies this tension. The intellectuals of liberal enlightenment, the radical romanticists, reactionary modernists, third worldists, socialists, have all, in different ways, written the story of how modernity came into being, its purpose, its ends, and so on. Against whichever surface it brushes its universal yet malleable form, a slew of new stories regarding its origins proliferates. Most of these stories live a strange and hidden life in the shadow of the standardized, self-appointed "scientific" version of modernity and its unique origins developed in the West. Yet, against the backdrop of a profound crisis in the discourse of Western objectivity and authority, as the totalizing hierarchies and dogmatic singularities of interpretation that accompanied the colonial, imperial, and bipolar superpower political eras slide away, an ever increasing proliferation and influence of multiple narratives points towards a more diversified, far less predictable, perhaps more "dangerous," at least as hopeful, and above all utterly irreversible phase in the stories of modernity. To whatever extent these stories may or may not conform to the "facts" – indeed, they often fly on the wings of imagination – we may certainly venture that they nevertheless contain within their imaginings the true, unacknowledged history of modernity as it has never before been allowed to voice itself.

The trajectory of the work

Modernity, as articulated since the Enlightenment by intellectuals such as Montesquieu, Hegel, Marx and Weber, depends for its self-definition as rational, universal and enlightened on the presence of an "other." In chapter 1, I present detailed critiques of their writings, showing how an "Oriental" other, passive, traditional and irrational, is contrasted to the modern world of the "West." Deep within the discourse of modernity we find a hostility to non-Western cultures that both operates to exclude them from the realm of meaningful participation in the making of the modern world, and positions them as in dire need of whitewashing and "civilizing" by the West. Instrumental in the ideology of colonialism, this configuration continues to wield a powerful influence in contemporary theories of the Orient and of modernity, such as Bernard Lewis's theorization of an Islamic Mind, consumed by the rage of ancient hostilities. This quintessential modern binary between an essentially un-modern and irrational "East" and the heroic, enlightened "West" has only gained strength in the wake of the Iranian Revolution and the rise of so-called

"Islamic Fundamentalism," leading Samuel Huntington, among others, to characterize the future as a "clash between civilizations."[33]

Yet, the Iranian encounter with modernity – the major subject of this study – is both temporally significant (spanning a century and a half) and too complex to be characterized in the dramatic and militaristic language of a "clash." Chapters 2 and 3 offer studies of Iranian intellectual and social movements from the constitutionalist movement of the beginning of the twentieth century up to the Islamic Republic of today, the establishment of modernity, and the question of the Iranian accommodation of modernity as the central pillar of Iranian intellectual efforts in the nineteenth century. For my purposes, three phases of Iranian modernity are particularly important: (1) an uncritical embrace of modernity as a Western model designed to totally replace Iranian culture; (2) a shift to a leftist paradigm of modernity critiquing imperialism and capitalism; and (3) the turn towards Islamist discourses of authenticity.

The Shah's decidedly unpopular "modernization" projects, the consolidation of an authoritarian state apparatus, and the subsequent massive social upheaval, severely recontextualized the meaning attached to "modernization" and "modernity" in Iran. The systematic suppression of secular opponents created a political vacuum for the emerging Islamic movement, and its attempts to articulate an alternative to oppressive Western models of modernization. Chapter 3 explores the social conditions leading to this vacuum, and the process of the politicization of Shi'ism as a revolutionary ideology. The ideology of the Iranian Revolution, when viewed in detail, emerges less as a monolithic clash between "modernity" and "tradition," than as an attempt to actualize a modernity accommodated to national, cultural and historical experiences.

Chapter 4 continues and extends the argument that political Islam is best interpreted as an attempt to reconfigure modernity by focussing on two of the most prominent intellectuals of contemporary Iran, Jalal Al-e Ahmad and Ali Shari'ati. Al-e Ahmad developed the concept of *Gharbzadegi* ("Westoxication") and a powerful call for redeveloping a romanticized "authentic" Islamic identity. Al-e Ahmad, however, did not reject the project of modernization, but argued that such modernization should take place under the cultural and ideological base of an "authentic" Islamic culture and government. Ali Shari'ati's intellectual project was likewise an effort to reconcile Shi'i Islam with modernization. Shari'ati contended that a nation must regain its cultural and religious traditions as a precursor to modernizing on its own terms. Both Al-e Ahmad and Ali Shari'ati construct a "local" image of Iranian culture in opposition to the "universal" West, but do so from within modernity, not from a "resurgence of ancient impulses" or "religious fanaticism."

Chapter 5 offers a comparative study of the "discourse of authenticity" as a response to modernization by examining the works of German writers and philosophers in the 1920s, showing that the politicization of the "local" in Iran is not a unique occurrence, but part of a pattern of responses to modernity. Friedrich Nietzsche, Ernst Junger and Martin Heidegger receive particular attention, as their works helped to shape many of the Iranian intellectuals discussed in chapters 3 and 4.

Chapter 6 has a double function, showing first the depth of the Left tradition in the modern Iranian political setting, and secondly how the failings of the Left resulted from a dogmatic refusal to see beyond the limits of their ideological scheme. This amounted to a naive support of Islamic politics, by some leftist organizations, based on a mistaken belief that religion could never constitute anything more than a peripheral element in popular struggle. Ironically, this blindness to the momentous power of religious politics – based on "modernist" certainties – was all but a reflection of the Shah's own dogmatic refusal to see a reality unfolding before his eyes but beyond the limits of his overly confident conceptions. The chapter documents in close detail the rise of the Left in Iranian politics throughout the twentieth century, examining its social bases in the period leading to the Revolution and after. It also relates the emergence of new radical discourses in the modern era to the rise of modern social classes, expanded education, and international communication. All of these developments are considered in relation to Islamic political discourses and ideologies, taking note of the tendency for Islamic ideologies to freely appropriate the ideas of the Left – ironically, in a far more flexible, pragmatic and creative way than the Left itself was ever able to manage. Finally, the chapter traces the role of the Left in the Revolution of 1978–79, leading to its being politically crushed in the revolutionary aftermath, and its subsequent efforts to reorganize either in Iran or abroad.

Beginning with interviews with Iranian intellectuals conducted in Tehran in 1995, the final chapter explores the possibilities of plurality in modernist narration. Contrary to Orientalist assumptions, the "Islamic Mind" is shown to be open to, interested in, and committed to an appropriation of modernity into a "local" context of Iranian culture and history. A reconfigured modernity, open to the experiences of those long considered as marginal or outside the pale shadow of modernity altogether, and capable of escaping the universalist trappings of current models, is necessary to assure that the positive qualities of modernity will survive. In conclusion, I assess the possibilities of secularism and democracy in the Middle East generally, and Iran in particular.

1   Western narratives of modernity

What does need to be remembered is that narratives of emancipation and enlightenment in their strongest form were also narratives of *integration* not separation, the stories of people who had been excluded from the main group but who were now fighting for a place in it. And if the old and habitual ideas of the main group were not flexible or generous enough to admit new groups, then these ideas need changing, a far better thing to do than rejecting the emerging groups.

Edward Said, *Culture and Imperialism*, p. xvi

Introduction

As recent debates surrounding the phenomenon of "post-colonialism" have amply demonstrated, the European "other" played an important role in Western self-definition of its modernity. In order to understand the complex dialectics of modernity in Iran, it is essential to explore the Eurocentric and imperial narrative entrenched deep within its liberatory promises. This chapter, through readings of Montesquieu, Hegel, and Marx, explores how modernity created and preserved a conviction that the non-Western world could exist only as modernity's other. Although this narrative has recently come under serious challenge by critics such as Edward Said, Timothy Mitchell and Gayatri Spivak, it continues to hold remarkable hegemony in the media, popular culture, and among academics. As I show in my interpretations of Samuel Huntington's "clash of civilizations" thesis, and Bernard Lewis's explication of the "roots" of Muslim rage, efforts to re-envision modernity will be doomed to failure unless modernity's troubled genealogy is acknowledged, critiqued, and engaged.

Orientalism and the Occidentalist discontent

The publication of Edward Said's *Orientalism* in 1978 marked an important intellectual challenge to the then prevalent Eurocentric scholarship in Middle Eastern studies.[1] Functioning as a powerful trigger for self-criticism within the academic community, Said's critique of Orientalism provoked many scholars of Islam and the Middle East to reevaluate long held precepts concerning the relationship of scholars to their texts.[2] More specifically, Said challenged Orientalists to reexamine the role of representations in the production and legitimation of political and cultural supremacy, and in the practice of excluding non-Western cultures and peoples on the basis of essentialized difference. Upon subjecting their own studies to Said's critique, some serious scholars of the Middle East found it difficult to acknowledge their deep entanglement in a dubious political tradition and to offer their studies as "objective" representations. A long established and unchallenged discursive tradition suddenly found itself reeling with criticisms and undergoing fundamental reevaluation. Even contemporary Orientalist scholars, such as Bernard Lewis, became self-conscious of the hitherto hidden implications of their positions as Western scholars and felt compelled to explain their thinking about the Middle East. One may even say that there was hope in the air in the early 1980s that scholarship critical of Orientalism would become the dominant mode of writing with regard to Middle Eastern issues, after a long century framing analysis around stony, unyielding, and unassailable "objective certainties."

Yet, as Said points out, critical writings on Orientalism did not effect profound changes at the public level.[3] While academia began to dismantle Orientalism there occurred a simultaneous and energetic resurgence of stereotyping and ridiculing of Muslims and Islamic societies in the media and popular culture. Representations of Islam and Muslims on television, in newspapers, films, and other arenas of popular culture reinforced tacit Orientalist notions of Middle Eastern people as fanatically Islamic, portraying Islam itself as essentially irrational, antagonistic to change, and incompatible with the modern world. Intellectuals, poets, artists, and other professionals in the mainstream of public culture revitalized Orientalist images of the Middle East as the West's inferior "other."[4] How can the ironic discrepancy between academic efforts at self-reform and the fanning of these fires of public prejudice be explained? Said has pointed to a revival of colonialist nostalgia among the literate public:

In England, France and the U. S., there had been a fairly massive investment in colonialist nostalgia – the Raj revival stuff like *Jewel in the Crown* and *Passage to India*, the film *Out of Africa*. It is a simple, colorful world with heroes and prototypes of Oliver North – the Livingstons, the Stanleys, the Conrads and Cecil Rhodes.[5]

The literary and artistic intelligentsia, more so than academics, draw upon this romanticized colonial memory and glorify colonialism in the context of the tragedy of post-colonial realities. Political violence, communities in conflict, and the collapse of nation-states are often contrasted to the "tranquility" of colonial order. It may be that the call for the "good old days" of the colonial past reflects a desire to reinvent or revitalize earlier modernist certainties.

The regeneration of intense Orientalist rhetoric in Western popular culture foreshadowed the tenacity of Eurocentric structures of knowledge. The Iranian Revolution, and the subsequent rise of Islamic movements, exploded at about the same time that Said's book appeared, posing a different type of challenge to the West and its intellectuals. The media, academia and public were overwhelmed by the vision of a modernizing and pro-Western monarchy being overthrown by a mass movement under the leadership of men whose image matched the most deeply entrenched Orientalist stereotypes. The self-reflection spurred by Said's text largely collapsed, as Western intellectuals reverted to interpretations of contemporary Middle Eastern politics heavily indebted to Orientalist presuppositions. The nature of this revolutionary movement had the unfortunate effect in the West of unleashing a conservative modernist backlash which suppressed critical thought about the troubled genealogy of modernization in the Third World. A number of other events that followed, such as the collapse of the Soviet Union and its periphery, and civil wars and conflicts in Africa, the former Soviet Republics, and Afghanistan, seemed to justify empirically the call for a return to the "serene" and manageable world of colonial times. The traumatic and rapid intensity of such events exacerbated already existing Western anxieties over the order of things in the post-Cold War world. Not only were these events difficult to access using the conventional models of analysis, but more importantly they pointed to the general unfolding of a new global situation with unforeseen and relatively unknowable consequences. The reserve of myths which form a culture's "instinctive expression of self"[6] come to the surface above all to cover any complex or threatening situation *in order to cover up* what the "experts" don't comprehend but feel compelled to. The types of crisis that shake a world provide a perfect location for viewing the intersection between "scientific apprehension" and the mythical substrata of historical existence applied on a global scale. Prevalent Western reactions to these events set the context for the analysis that follows and the ingrained precepts we intend to disclose within the conventional narratives of modernity. These precepts – ostensibly concerning the "other" yet reflecting fatally back on oneself – reveal a legacy of exclusion and domination which survives to this day (and certainly not only in the West). Such precepts must be called into question.

The discourse of modernity, as a self-defining project in the West, encompassed a wide diversity of purposeful interests; yet the construction of an imagined "Other" endured as an availing and fundamental tool in nearly all of these proceedings. The writers in the following study provide seminal examples of this tradition. Their work will be viewed in the political context of their time, especially the expansion of imperial empires unprecedented in scope and power. This development climaxed in the period between the 1880s and World War I, with 85 per cent of the world's surface under Western domination on the eve of World War I. The writings of Edward Said, Timothy Mitchell, and Thierry Hentsch have demonstrated how "Orientalist" discourse functioned to shape the Western imagination in order to establish a normative framework for imperial practices. To an equal degree such discourses – particularly in the context of "modernist self-understanding" – have served to consolidate a sense of "Western identity" in the context of a tumultuous world in permanent transformation. We can trace this self-defining mechanism back to "modernity" at its very inception, at the site of the West's sudden and urgent need to consolidate an identity in the face of its own experience of modernization. In multiple and fundamental discourses, a new identity was seized by means of *contrast*: a totalizing ideology was constructed upon the notion of a non-Western Other in the defining moment of modernity itself. Modernist self-understanding established the dialectical presence of this "Other" as a prerequisite for the internal solidarity and durability of its own innermost structure. This is the dark side of modernity, both intellectually and politically. Most scholars who emphasize modernity's universalism point to modernity's democratic qualities. I do not deny these qualities; however, a glimpse into the systematic imperial practices of modern Western states shows the very opposite of these qualities inflicted upon vast sections of the world. The ascent of modernity, in its imperial dimension, has depended on a deep entanglement with those authoritarian values which are allegedly the very opposite of its most cherished democratic ideals.

Diverse responses to this mythical tower of reason have emerged in the context of anti-colonial struggle and post-colonial social reconstruction. In many cases the paradigm of modernity has been preserved, yet relativized with its diffusion among different cultural subjectivities. Specific cultural/moral meanings, from diverse local/historical contexts, have replaced the spatio-temporal "neutral" core which professed a universal rationality, while covertly privileging European culture. Frequently modernity has been retained in form, yet transformed into a weapon of emancipation against those who initially conceived it. In certain cases – as with Iran – there have been vain efforts to dispense with this "totalizing" paradigm altogether.

Montesquieu's *Persian Letters*

Long before the paradigm of modernity was enshrined in the positivist-scientific discourses of, for example, Max Weber, the intellectual foundations for its empirical constructions were laid down on a more abstract level in the rationalist discourses of the Enlightenment. Whereas positivism requires the furnishing of proof (albeit selectively and in patterns designed to reproduce preconceptions), rationalist discourse is more at liberty to employ the imagination as a means of confirming imagery. The Enlightenment set universal and normative standards of human behavior and ethics based on a rational, democratic, and humanist model of society. One of the ways that the Enlightenment discourse legitimized its discourse of modernity was to construct the Enlightenment's "Others." Among the most influential of Enlightenment thinkers was Montesquieu, whose *Persian Letters* brilliantly imagined an essential interconnection between the religious forces of reaction in European society and the fanatical world of the Muslim Orient. In the context of a dawning age of Reason which promised to give birth to a new world, his work vividly invoked the Orient as the culmination of the Irrational in history and hence the antithesis of the emerging spirit of freedom in the West. The true brilliance of Montesquieu's story lies in its power to insert the voices and opinions of Frenchmen into invented Persians, who thus inevitably "discover" the ultimate superiority of Western modernity over their traditional homeland. The odyssey of consciousness experienced by these Persian characters is an almost Hegelian articulation of modernity, in which the "Eastern mind" realizes through a series of rational steps that the truth is to be found only within the narrow limits prescribed by Western modernity.

The *Persian Letters* weaves a cast of characters in an imagined world, known to the reader through the constellation of letters they exchange. Set between 1711 and 1720, the voices circulate in an orbit between Paris, France and Ispahan, Persia, with reports from various locales along the way. The book centers on two Persian friends, Usbek and Rica, as they embark on a nine-year migration to the West ostensibly for "love of knowledge" and so they "should [not] see by the light of the East alone."[7] Over the course of their journey from Persia to France, their letters become the camouflage for Montesquieu's own critical observations of Oriental stagnation and decline, particularly with regard to the Ottoman Empire. Upon arrival in Paris, their voices become the author's covert mouthpiece for criticisms and praises within his own society. These criticisms and praises are addressed from a supposed "Oriental perspective," making full use of the Orient as a negative model of comparison for praising incipient democratic elements in French society and chastising intransigent authoritarian ones. Montesquieu aligns himself within the contending social forces of his time on the side of modernist secularism, and the *Letters* are used to combat the overbearing religious power in

French society. The "Oriental voices" therefore become the cheerleaders of European modernity in opposition to blind tradition, condemning despotism in their native land and implicitly in France. The utility of this "Eastern model" in launching his attack is not incidental: by making the comparison, Montesquieu equates the forces of reaction in his own society with an "Orient" that runs deep in the Western imagination.

The main character, Usbek, presents all the essential qualities of "modern man." Despite his inner resistance, he finds himself estranged from the spirit and institutions of his native culture. His departure is prompted in equal part by malaise within his harem at home, and indignation at the corruption and flagrant vice of the court in his public life. These twin factors – private and public – drive him to devise the pretext of leaving his own country to instruct himself in Western knowledge. This initial pretext conceals the instinctive desire to embark on a "quest for self," to locate a system of meaning which will transcend the disappointing and rotten structure which commands his home country. His adventure is in principle a leap from tradition into the flow of "modernism," as defined by Jonathon Friedman:

Modernism can be defined in Goethean terms as a continuous process of accumulation of self, in the form of wealth, knowledge, experience. It is a dangerous state where in order to survive the person must be in constant movement. It is an identity without fixed content other than the capacity to develop itself, movement and growth as a principle of selfhood.[8]

Usbek leaves behind the traditional world of Islam, with its complexities of predetermined social roles and rules located within elaborate institutional machinery. His immersion in the headlong "modernizing" process dissolves his blind obedience to custom and carries him across the world to an ultimate realization of Western superiority over the East. His embrace of reason leaves him no choice but to concede this "reality," and we are meant to believe that any thinking person would have no choice but to do the same. Yet even this realization cannot prevent him from being sucked back into the vertiginous and licentious demise of the harem, when from afar his inexorable "Oriental sensibilities" inflict bloody havoc on the world he has attempted to leave behind.

Usbek's journey begins with a conventionally modernist "crisis of conscience." His doubts concerning the validity of his own society gradually swell into a full-blown rationalist critique once he experiences Parisian intellectual life. This development is frequently kindled by the intervening voice of an important character known only as "an intelligent European" or "a man of sense." No details, names, or even any context are provided for this repeated encounter; the disembodied voice simply materializes to highlight the general supremacy of the West. Usbek never once challenges or takes exception to these proclamations. Instead, he relates them to his friends in letters in overwhelming detail:

A man of sense said to me the other day: "In France, in many respects, there is a greater freedom than in Persia, and so there is a greater level of glory. This fortunate peculiarity makes a Frenchman, willingly and with pleasure, do things that your Sultan can only get out of his subjects by ceaseless exhortation with rewards and punishments . . .

"The difference between French troops and your own is that the latter consists of slaves, who are naturally cowardly, and can overcome this fear of death only by the fear of being punished, which causes a new kind of terror in their souls and virtually stupefies them; whereas ours gladly face the enemy's attacks, banishing their fear by a satisfaction which is superior to it."[9]

This classic conception of "Oriental despotism" – that no relation exists between individual subjectivity and external authority in the East – is but one of the illuminations bestowed upon Usbek by the mysterious voice. On another occasion an "intelligent European" tells him: "People are surprised that there is scarcely ever any change in the methods of government used by oriental sovereigns: what other reasons can there be except that their methods are tyrannical and atrocious?"[10]

After this remark the voice continues to tell him that change in the Orient is impossible because the sovereign's power is unlimited. Yet this "unlimited power" can be freely exchanged from individual to individual, based on whoever is ruthless enough to seize it by force of violence. Finally, the voice says, people in the country will not recognize any difference between one ruler and the next: "If the detestable murderer of our great King Henri IV had carried out his crime on some Indian king, he would have been in control of the royal seat, and of a vast treasure accumulated."[11] This exaggerated caricature is less interesting for the fact that it is inaccurate than because it shows the use of "the East" as an imagined world in rationalist discourse. A world at once geographically distant yet imaginatively charged can be manipulated with unrestricted freedom and for any purpose. In this instance, it is used to evoke an entire world where unbridled brutality and power reign supreme, and as an omen should certain forces gain ascendancy.

We are supposed to believe that Usbek experiences these caricatures as enlightening remarks on his native society. Yet it seems that Usbek's "Western sensibilities" lay tacit in his mind even prior to his arrival and "enlightenment" in Paris. His letters concerning the journey through the Ottoman Empire reveal a perspective which resounds with the imperial appetites and prejudices of a colonial administrator, rather than those of a Muslim traveler who has yet to tread foot on European soil:

I was amazed to see the weakness of the Ottoman Empire. It is a diseased body, preserved not by gentle and moderate treatment, but by violent remedies which ceaselessly fatigue and undermine it . . . These barbarians have paid so little attention to technical knowledge that they have even neglected the art of war. While the nations of Europe advance further every day, they remain as ignorant as they always were, and never think of taking over new European inventions until they have had them used against them thousands of times . . .

They are incapable of carrying on trade, and it is almost with reluctance that they permit Europeans, who are always industrious and enterprising, to come and do it; they think they are doing a favor to these foreigners in allowing themselves to be enriched by them.[12]

It is not long after his arrival in Paris that Usbek begins to write impassioned letters mocking the superstitions of Islam and Iranian culture, and exalting the greatness of the West, particularly of its political institutions. The hero is at once over-awed by the greatness of the West and haunted by the cruelty and strangeness of the Persian customs he has left behind. Just as his letters make constant comparisons between Eastern and Western forms of government, so the reader is invited to make comparisons between the "despotic East" and forces of reaction in French society. The result is an implicit construction of "enlightened modernity" standing in confrontation with an entire world of hostile delusion and irrational superstition.

The candid remarks of these Persian wanderers should also echo in the minds of Europeans, reminding them of the irrelevant old "idols" who still wield authority and mire them in superstition:

The Pope is the chief of the Christians; he is an ancient idol, worshiped now from habit. Once he was formidable even to princes, for he would depose them as easily as our magnificent sultans depose the kings of Iremetia or Georgia. But nobody fears him any longer. He claims to be the successor of one of the earliest Christians, called Saint Peter, and it is certainly a rich succession, for his treasure is immense and he has a great country under his control.[13]

Elsewhere, the Pope is referred to as a "magician" who "controls [the king's] mind as completely as he controls other people's." This magician has the power to fill minds with irrational illusion, for he can "make the king believe that three are only one, or else that the bread one eats is not bread, and that the wine one drinks is not wine, and a thousand other things of the same kind."[14]

For Montesquieu, the image of the harem – the only Islamic image presented in detail – symbolizes the condition of human relations in the Orient. The harem is the site of a bitter and brutal struggle for domination set within a rigid and changeless form. The eunuchs who guard "chastity" employ the rhetoric of virtue to impose arbitrary and spiteful restrictions upon the women; while the women use the persuasive "pleasures of the bedroom" to induce their husband to wreak vengeance upon the eunuchs. At the same time the different wives are engaged in vicious rivalry with one another. Yet in this world of seething passions, life is "equable" and "without stimulus": "Everything is based on subordination and duty. Even pleasures are taken seriously there, and joys are severely disciplined; they are hardly ever indulged in except as a means of indicating authority and subjection."[15]

As a social device for controlling human passion, it depends equally on every component to perpetuate itself, and Usbek's absence destroys the functioning of the machine. The very structure itself initially undermined his love for his wives and seeded a tyrannical and vindictive wrath in its place:

> But what troubles my heart above all is my wives: I cannot think of them without being eaten up with worry.
> It is not, Nessir, that I love them. I find that my insensibility in that respect leaves me without desire. In the crowded seraglio in which I lived, I forestalled and destroyed love by love itself; but from my very lack of feeling has come a secret jealousy which is devouring me.[16]

When the chief eunuch sends a letter revealing the multiple transgressions of his wives, Usbek's jealousy develops into an obsession. He immediately sends a letter giving the eunuchs unlimited power over the harem: "let fear and terror be your companions; go with all speed to punish and chastise in room after room."[17] The obsession dominates his mind and he finds himself longing for home yet dreading what he will find. France is suddenly a "barbarous" and "oppressive" region. It seems most likely that Usbek is experiencing a resurgence of lust for power; even as Usbek embraces the supposed universal rationalism of Western modernity, we find him unable to extend its emancipatory politics to his wives in the harem. It is his furious jealousy which binds his nature to the Orient he has left behind, and to all of its concomitant excesses against human freedom and dignity.[18]

The ensuing clampdown by the eunuchs and resistance by his wives results in the complete dissolution of the harem, as this traditional structure explodes into a murderous and traitorous chain of events. The final condemnation made by Usbek's youngest and most favored wife, as she commits suicide, takes him to task for violations of humanity which contradict every highbrow principle he avowed throughout his heady self-exile in Europe.

We are now in a position to discuss the implications of this epistolary epic in relation to the subject of modernity. It is a perfect account of a

European writer inventing an "Oriental" subjectivity, showing the deplorable character of non-Western society through his eyes, and finally affirming the superiority of Western modernity through those same eyes. In this case, the task of the writer is to oppose non-secular forces – opponents of modernity – within his own society. The underlying model of reality attaches the waning religious forces of tradition within French society to the larger non-Western world of "irrational tradition." Finally, Montesquieu asserts that the modernizing forces which he espouses within France possess the authority of scientific truth. In this way, he creates a totalizing dichotomy between himself and his opponents and helps fashion a cardinal tendency in the Western paradigm of modernity persistent to this day.

Hegel: the colonization of world history

Although works such as *Persian Letters* helped to create an essential differentiation between modernity and its Other, it was not until Hegel that the concept of modernity became intellectually transformed into an overarching, totalizing, and universalizing historical system powerful enough to cover the entire world and its history. Hegel assembled the totalizing elements implicit in Enlightenment conceptions of modernity within a massive frame in which all civilizations were consolidated inside the West's orbit. The West, inscribed as the center and controller of every one of them, emerged with the power to assign them placement within a scheme where they could only count as peripheral and tangential. According to Jurgen Habermas, "Hegel was the first philosopher to develop a clear concept of modernity."[19] Certainly, the power of compartmentalization immanent in this universal Western gaze created a revolution in thought that virtually all thinkers have been in intrepid dialogue with ever since. In the deconstructive efforts of thinkers like Nietzsche and Foucault, the post-Hegelian metanarrative of Marx, and the pre-Zionist Hegelianization of Jewish history in Nachman Krochmal's work, we find that intellectual divisions are split along the cracks imparted by Hegel's prodigious impact. As Peter Singer has claimed, "[W]ithout Hegel, neither the intellectual nor the political developments of the last 150 years would have taken the path they did."[20] And as with all debates involving Hegel, it often seems as if neither his friends nor opponents can resist falling within the boundaries and implicit categorical limitations of his system of thought.

Hegel is interesting for us because, in his lectures on the *Philosophy of History* above all, he articulates the *story of modernity* from his European gaze. His narrative is presented as anything but a personal tale; it assumes a transcendental voice of "universal" proportions, speaking for history and "Ultimate Reality" as such. In the process it assigns value to the world's peoples and cultures in relation to their place in the Universal Historical Scheme. The scheme is not moved by contingency or chance, but glides along the rails of unalterable Fate. His narrative succeeded in consolidating age-old myths and prejudices in the granite binary categories which thwart dialogue and understanding to this day. As the intellectual fountainhead of the dominant systems of modernist thought, from Marxism to Fascism, to the liberal developmentalist and nineteenth-century colonialist theories of "progress," Hegel's thought has incited all manner of controversy and polemic. Yet, the essential inbuilt assumptions concerning those cultures within and without history – until fairly recently – have remained habitually uncontested.

Arguably, it is not a mere story. Hegel himself went to great lengths in reassuring the reader that he would remain true to the "nature of philosophical science,"[21] and refrain from making "appeals to belief" which might violate this principle. In his introduction he strives, in the very language he uses, to drape an aura of scientific authority around the astonishing fable he is about to recount.

The vision of modernity expressed in Hegel's work is not a *reflexive* one; he doesn't write of his particular experience, but evokes a "universal narrative." In essence, he transforms his voice into the "voice of history" itself. The manner in which he represents his voice impresses the reader with an uncanny sense of supernatural communication. Between the pages of the book, the overwhelming heterogeneity of history is manifesting itself to our mind's eye in a unitary and authoritative essence, as a *voice*.

Hegel's style of expression combines two implicit claims to authority: the claim to scientific legitimacy and the claim to the mythic voice. In as much as Hegel's system explains the structure and purpose of the universe, reinforcing the cultural bonds and social ties of "a people" within the context of that universe, the system adopts a mythic function. Yet in writing a self-consciously modernist myth, Hegel understands the necessity of wedding this myth to scientific legitimacy and of discouraging any mythical interpretation of it by the reader.[22] The legacy of this endeavor was to advance the consolidation of a modernist self-understanding in the West, using the force of imagination to raise subjectivity to near monolithic proportions out of a disparate and conflictual geographic confinement. The call for this reconceptualized identity came in the context of the widespread and unprecedented social upheaval which ushered in European modernity. Hegel answered the call with his philosophy, fueled jointly by his personal crisis and resolute optimism in experiencing German efforts at modernization. He sought above all to instill authority, norm, and design upon a world otherwise collapsing into turmoil and uncertainty.

We can say, then, that the question of modernity is not peripheral in Hegel's system of thought. On the contrary, he was a living witness to the birth of modernity in Europe, and his philosophy was the expression of this social and cultural upheaval. Habermas has located "the fundamental problem of Hegel's philosophy" as "the problem of modernity's self-reassurance."[23] He describes the way in which the destruction of the past inflicted by modernity expands the difference between experience and expectation. In the face of this dilemma, philosophy is called upon to create teleological constructions of history to close off the future as a source of disruption:

Modernity's specific orientation toward the future is shaped precisely to the extent that societal modernization tears apart the old European experiential space of peasants' and craftsmans' lifeworlds, mobilizes it, and devalues it into directives guiding expectations. These traditional experiences of previous generations are then replaced by the kind of experience of progress that lends our horizon of expectation (till then anchored fixedly in the past) a "historically new quality, constantly subject to being overlaid with utopian conceptions."[24]

In the absence of a visible material legacy from the past, modernity must "constantly take its normativity from mirror images of pasts whose services are enlisted for this purpose."[25] For Hegel, this reveals the need for philosophy. In his particular manner, he helped establish the modernist propensity and potential for the reinvention and reappropriation of the past.

Hegel's task of reassuring modernity transpires on two levels which exist simultaneously: (1) in the context of Germany's place in Europe during his lifetime (1770–1831), and (2) in the context of Europe's place in the larger world as a rising colonial power. The two domains are profoundly interlinked and find themselves in a curious configuration in Hegel's philosophy of history.

Let us briefly map out this system of relations as they pertain to Hegel's view of modernity. With regard to Hegel's own nation, Robert C. Solomon has pointed out that in Hegel's time "Germany was not yet Germany," but rather 234 fragmented petty states which "considered themselves part of the 'East', a synonym for 'backward' throughout most of the 'West.'"[26] Before Germany could follow the modernizing path of its Western neighbors, it needed initially to establish itself as a unified cultural and national entity. Modernity was thus something vividly imagined, based on comparative observation, well before it was realized. The struggle for this vision began in the world of literature: a vast and powerful feat of the imagination was required to transfix the

German nation uniformly under a single national identity. Many Germans still identified with their town or province. The king of Prussia could only speak French and indulged in French fashion and decor. As head of the largest German state, he hardly served as an inspiring symbol of national unity.

In his thirties, Hegel saw German society crushed by Napoleon's forces. For many young Germans including Hegel, "after years of despair and looking in envy across the French border," Napoleon appeared as "their instrument of destiny, clearing away the corrupt and stagnant structure of a still feudal Germany" to bring a modernized and revitalized Germany.[27] However, by 1823 Germany had started to drift back into political reaction, and for all the trauma of Napoleonic invasion it failed to institute "social enlightenment." Given these circumstances, we may speculate that Hegel's conception of the centrality of his own nation in the context of the modern world was not entirely unequivocal. Hegel called the quest for identity "worthy of self respect";[28] the social revolutions transpiring in the more developed Western nations found their equivalent in Germany's struggle for cultural independence upon the terrain of poetic, literary and philosophical self-realization. When Hegel undertook the challenge of "modern German identity," he did so under the exhilarating influence of Enlightenment ideas. He resolutely sought a "universal" truth about the world and humanity, and crafted a resolution for Germany's specific dilemma only within that context.

Hegel's philosophy of history is one of human development. Advance, or "Development," is to be understood in terms of "grades" – that is, higher or lower grades of society. The Spirit moves in dialectical ascent through various civilizations, following a westward migration. In tracing this migration Hegel maps out a hierarchy among cultures. The odyssey of Spirit traverses historical space and time, breaking into binary structures corresponding to Hegel's assertions about culture. In Hegel's system, space is divided between the West and the Orient; time is divided between Universal History and the "world of nature" which lies beyond its parameters. Essential conditions exist for both worlds. Thus, in its migration through the Orient the Spirit moves under certain limits and restrictions that Hegel ascribes to the intrinsic limits of "Oriental nature." These limits are the basic essence shared among all Oriental nations. Human history is the agent for the Spirit's self-realization, but there are qualitative differences among human groups based on geography and culture. These spatio-temporal divisions function as the motor of Hegel's system of historical development.

There is a more fundamental axis upon which these categories operate.

At the most basic level they advance upon the rails of a scheme which begins in the "state of nature" and progresses across the entire trek of history to so-called "Absolute Spirit." Only at the gates of the West is nature eventually shrugged off. Hegel's conception of nature – and the manifold ways it is used in his text – deserve our attention. Three aspects of dialectical movement are relevant for our purposes. (1) We will show the scheme of humanity emerging from the yoke of nature, the construction underlying the vision of historical development. It is in terms of this trajectory that questions concerning the Orient and the West can be clearly understood. (2) We will define Universal History in relation to its outer limits. It is not synonymous with "contemporary reality" because there are large parts of the contemporary world which explicitly fall outside of its scope. The two worlds interact dialectically in the progress of history. We will define the essential qualities of the world within Universal History and the world which falls outside of it. This depiction will reveal the nature of time within these two worlds. While Universal History is a world forever pressing into the future (towards its ultimate goal), the other world remains "stuck in time" under the yoke of nature's endless cycles. In the context of this split, we find the later world becomes the living embodiment of a past which is culturally inferior and in need of "emancipation." (3) We will show by what means Hegel's dialectic brings these two worlds into a synthesis, as Universal History penetrates the other. This will raise the problematic issue of "emancipation" as Hegel views it in his determinate historical scheme.

The subject of nature in Hegel's historicism cannot be easily untangled from the essential East/West binary; indeed, it forms the foundation for this binary. Prior to examining this entanglement in detail, I shall make two observations about Hegel's understanding of nature. Initially, nature, in its external and alien state, is to be overcome. Nature is the most formidable barrier on the path to Spirit's self-realization. The "state of Nature" is a world of "injustice and violence, of untamed natural impulses, of inhuman deeds and feelings." The task of Universal History is to transcend and overcome this condition: "The History of the World is the discipline of the uncontrolled natural will, bringing it into obedience to a Universal Principle and conferring subjective freedom."[29] Secondly, Spirit manifests itself in Universal History. Nature and Spirit must be understood as existing in two separate realms. While both embody reason, each moves according to a fundamentally different logic. Nature enacts cycles in eternal repetition, while Spirit *develops* and *progresses*. The East embodies the former while the West corresponds to the latter, as in this remark on India: "Where that iron bondage of distinctions derived from nature prevails, the connection of society is nothing but wild arbitrariness – transient activity – or rather the play of violent emotion without any goal of advancement and development."[30]

The Spirit moves from civilization to civilization, each time undergoing a further transformation towards freedom. The restricting mire of nature is finally shaken off at the gates of the West. However, the Oriental world, left behind in the Spirit's wake, remains essentially unchanged even as the Spirit moves on and attains its ultimate perfection in the West. Hence, at this seminal juncture the contemporary world is split in two. The "point of separation between East and West" congeals. In the West, "Spirit descends into the depths of its own being, and recognizes the fundamental principle as the Spiritual." The result for the West is that nature is "depressed to the condition of a mere creature" and "Spirit now occupies first place," while for the East nature remains as "the primary and fundamental existence."[31] At this point, according to Hegel, the very substratum of life in the East becomes merely one object among others available for rational manipulation and contemplation by the West.

Hegel tells us: " . . . as Europe presents on the whole, the centre and end of the old world, and is absolutely the *West* – so Asia is absolutely the *East*."[32] Having arrived at this great historical and geographical (and above all imaginative) fissure in the Spirit's trajectory, let us pause for a moment to explicate the essential differences between these two worlds as Hegel understood them. Historical form is dialectical, but the content within the form follows certain generalizations. Oriental society is *static* because it remains firmly within the grip of nature. Oriental minds are *irrational*, lacking the power to transcend their immersion in nature. Their political structures are intrinsically *despotic* because they lack the level of self-consciousness necessary to become free. Above all, their belief systems, restrained by their immersion in nature, are invalid. Though each of these societies somehow forms a link in the chain of development, these general qualities which Hegel depicts embody the antitheses of Hegel's contemporary Historical ideal. The fact that their existence has remained static since their brush with the Spirit throws them in a contemptible light as far as the contemporary world is concerned. Hegel is aware of this; he says explicitly that the value of these societies lies only in their *past*, and even then only as a means to a future Western end. With regard to this matter, he tells us: "It is only when dead that the Chinese is held in reverence."[33] Chinese in the contemporary world exist only as incarnations of a retrograde past in Hegel's system.

Historical development occurs in terms of various grades in the consciousness of freedom. As the ultimate purpose of History, the eventual realization of freedom is identical with the Spirit's achievement of Absolute Knowledge. Freedom appears, in an incomplete form, for the first time in Greek society. Upon arrival in Greece, Hegel tells us, "we feel immediately at home, for we are in the region of the Spirit."[34] In the Spirit's passage through the Oriental world there are several forms of gradation, but freedom does not yet exist: "The Orientals have not attained the knowledge that Spirit – Man as *such* – is free; and because they do not know this, they are not free."

Only the Despot himself is free, and this is not true freedom because it is "only an accident of Nature."[35] The corruption of Oriental political structures and belief systems can be traced, once again, to the taint of immersion in nature. Political servitude exists in China and India because "obedience is purely *natural*, as in the filial relation" and is "not the result of reflection and principle." As others have noted, these claims amount to the charge that these people can in no way think for themselves. Furthermore, the systems of belief in these societies are inherently flawed because their beliefs are "only a unit of the Spiritual and the Natural."[36] Thus, Hegel has the temerity to remark that: "The Indian view of things is a Universal Pantheism, a Pantheism, however, of Imagination, not of Thought . . . The Divine is merely made bizarre, confused, and ridiculous." Or, with regard to China: the "distinguishing feature [of the Chinese character] is that everything which belongs to Spirit – unconstrained morality, in practice and theory, Heart, inward Religion, Science and Art properly so-called – is alien to it."[37] I cite these passages not merely to lambast Hegel, but to show how his system is shot through with hostility toward non-Western culture as such, and how he interweaves Eurocentric arrogance into the rudiments of his metanarrative. Hegel's vision of "the progress of freedom" has a totalizing cultural thrust buried within it, though it hardly takes mental fingers of steel to dig it up. Eurocentric imputations are grating, but in themselves might be disdainfully overlooked. However, it becomes plain that Hegel's remarks on "the Orient" were not limited to mere historical observation; he was making a statement about the Orient in his own time. He sums up China from its ancient history to the present with the remark: "The East knew and to the present day knows only that *One* is Free." We should not be surprised by his sudden descent from the aloof philosophical plateau to questions of colonial policy: "[In India] [t]he English, or rather the East India Company, are the lords of the land; for it is the necessary fate of Asiatic Empires to be subjected to Europeans; and China will, some day or other, be obliged to submit to this fate."[38]

Hegel was a humanitarian thinker in the Enlightenment tradition. When he thunderously exclaims that "the German World knows that *All* are free," we should probably believe him. He may have subscribed to this view in principle. What we must ask, however, is: what are the conditions for this "freedom"? There is abundant evidence to answer this question in *The Philosophy of History.* Answering it will take us to the heart of the intersection between Universal History and the world supposedly arrested in the grip of nature.

Let us begin by briefly sketching the border line where these two worlds brush shoulders. First, we shall conclude our survey of the Orient's bondage to nature. In India and China, "every change is excluded" and "the fixedness of character which recurs perpetually takes the place of the truly historical." Therefore, "China and India lie, as it were, still outside the World's History."[39] Persians, however, were "the first Historical People" because a shared general principle, rather than naked external authority, was the basis for their social order. Externally, it followed the pattern of "Eastern Despotism" but Hegel views it as an "elevation . . . from the merely natural." Yet even so, Persia was still bound to nature (and remains so) for the general principle was still "a dictum of mere Nature."[40] The culmination of this Eastern oscillation with nature occurred in Egypt, where the yearning of the Spirit for transcendence from this brute existence manifested itself in colossal artistic endeavors.

The Sphinx may be regarded as a symbol of the Egyptian Spirit. The human head looking out from the brute body, exhibits Spirit as it begins to emerge from the merely Natural – to tear itself loose therefrom and already to look more freely around it; without, however, entirely freeing itself from the fetters Nature has imposed.[41]

However, despite this strenuous effort to transcend nature, Hegel parts company with the Egyptians, saying, "[T]he Egyptians are vigorous *boys*, eager for self-comprehension, who require nothing but clear understanding of themselves in an ideal form, in order to become *Young Men.*" Even as the Spirit makes its exit from the Oriental world, the persistence of nature's bondage has not diminished. Thus: "In the Oriental Spirit there remains as a basis the massive substantiality of Spirit immersed in Nature."[42]

In his parting shot, then, Hegel leaves us with a vision of the modern West confronting a vastly larger Orient whose people are inherently unthinking, servile, and imprisoned by limits of their own making. The greater share of Spirit's ultimate "home coming" occurs on the religious plane. Once again, the essential truth of Western religion is contrasted with the inferiority of Eastern attempts at realizing God:

What we call God has not yet in the East been realized in consciousness, for our idea of God involves an elevation of the soul to the supersensual. While *we* obey, because what we are required to do is confirmed by *internal* sanction, there the law is regarded as inherently and absolutely valid without a sense of the want of this subjective confirmation. In the law men recognize not their own will, but one entirely foreign.[43]

Here we find Hegel once more wrapping his Eurocentric assumptions in the gauze of his Universal philosophy about the historical attainment of "unlimited immanence of subjectivity."[44] I would like to call attention to an interesting dialectical opposition permeating his philosophy and evident in this passage: the dialectic between "home" and "foreignness." Hegel's injunction for human freedom is based on the repeated claim that non-Westerners live under their own political and cultural systems but recognize them as entirely foreign. Having mapped out the elaborate field of errors and limits which ensure the corruption and alienation of their world, Hegel points to only one way "home." This home could only be where the Spirit itself finds home. This, we are reminded in no uncertain terms, is the modern Christian West. Therefore Islam is foreign even to those who believe in it; Muslims know in the depths of their souls that home may only be attained by accepting the Universal truth.

It would seem, in a grand global dialectic of "home" and "foreignness," that the Spirit only finds home when Europe has ascended world hegemony. Hegel was in no short supply of advice for those who would build a global empire. His remarks on the Persian Empire, bemoaning their inability to fundamentally transform their subjects in mind and body, show Hegel at his most insightful in summing up the essence of the colonial mentality with regard to the diversity of world cultures:

[T]his is the side on which Persia itself shows weakness as compared with Greece. For we see that the Persians could erect no empire possessing complete organization; that they could not "inform" the conquered lands with their principle, and were unable to make them into a harmonious Whole, but were obliged to be content with an aggregate of the most diverse individualities. Among these nations Persians secured no inward recognition of the legitimacy of their rule.[45]

Hegel finds fault with the Persian Empire for not consolidating a grip on the cultural imagination of the diverse peoples within its Empire, in the unique manner of imperial modernity. Here, then, Hegel takes us a step further into what constitutes the ultimate self-realization of Absolute Spirit.

Strictly speaking it would be untrue to say that the Spirit, prior to its full self-realization in the West, was foreign to itself. It is true only in the sense that the societies through which it passed contained people who as yet did not realize themselves as one with the Spirit, and were thus inhabiting a world that appeared alien and "external." There is in fact no distinction between the Spirit and the world, but a precondition for its materialization in human society and history as a controlling power was a

long period of human illusion. This, we call history before the advent of
Absolute Spirit – history as accident and contingency, the brutal hand of
chance thwarting our most well thought out endeavors. The Spirit was
never divided from itself except in human terms – it would be more correctly said that humans remained divided from themselves while the
Spirit remained forever whole. The social world emanating from this self-
delusional split was inevitably false. The cultures themselves were emana-
tions of an imperfect form of humanity. The despotical political systems
of the East emerged on account of this split. The religious life was essentially godless and misguided. The Spirit only found its "home" in the
West, and attained its perfection in Western cultural and political formations. The Oriental world left in the Spirit's wake remained essentially
unchanged even as the Spirit attained its ultimate perfection in the West.
Hegel tells us in no uncertain terms that the East lacks the human and
cultural qualities necessary to attain "freedom" on its own. It thus
becomes the ironic burden of the West to dominate and enslave these
Eastern cultures in order to emancipate them. According to Hegel, their
indigenous state of servitude, based on their own internal limits (of
"mind" and "culture"), is far worse than any bondage the West could
inflict upon them. More importantly still, it is their only possible access
point for entering Universal History and a superior cultural world.

The word "home" is very significant. The Spirit found its home in
Europe. This implies a former condition of exile. The Spirit existed in
exile throughout human history, gradually working its way back into the
world through its manipulation of human bodies (historical events) and
minds (for at least half of its struggle occurred inside people's minds).
Hence Persia as the unchanged external Eastern Despotism but internal
Spirit transformation. The Orient is materially unchanging and Spirit
finds its way through the darkness of people's minds. The mind finds itself
at home only in Western culture.

Taking this dizzying vision of power into account, this centering of
European subjectivity as the culmination of a divinely willed historical
process, let us now consider some of Hegel's charitable speculations on
the prospects for development. The question of development in Hegel
can be understood in terms of his vision of penetration of the "world of
nature" by Universal History. The dialectical ramparts connecting the
two worlds, like the overall structure, are conceived in terms of gradation.
The elementary assumption, in this confrontation between the dynamic
and the static, is that "the 'Natural Condition' itself is one of absolute and
thorough injustice." This provides the complete antithesis of History's
ultimate goal, which is Absolute Freedom. On these stark and unequivocal grounds, Hegel can confidently proclaim that (for Africans) "slavery

is itself a phase of advance from the merely isolated sensual existence – a phase of education – a mode of becoming participant in a higher morality and the culture connected with it." The ramparts of gradation within the dialectic will inevitably prove painful for those attempting to ascend from the "state of nature" to the illustrious vessel of Universal History: "Every intermediate grade between this [state of nature] and the realization of a rational state retains – as might be expected – elements and aspects of injustice."[46]

Though ascending the rampart may prove painful, Hegel's canny voice reassures us that as "bad as [enslavement] may be, their lot in their own land is even worse, since there a slavery quite as absolute exists; for it is the essential principle of slavery that man has not yet attained a consciousness of his freedom, and consequently sinks down to a mere Thing – an object of no value."[47] More importantly – with regard to preserving Hegel's credentials as one of the great modernist philosophers of freedom – we have ample evidence that Hegel envisioned a pathway out of the inferno of a mind and soul conditioned by nature's paralyzing touch. Even though for Africans the "want of self-control" creates a condition "capable of no development or culture," and even though "the entire nature of this race is such as to preclude the existence of [political] arrangement," Hegel brightly informs us that for all this, "Negroes are far more susceptible of the European culture than the [American] Indians." There are reported instances of Africans having become "competent clergymen, medical men, etc."[48] In such remarks it is revealed what Hegel truly envisions at the summit of the dialectical scaffold for those "outside history," should they be fortunate enough to survive: the utter adoption of the superior and Divinely ordained culture of Europe. Resistance to this means death; hence, Hegel expresses regret at the African contempt for life when they "allow themselves to be shot down by the thousands in war with Europeans." And while some cultures enjoy the remote prospect of assimilation, others are not so fortunate. Hence, Native American culture in its isolation from the Universal "must expire as soon as Spirit approached it," and Hegel is able to casually remark that "the original nation [has] vanished or nearly so."[49]

In a very interesting passage Hegel reveals the thought process behind this seemingly genocidal disposition. He tells that because the African world is inherently suffused with slavery, "the bonds of moral regard which we cherish towards each other disappear, and it does not occur to the Negro mind to expect from others what we are enabled to claim."[50] In this remark lurks the morally poisonous essence of Hegel's philosophy. He is a humanist philosopher extolling the greatness of human freedom and the Enlightenment tradition; yet based on concocted intellectual categories he erects an essential division between the "European mind" and the "Negro mind," and claims that morality exists in two separate spheres for "Us" and "Them." Based on this reasoning, "we" are to promote liberal political and social values at "home," and are simultaneously perfectly within our rights (and the restraints of "reason") to invade, occupy, and destroy foreign peoples because that is congruent with their mental state and they could not have it otherwise. This tiny passage raises to the surface of Hegel's obscure prose the sentiment behind the Other face of modernity, the side the West would like to hide, but must ultimately face. Two systems of morality coexist within modernity, one for "us" and the other for "them." All of the "liberal," "enlightened," and "progressive" triumphs in Western modernity have had their interdependent counterpart in utterly illiberal, violently totalizing, and destructive assaults upon other peoples.

There is one more point to be observed about the parameters of the Spirit. Hegel tells us that "Africa" is "no historical part of the World," but that "Historical movements [in its northern part] belong to the Asiatic or European World."[51] This provides an interesting insight into the nature of Spirit and Universal History. It is indeed cosmopolitan, if only in the sense that "historical movement" is not bound regionally. Entire regions, including those who are native to them, simply "belong" to anyone with the military prowess to come and take them.

The ghost of Hegel will probably never be laid completely to rest. His brilliance as a philosopher will probably hold imaginations captive as long as there are minds to read his books. However, Hegel's narrative of modernity does not contain harmless intellectual ideas. We must learn from his ideas in many cases about what not to do. The rudiments of the historical scheme in his book are totalizing and ultimately racist in practice. To conceive the world in terms of sequences of gradation towards a single uniform goal is unhelpful. Civilizations of transition are perishable. For those at the summit, "their" history becomes "ours"; they were only a means to us. And just as we were able to take their history and make it our own, so we are able to take their world and declare it our belonging.

Modernity was not a divine Spirit that "chose" Europe. There was no Spirit secretly European in nature, using the world's peoples in its ascent to the summit of subjective self-realization. The human world is not a tool box for manipulations by a single overarching Cosmic Consciousness, especially when that gigantic mask can be shattered to reveal the ordinary, self-interested men who stand behind it. Modernity – if it is not to perish on the sharp rocks of human corruption and ruthless self-interest – must open its spirit to a limitless diversity of voices, and make this the focus of its self-understanding.

Karl Marx: the materialist narrative of modernity

When Karl Marx was asked by his daughter to write down on a piece of paper the vice he most detested, he wrote "servility."[52] A passion for human emancipation characterizes the spirit and content of his writings. The dominant conception of modernity in Marx's materialist inversion of Hegel's idealist dialectic undergoes more than the simple reproduction of Hegel's constricting parameters with regard to non-Western potential for emancipation and development. There is evidence of a will to perceive colonized peoples as capable of empowering themselves and effecting their own liberation, rather than being the innately passive fodder of the West's own "spiritual" progress. It is this conviction which entailed the possibility of a radical shift in the construction of modernity – its nature and potential – along Marxist lines. The significance of this shift has been exhibited dramatically in the widespread and revolutionary appeal of Marxism in struggles for liberation and national self-determination in the Third World.

The key to this shift in the Marxist paradigm of modernity is its materialist approach. The materialist alternative to Hegelian idealism makes the project of self-liberation available to all societies irrespective of their geographical location or cultural identity – it is not a question of possessing the "Spirit." It is for this reason that we can read Marx as a shift away from the Eurocentrism which characterized Hegel. Moreover, Marx perceived the brutality of colonialism as concomitant with the brutality of capitalist society in the industrialized West, and anticipated the overthrow of the capitalist system on both fronts.

Yet, for all the theoretical innovations and emancipatory inclinations in Marx's work, we can see in both theory and practice how his materialist system falls right back in step with several of Hegel's most egregious historical-metaphysical categories. This inadvertent lingering of Marx's radical critique within the boundaries of the Hegelian paradigm of modernity reflects his apparent underestimation of the power latent within the broader cultural and intellectual construction. It begs the question: how can Marx's deeply conceived and radical critique of Western society proceed to ultimately reproduce the same historical metaphysics of development as Hegel? How is it that the Marxist line on modernization and the neo-liberal line are virtually indistinguishable in their attitudes to the issue of transcending local tradition in favor of achieving a universal culture of modernity, which all too often amounts to a reproduction of European cultural forms? To answer these questions is also to point out the significance of apprehending modernity as a focus of analysis for understanding developments in Iran and Third World politics more generally. The paradigm of modernity provides the overarching frame for analysis on a broad spectrum encompassing thinkers of both the Right and Left, and its relative invisibility only strengthens the strings by which it is fastened to the theoretical mind.

A reading of Marx's two short essays on the British colonization of India goes a long way in exhibiting where Marx's thought slides back into step with Hegelian historical metaphysics. At the outset, Hegel's depictions of "Eastern characteristics" are reproduced in almost identical form yet provided with a material rather than spiritual basis. We are told that India – and "Oriental society" as a whole – is unchanging, without history, despotic, mentally rigid, bound by superstition and tradition, restrained by nature's yoke, and fated to be conquered by the superior civilization of the West. Marx, influenced by Orientalist writings of his time, observes that although we may feel emotionally distraught at the sight of ancient traditions ground underfoot, we must recognize rationally that no other means of emancipation is possible. Up to this point, Marx's argument is fairly consistent with Hegel's, although the terms he uses to describe these events are "empirical" rather than "spiritual." It could be said that he contrives to reduce these concepts to their secular basis. Indeed, his empirical observations are reasonably sound. Yet the preeminence ascribed to his particular body of evidence stems from its consistency with the concepts wielded by Marx from the outset.

Where Marx parts company with Hegel, initially, is in criticizing the British for being motivated by "vile interests" and for conducting their enterprise in a "stupid manner." Let us consider what underlies this point of divergence more closely. India is conceived by Marx as existing on a flat and unchanging plane throughout the whole of history: "All the civil wars, invasions, revolutions, conquests, famines, strangely complex, rapid and destructive as the successive action in Hindustan may appear, did not go deeper than its surface." However often political transformation has swept the country, the "social condition has remained unaltered since its remotest antiquity."[53] Eastern social conditions, the "village system," are founded upon the Oriental situation where "civilization is too low and the territorial extent too vast" to inculcate the private enterprise leading to capitalist/class society, and the coinciding class tensions which stimulate historical motion and progress. The result is that the burden of providing public works falls exclusively upon an overarching central government, while the nation is otherwise composed of a dispersal of small villages, each with its own independent system of organization and mode of life. These "idyllic village communities," we are told, "inoffensive though they may appear, had always been the solid foundation of Oriental despotism, in that they restrained the human mind within the smallest possible compass, making it the unresisting tool of superstition, enslaving it beneath traditional rules, depriving it of all grandeur and historical energies."[54]

This historically static surface has been penetrated for the first time by British colonialism. From out of this tumultuous yet fundamentally unchanging condition, British colonialism has inadvertently ushered in the first and "only social revolution ever heard of in Asia" by destroying the traditional economic base with the introduction of free trade. Therefore, although we may recognize British colonialism as unjust and even "vile," on a higher level this injustice forms the precondition for India's emancipation (from its own Oriental backwardness) and for human emancipation as such:

> England, it is true, in causing a social revolution in Hindustan, was actuated only by the vilest interests, and was stupid in her manner of enforcing them. But that is not the question. The question is, can mankind fulfill its destiny without a fundamental revolution in the social state of Asia? If not, whatever may have been the crimes of England she was the unconscious tool of history in bringing about that revolution.[55]

It is therefore the "fate" of India, and societies like it, to be conquered. Marx points out that India's entire past is the mere "history of the successive conquests she has undergone" (and that "she" therefore "has no history at all").[56] Given this society's destiny as a conquered people, Marx decides that the fundamental question is "whether we are to prefer India conquered by the Turk, by the Persian, by the Russian, to India conquered by the Briton." Marx makes this decision based on "an eternal law of history" wherein "barbarian conquerors" are "conquered themselves by the superior civilization of their subjects." All previous conquerors were swiftly "Hinduized," but Britain was the first conqueror "superior, and, therefore, inaccessible to Hindu civilization." With this immunity to the bewitching seizure of Hinduization, only Britain is qualified to construct the foundations for India's emancipation from its own cultural and social constraints. England, therefore, "has to fulfill a double mission in India: one destructive, the other regenerating – the annihilation of old Asiatic society, and the laying of the material foundations of Western society in Asia."

We should take note of three issues at this point: (1) by calling England the "unconscious tool of history," Marx evokes history as a subject acting upon the short-sighted myriad of human activities with a higher purpose in mind. This reification of history as a subject of loftier design than mere human intentionality echoes all too resoundingly of Hegel's similar rationalizations for European intervention in non-Western societies. (2) Marx speaks repeatedly of the "Orient" as a monolithic entity, and ascribes to it a set of essential characteristics – all of them negative – which can only be overcome through Western intervention. He makes no discriminations regarding Oriental society, but repeatedly proclaims its unity, implying that all Asian societies are candidates for similarly intrusive treatment. (3) The most important and progressive contribution that Britain will make to India – and where other Asians could never succeed – is in the destruction of traditional forms of society to make way for the birth of a new world. Moreover, where Marx talks of the modernization of India, he describes this process as being interchangeable with Westernization. India will, indeed, "be actually annexed to the Western world."[57]

The second major point of diversion between Hegel and Marx lies in their treatment of European colonialism. Although Marx tells us that British colonialism is a necessary prerequisite for India's emancipation from itself, he does not rule out the possibility of Indians effecting their own liberation from Britain. Indeed, he informs us with a sort of relish that with the modernization of India through internal communication, irrigation, railways, roads, industry, and knowledge of its application, "now the tables are turned." It is clear that with the experience of colonization, in conjunction with the class stratification imposed by modernity, the necessary tensions for class struggle and hence eventual socialist revolution – what Marx calls mankind's destiny – will be introduced. Although this rupturing of traditional social structures (i.e. castes) to make way for modern class society will be painful, it is a necessary stage in the universal scheme of history: "Has the bourgeoisie ever done more? Has it ever effected a progress without dragging individuals and peoples through blood and dirt, through misery and degradation?"[58]

The question of India's revolution against British rule is somewhat ambiguous in Marx's view. In one passage, we are told that "[the] Indians will not reap the fruits of the new elements of society scattered among them by the British bourgeoisie, till in Great Britain itself the now ruling classes shall have been supplanted by the industrial proletariat, or till the Hindus themselves shall have grown strong enough to throw off the English yoke altogether."[59] Yet only two pages later this flexible view of the future's potential is inexplicably thrust aside in favor of a more rigid proclamation about the proper order of things to come:

When a great social revolution shall have mastered the results of the bourgeois epoch, the market of the world and the modern powers of production, and subjected them to the control of the most advanced peoples, then only will human progress cease to resemble that hideous pagan idol, who would not drink the nectar but from the skulls of the slain.[60]

This very dramatic paragraph seems to restore once again the role of human liberation to the European proletariat, since Marx is presumably referring to Europe when he speaks of the "most advanced peoples." The possible Indian revolution referred to earlier in the essay, then, could in itself not constitute the fullest stage of human emancipation, but functions as a mere prelude to the "absolute" revolution still to come. The scheme of historical gradation implied in this narrative forecloses the fullness of historical possibility by insisting on the adherence of human practice to an abstract, allegedly scientific, scheme of historical progress. The sheer narrowness implicit in this design, not to mention its Eurocentrism, is unspoken but implicit, not least of all because it receives its boundaries from a tradition established most spectacularly in Hegel, but certainly also elsewhere in the European discourse of modernity. The very "narrative of materialism" in itself constructs specific elements of the material environment – economic forces, class identity – and crowns them as primary, energetic, progressive, while denigrating others – tradition, religion, small communities – as indisputably obsolete, half way to the grave, and certainly lacking the type of internal dynamism necessary to mobilize a people in mass social revolution and self-emancipation. History has radically proven otherwise. These indisputable "certainties" of the Marxist narrative of materialism betray the fact that a materialist narrative in itself inevitably confers subjective judgments and thereby constructs "objective" limits where material reality may – and most often does – launch itself full-bodied beyond the confining expectations of such a discourse. And in the face of such betrayals by "reality," it is all too often the tactic of such discourses to seek ulterior explanations in terms of their own principles and their accompanying systems of logic. These efforts to cover up for the failure of a materialist narrative to conform to material reality seldom inflict as much suffering on the "reality" – though this by no means implies that its inhabitants escape the dire consequences of such illusion – as they do on the dogmatic minds who perpetrate them.[61]

The "popularization" of the Islamic Other

When the respected and learned Orientalist Bernard Lewis wrote his article on "The Roots of Muslim Rage," first delivered as a prestigious lecture, and later published in the *Atlantic Monthly*, one might have hoped he would reveal something about Islam to the American public beyond reiteration of already ingrained prejudices. The blurb at the top of the page suggests that this expert, with a deep understanding for Islamic society and culture, will perhaps impart some illuminating Islamic perspective and provide a context for a fleeting empathy where Americans will understand "Islamic resentment" through "Muslim" eyes. The article does indeed apparently aim to do precisely this. The article asks us to empathize – if only for a brief moment – with a people who are irrational, bound to the ancient past, fanatically religious, gullible and assorted other dubious qualities which Lewis indirectly imputes to them.

Lewis begins by posing the question: "Why do they hate us?" By asking the question in this way, Lewis could seem to be inviting us to reflect upon the fevered emotions of an irrational people. The assumption that the issue is not self-evident and therefore needs to be discussed and a cause searched for like a needle in a haystack, itself conjures up the image of extremes of emotion with no empirically grounded base. It implies that whatever the factors were that motivated the Iranian Revolution, for instance, they were not accessible to any Western mind or sensibility. They could only be understood in terms of the "Islamic mind," which operates on purely religious terms in a realm completely outside of the considerations which might induce a Westerner to rebellion (i.e., social and economic injustice). Moreover, these motivations stem from ancient beliefs and loyalties first, and contemporary conditions only provide a secondary motivation in relation to them. We are therefore presented with a being motivated by purely religious concerns, and a being fundamentally attached (and comprehensible only in terms of) the ancient past. What is notable about Lewis's exposition is that there are no references to the historical events or political information that might help answer the "question" and the reader is instead dazzled with a show of knowledge which simply affirms already existing Western precepts and prejudices. The spirit of simple good will that appears to pervade the argument should not lead us to the wrong conclusion: this argument is a brilliant and succinct fusion of historical and scholarly knowledge with a well-established precept.

We might call the general thesis of the argument the "something deeper" claim. It is certainly this point that Samuel Huntington picked up to exploit the myth of the monolithic Islamic essence in order to secure his vision of the West's new global rival.[62] We are asked by Lewis to go deeper than the supposedly irrelevant historical details of Islamic societies in the twentieth century; deeper than any culturally or historically specific observation of contemporary Muslim life; to a mysterious transhistorical essence by which Islamic behavior and thought can be explained in regions as diverse as Nigeria, the former Yugoslavia and Paris. By imparting an irrational and metaphysical mode of being to the Muslim, we may thereby freely launch ourselves from our rational plateau into the most mystifying assertions, all of which are justified when we concede beforehand that his motivation cannot be comprehended in reasonable terms.

The argument moves in the form of an implicit comparison between the secular, rational, and modern West and an inexplicable, volatile Islamic essence. We are initially presented with a commonplace depiction of the historical rivalry between the Christian West and Islam as the two great contending monotheistic religions. This is followed by a "benevolent" passage expressing the author's admiration for Islam, but also expressing regret that a few bad apples are currently spoiling the barrel and inspiring a "mood of hatred and violence": "It is our misfortune that part, though by no means all or even most, of the Muslim world is going through such a period, and that much, though not all, of that hatred is directed against us."[63]

We are subsequently told that this "surge of hatred distresses, alarms, and above all baffles Americans." Any fears or suspicions that this "hatred" may actually have to do with us are immediately allayed. Not only is this extreme emotion utterly disconnected from anything we may be held accountable for, but it is also disconnected from any tangible, rationally perceived cause. Their hatred, he tells us, came seemingly out of the blue. It materialized without visible or self-evident cause. He leads us back to a harmonious era prior to the explosion of this groundless emotional ferment:

For some [in the Islamic world], America represented freedom and justice and opportunity. For many more, it represented wealth and power and success, at a time when these qualities were not regarded as sins or crimes.

And then came the great change, when the leaders of a widespread and widening religious revival sought out and identified the enemies of God, and gave them a "local habitation and a name" in the Western hemisphere. Suddenly, or so it seemed, America had become the archenemy, the incarnation of evil, the diabolic opponent of all that is good, and specifically, for Muslims, of Islam. Why?[64]

This statement does not refer to any specific society, and evokes something like a free-floating Islamic spirit undergoing this mystifying transformation in a vacuum. Yet we can be sure that placed in context, the development would appear nowhere near as arbitrary. It would not be unreasonable to speculate that Lewis is in part referring to Iran in this passage; and this being the case, the conspicuous omission of crucial and relevant information is unpardonable.

Having therefore evoked his enigmatic Eastern puzzle, Lewis proceeds to seek possible explanations in the manner of a master detective. By implication we are dealing with something profoundly irrational; even he, the expert scholar, cannot easily discern the underlying motor of Islamic behavior in this instance. He goes deep back into history. He finds reasons for Islamic hatred in doctrinal ideas about the "cosmic clash of good and evil"; in the identity of the Prophet as a soldier; he proposes that many

Muslims, in the face of Western superiority and influence, are "returning" to "the classical Islamic view" in which "the duty of God's soldiers is to dispatch God's enemies as quickly as possible to the place where God will chastise them – that is to say, the afterlife."[65] Ultimately, by his ancient perusal, he unearths a metaphysical world in terminal combat, Islam and the West, and Lewis calls this the clash of civilizations.

The clash of civilizations sets the context for the implicit comparison between the West and Islam. Lewis depicts this clash as transcending the particularities of politics and history in the twentieth century (conveniently), and transpiring on a deeper, ancient level:

We are facing a mood and a movement far transcending the level of issues and policies and the governments that pursue them. This is no less than a clash of civilizations – the perhaps irrational but surely historic reaction of an ancient rival against our Judeo-Christian heritage, our secular present, and the worldwide expansion of both.[66]

Following this remark, Lewis appeals to our reason that we may not behave likewise: "It is crucially important that we on our side should not be provoked into an equally historic but also equally irrational reaction against that rival." This appeal to Western reason – and the fact that no such appeal holds sway for those in the grip of ancient history and irrationality – is predicated, according to Lewis, on certain historical progressions which allowed the West to break its attachments with the ancient forces of bloodlust and religious fanaticism:

Only by depriving religious institutions of coercive power, it seemed, could Christendom restrain the murderous intolerance and persecution that Christians had visited on followers of other religions and, most of all, on those who professed other forms of their own.[67]

The "clash of civilizations" is meant to account for contemporary Islamic unrest. Though it is perennial in essence, the West experiences the clash as a disturbing, yet hardly central, preoccupation, while for Islam it has remained an overwhelming and debilitating obsession. We therefore have a West that has matured, outgrown childhood temper tantrums and resentments, and who looks down upon its immature sibling – Islam – with a mixture of fond concern and uncertain trepidation. This is assuming we accept Lewis's claim that the roots of Muslim rage lay deep in the past and are only tangentially exacerbated by the strain of modern conditions. The rage directed at the West (especially America) is above all undeserved, yet can and should be taken in stride just as an upright citizen would ignore the drunken abuse of a beggar in the street, while harboring secret hopes for the beggar's eventual moral rehabilitation.

Lewis sympathizes with the suffering of the Islamic world in the face of modernity, attributing that suffering to an ineptitude in dealing with modern implements and methods:

Even the political institutions that had come from the West were discredited, being judged not by their Western originals but by their local imitations, installed by enthusiastic Muslim reformers. These, operating in a situation beyond their control, using imported and inappropriate methods they did not fully understand, were unable to cope with the rapidly developing crises and were one by one overthrown. For vast numbers of Middle Easterners, Western-style economic methods brought poverty, Western-style political institutions brought tyranny, even Western-style warfare brought defeat.[68]

We are led to believe that the political failures of modernity in the Middle East occurred in a sealed vacuum, where well-intentioned reformers strived to bring democracy, while the West could only stand by and watch bereavedly as these efforts were thwarted by inexperience and naive enthusiasm. Such an account, of course, is outrageously inconsistent with the actual political realities of modern times. However, it helps to consolidate Lewis's claim that the crisis in Islamic society is purely self-induced, while the West has only inflicted damage by the magnitude of its own success and therefore fueled a resentment for which it is the scapegoat. The venturing of the "clash of civilizations" thesis depends upon the assertion that the hatred felt by Muslims has relatively little to do with any violation on the part of the West, and a great deal more to do with an ancient and almost supernatural form of enmity.

Yet prior to making this assertion, Lewis does entertain the possibility that late twentieth-century Islamic rage towards the West does have something to do with Western behavior in the twentieth century. Although he concludes that none of these factors are sufficient in themselves for explaining Muslim rage, and must therefore be laid aside in order to search for "something deeper than these specific grievances,"[69] it is worth considering Lewis's treatment of the alternatives to his atemporal "clash of civilizations" thesis. He considers the primary factor as the unfortunate influence of certain bad books coming from several German writers: Ernst Junger, Martin Heidegger, Rainer Maria Rilke. There was also the bad influence of Communist ideas spread from the Soviet Union, and finally the bad influence of Third Worldist ideas. In his description, ideas seem to float freely without any social context. Not only is his vague description of social conditions postponed until later in the essay, but he also omits to relate the interpretation of these ideas by the Muslims who read them; how they were perceived as relating to the social context and why; or which members of society received them and who they were transmitted to. It is as if the interpretation of the ideas is irrelevant, and the "badness" of the ideas suffices in itself to explain the turn of events. His emphasis on the "badness" of the books, rather than on people's interpretation of them, seems to imply a paternal figure disgusted by the discovery of an impressionable youth reading corrupting literature. He claims that the anti-American content of the books is a major factor in fermenting anti-American feeling, while disregarding the possibility that something in people's experience had paved the way for their embrace of these ideas.

This extended and acontextual representation of ideological influence is followed by an unsatisfactorily brief consideration of other factors including European colonialism and Western support for hated regimes in the Middle East. Colonialism is dismissed almost instantly as a central factor because it is "over," and therefore cannot be of significance. There is no consideration given to the legacies of colonial rule. This silence in itself constitutes a disservice to truth. The second factor is dismissed as insufficient because, we are told, it has been limited in both extent and effectiveness. There is no argument or any kind of evidence provided for either of these assertions. Yet Lewis's entire treatment of the twentieth century in this essay could not really be called an argument. At best, you could say he omits reference to incredibly important information and thereby demonstrates his case on the basis of other people's presumed ignorance. Having, then, dispensed with the "familiar accusations," Lewis informs us that it is time to dig deeper: "Clearly, something deeper is involved than these specific grievances, numerous and important as they may be – something deeper that turns every disagreement into a problem and makes every problem insoluble."[70]

This remark, to say the least, impresses us with a sense of pessimism with regard to the secret which is about to be disclosed. This ominous "something," it is already implied, will only lend ultimate confirmation to the essential difference between the Muslim and Western minds. We find out, in the context of an impassioned general defense of the West against all of its critics, that the essence of Muslim rage is to be found in the Islamic conception of "imperialism":

In many [Islamic fundamentalist] writings the term "imperialist" is given a distinctly religious significance . . . One also sometimes gets the impression that the offense of imperialism is not – as for Western critics – the domination of one people over another but rather the allocation of roles in this relationship. What is truly evil and unacceptable is the domination of infidels over true believers.[71]

This remark lays bare the "Islamic mind" in two important respects. The Muslim does not experience oppression in a manner similar to the Westerner. Their hearts are not aflame with yearnings for justice, or aching with sorrow for the sufferings of their fellow human beings. They have no social vision of a world emancipated from servitude. Further, they feel no intrinsic objection to servitude in itself; only an objection to servitude when it is not being enforced by Muslims upon other Muslims and, ideally, upon "infidels" alike. The motivation, then, for Muslim insurgents is a single-minded devotion to domination of the world along Islamic lines. This essential principle, Lewis tells us, can be applied to make sense of any situation in the world where Muslims are causing trouble:

[F]or misbelievers to rule over true believers is blasphemous and unnatural, since it leads to the corruption of religion and morality in society, and to the flouting or even the abrogation of God's law. This may help us to understand the current troubles in such diverse places as Ethiopian Eritrea, Indian Kashmir, Chinese Sinkiang, and Yugoslav Kossovo, in all of which Muslim populations are ruled by non-Muslim governments. It may also explain why spokesmen for the new Muslim minorities in Western Europe demand for Islam a degree of equal protection which those countries no longer give to Christianity and have never given to Judaism.[72]

This "insight" apparently presented as a universal truth might be contended as being one of the most blatant misconstructions of reality yet conceived by an Orientalist. By reducing the complex of social, cultural and economic problems in each of these disparate situations to this untenable thesis, Lewis shows a taste for simplification, branding Islam as incompatible with the realities of the modern multi-ethnic society. This is something said implicitly here, which is articulated explicitly in the final course of the essay. We are told that the two primary enemies of "Fundamentalism" are secularism and modernism. This allegation of a revolt against modernity is worth closer attention. Fundamentalism, we are told, wages "a war against modernity [which is] for the most part neither conscious nor explicit, and is directed against the whole process of change that has taken place in the Islamic world in the past century or more and has transformed the political, economic, social, and even cultural structures of Muslim countries."[73] By this account, then, so-called Islamic fundamentalism is a revolution effected in a state of blindness even by those men who organize and lead it. They act without reflection or consciousness upon the savage current which runs through and paralyzes their entire culture. Lewis makes a distinction between leaders and masses in the fundamentalist movement. The masses have a curiously ambiguous relation to their leaders, because while on the one hand "it is (more than ever before) Western capitalism and democracy that provide an authentic and attractive alternative to traditional ways of thought and life," there is also an accumulated history of "aimless and formless resentment and anger of the Muslim masses" against the

West.[74] Fundamentalist leaders, Lewis says, perceive the attractions of Western capitalism for the masses and feel compelled to intervene so as to protect the ancient order they so deeply desire: "Fundamentalist leaders are not mistaken in seeing in Western civilization the greatest challenge to the way of life they wish to retain or restore for their people."[75]

These fundamentalist leaders, by this account, succeed in winning influence over the masses by giving "aim and a form" to their alleged resentment and anger.[76] The scenario depicted is therefore one in which (1) an entire society lives enslaved in the ancient grip of irrational and fanatical hostility based on the internal shortcomings of their religious tradition; (2) these masses perceive a superior way of life in the modern capitalist West and a part of them yearns to attain it; (3) certain evil-minded individuals perceive this situation and willfully manipulate the first condition in order to restrain these masses from attaining their desire for freedom. By this account, then, the West is blameless with regard to the plight of the Islamic world, standing merely as a beacon of freedom. The major obstacle separating the Muslim masses from this freedom is, first, the enslaving atavism of their cultural heritage which distinguishes them in mind and spirit from the West, and second, the malicious men who manipulate this cultural defect in an attempt to drag them back into the darkness of the past. Hence, with regard to modernity, Islamic fundamentalism is merely a blind and visceral reaction rooted in ancient impulses, on the part of both its leaders and the masses who participate. Given that Lewis merely asserts these interpretations without reference to any particular social or historical context, it remains to be seen to what extent they conform to the actual realities in Middle Eastern societies. Later in this book, an in-depth and detailed study of Iran will be provided, mapping political developments in relation to modernity throughout the twentieth century. We will see, then, to what extent the opinions of this expert conform to actual events, individuals, literature, and complex social developments. By extension, we will also put to the test the views of modernity described by other modernist writers in this chapter, seeing how Lewis's categories so frequently fall in sync with Hegel's in regard to the binaries between East and West, tradition and modernity, irrational momentum and reasoned progress.

Let us now investigate the "clash of civilizations" thesis as adopted and utilized by Samuel Huntington in his essay on the shape of things to come in the post-Cold War world.[77] The central contention of the essay is that conflict in the post-Cold War world will cease to occur along ideological or economic lines, but will instead take place along great cultural "fault lines." The author uses the term "civilization" instead of culture for the most part, presumably so he can subsume diverse so-called "sub-civilizations" into larger civilizational units. In his mind, for example, Islam is one civilization, and therefore the Bosnian Muslims form one civilization with Muslims in Nigeria or the Sudan; on the other hand, Bosnian Muslims are in a separate civilization from Bosnian Serbs (who are Eastern Orthodox and hence count as "Slavic-Orthodox") and both of them are in a separate civilization from Bosnian Croats (who are Catholic and hence count as "Western"). Each group represents a different civilization from among the eight world civilizations. The other world civilizations include Confucian, Japanese, Hindu, Latin American, and African.

This crude system of classification presents serious problems. The simplistic reductionism collapses with even a mere brush against the inevitably more complex reality of any one of the situations that Huntington generically applies it to. Any reader who is even reasonably intimate with the situation in Bosnia, or Nigeria, or any of the numerous locations Huntington binds up in his thesis should rapidly see the contradictions proliferate as reality knocks the weak conception aside. We would prefer to devote less attention to exposing the already obvious conflation of contradictions that riddle Huntington's proposed system of explanation, and instead draw attention to the dubious underlying structure which articulates his idea.

To begin with, we may consider the apparent purpose behind his attempted prophecy. Huntington intends his prophetic system of analysis as a basis for reconstituting the Cold War in new form. He elaborates the system and then virtually in the next breath insists with a kind of zeal that it will lead to clashes (and where there have been clashes, he assigns this as the *a priori* cause). The inevitability of a specific type of conflict is established by listing six factors which supposedly make these clashes inevitable. Several are notable for their insistence on the rigidity and immutability of separate cultural entities and their values. A more interesting factor is the issue of modernization: we are told that as countries modernize, people are separated from their local identities, and religion provides the major substitute for this loss. Instead of following from this interesting observation to articulate its myriad of implications, positive or negative, Huntington inserts a thought-stopping abstraction into the text, invoking a familiar mood of paranoia. The fanciful evocation of a world-conquering Islamic fundamentalism is as baseless as it is sensational. This is characteristic of the whole piece. Huntington merely strings together an enormous list of "ethnic" conflicts in diverse regions, and then without looking at the historical specificities of any single one, he asserts that they exist to prove his clash of civilizations thesis. He does not provide any evidence for saying that ethnicity or ethnic values are the primary factor of motivation in any of these wars; he apparently expects us to take that for granted as if there were no other factors present. The predictable mood of unease conjured by these calculated abstractions form the only cohesion and persuasive power in Huntington's so-called "argument."

Following the elaboration of his six factors, Huntington tells us that the "fault lines between civilizations are replacing the ideological boundaries of the Cold War as the flash points for crisis and bloodshed."[78] This is not merely the substitution of one form of conflict for another; the cleavage between civilizations is far older and runs much deeper than any ideological difference. In a dramatic tone worthy of a circus ringmaster announcing the opening of an exciting and dangerous show, Huntington proclaims the rebirth of premodern, preintellectual forces of instinctive cultural animosity: "the great historic fault lines between civilizations are once more aflame." The motivations for these "cultural upsurges," he reminds us, cannot be perceived as part of any intellectual universe:

A Western democrat could carry on an intellectual debate with a Soviet Marxist. It would be virtually impossible for him to do that with a Russian traditionalist. If, as the Russians stop behaving like Marxists, they reject liberal democracy and begin behaving like Russians but not like Westerners, the relations between Russia and the West could again become distant and conflictual.[79]

The implication here is that any form of "traditionalist politics" is inherently unintellectual in itself, and even more so to anyone outside the tradition; that it is visceral and born of deeper instinctive potencies than the mind can conceive; that it is unable to communicate and inherently hostile.

Following the announcement of these "fault lines of fire," Huntington unfurls a dramatic evocation of the great historical rivalry between the West and Islam, culminating in the Gulf War. This familiar narrative of Islam and Christendom concludes with Huntington making the ominous remark: "This centuries-old military interaction between the West and Islam is unlikely to decline. It could become more virulent."[80]

We see the general strategy at work in Huntington's argument. He puts together extended lists of conflicts which all have some relation to a given topic – ethnicity, Islam – and then rather than analyze any one of these conflicts in detail or in its specificity he proclaims a unifying and singular cause for all of them based on a stereotype associated with this common topic. This is precisely his method of treating the non-Western world generally and Islam in particular. A strategy of triggering via association acts as a substitute for analysis. In order for the argument to carry conviction, such stereotypical imagery must already be well established.

It is not insignificant that he drew his main concept from Lewis's "The

Roots of Muslim Rage."[81] Indeed, Lewis's depiction of Islam in the modern context as a reactive and innately hostile force (especially to the West), irrational and fanatical, bent on world domination, bound in blindness by the immutable insularity of its ancient tradition, and above all completely unable to co-habit with other religions and peoples, paved the way for Huntington's remarkable effort to explain every single contemporary clash involving Islam in terms of a single "Islamic essence." After an exhaustive listing of conflicts involving Islam, the paragraph is concluded not by analysis of these conflicts but merely with a grim and sinister verdict – "Islam has bloody borders" – implying without actually saying that the bloodthirsty and fanatical nature of Islam is entirely to blame for all of them. This is the kind of evocative remark which lends Huntington's essay persuasive power while sparing him the difficulty of researching the actual details of the situation. It is only in this manner that he may cover such a broad scope in so short an essay and then baselessly attribute a single simplistic thesis to explain this multiplicity of events.

Under the pretext of scholarly objectivity, Huntington arrives at two central contentions: the first is that Islam is essentially other and antagonistic to the West, and the second is that the entire non-Western world is essentially other and at least potentially antagonistic to the West. What we see in Huntington's "revelations" about a "new world" are simply pieces of classic Orientalist rhetoric. The ontological East/West binary is reaffirmed, and everything to occur inside of a Muslim society is conceived as having purely Islamic motivation. There is only one considerable break with the "tradition" that, in most other respects, Huntington unreflectingly carries out to the letter. This is the renunciation of "universalism": modernization of the world, we are told, never will and never can be the equivalent of Westernization. Instead, the spirit of tomorrow will be "the West versus the rest." This is no prophecy of doom for the West: Huntington is implicitly saying that democratic principles of justice and equality are essentially Western, and we should practice them among ourselves. They are alien to other cultures, and we should therefore not bother with extending them "outside" unless it serves our interests to do so. Yet this does not mean that the West should cease to pay attention to the wider world. On the contrary: the West must take every measure to ensure its continued domination of the "other" world, yet with particular concern for economic advantage and without the burdensome consideration of "principle."

There is a creeping fear throughout Huntington's essay with regard to the "modernity" of non-Western "civilizations." While he notes that "the West is now at an extraordinary peak of power in relation to other civilizations" and may act through international institutions (with Japan) "to the exclusion of lesser and largely non-Western countries," there is also the threat of civilizations with fundamentally different values acquiring greater power through modernity:

Non-Western civilizations will continue to attempt to acquire the wealth, technology, skills, machines and weapons that are part of being modern. They will also try to reconcile this modernity with their traditional culture and values. Their economic and military strength relative to the West will increase . . . the West will increasingly have to accommodate these non-Western modern civilizations whose power approaches that of the West but whose values and interests differ significantly from those of the West.[82]

By Huntington's estimation, these new modernities are bound by their cultural dispositions to be lawless, authoritarian, and hostile to secularism:

Western concepts differ fundamentally from those prevalent in other civilizations. Western ideas of individualism, liberalism, constitutionalism, human rights, equality, liberty, the rule of law, democracy, free markets, the separation of church and state, often have little resonance in Islamic, Confucian, Japanese, Hindu, Buddhist, or Orthodox cultures.[83]

According to this interesting logic, which perceives culture (particularly religion) as the essentially determining factor in shaping a society, we are to believe by implication that Croatians are more prone to democratic politics (because they belong to the Catholic Western tradition) than the Muslims or Serbs who have come from the same historical-political experience of Yugoslav Communism. Huntington is not ambiguous about the significance of this division in separating the Eastern mind from the Western:

The most significant dividing line in Europe, as William Wallace has suggested, may well be the eastern boundary of Western Christianity in the year 1500 . . . In the Balkans, of course, this line coincides with the boundaries between the Hapsburg and Ottoman empires. The peoples to the north and west of this line are Protestant and Catholic; they shared the common experiences of European history – feudalism, the Renaissance, the Reformation, the Enlightenment, the French Revolution, the Industrial Revolution; they are generally economically better off than the peoples to the East; and they may now look forward to increasing involvement in a common European economy and to the consolidation of democratic political systems. The peoples to east and south of this line are Orthodox or Muslim; they historically belonged to the Ottoman or Tzarist empires and were only lightly touched by the shaping events in the rest of Europe; they are generally less advanced economically; they seem much less likely to develop stable democratic political systems. The Velvet Curtain of culture has replaced the Iron Curtain of ideology as the most significant dividing line in Europe.[84]

Huntington's tendency to establish false categories is matched only by his apparent reaffirmation of an essential East/West divide which marks certain people as more "promising" on account of their cultural heritage. But there is no grand synthesis of world culture along Western lines, as with Hegel. Huntington is fully prepared to concede that the "other" cultures are essentially antithetical to the West, and yet will still construct modernities in their own image. There is a certain melancholy, albeit with stiff upper lip, in his concession that the days of the West as center of all things are soon to be over:

With the end of the Cold War, international politics moves out of its Western phase, and its center-piece becomes the interaction between the West and non-Western civilizations and among non-Western civilizations. In the politics of civilizations, the peoples and governments of non-Western civilizations no longer remain the objects of history as targets of Western colonialism but join the West as movers and shapers of history.[85]

One is reminded of an old colonel, sent home from India, standing glassy eyed and unafraid as he watches his daughter marry a working-class hooligan, seeing the lost expanse of Asian horizons burned on the inside of his eyelids, wondering above all what has happened.

Huntington concedes the pluralistic potential of modernity. It is only the limitations of his own precepts, inherited from an old tradition of modernist thought, that make him see only doom and gloom beyond the controlling glove of the Western hand.

Conclusion

In this chapter we have looked at a body of thought which makes every effort to present a narrative of modernity which is unyieldingly Eurocentric and that denies all other cultures and histories any positive role in the making of modernity in the contemporary world. The traditional narrative presents non-Western culture as inherently passive, to be "saved" or "destroyed" depending on the circumstances. But its role within modernity is never conceived in a *positive, creative* sense. This passivity is always accounted for in terms of some thematized deficiency *vis à vis* the West: thus, for Hegel they lack the Idea (freedom) and for Marx they lack the material conditions (class, private property). It therefore becomes the "mission" of the West to impose it on them for their own good. The struggle and overthrow of colonialism – the production of pluralistic discourses – initiated and ensured the demise of such self-assured assumptions and the concomitant intellectual paradigms which necessarily accompanied them.

The narratives of modernity presented above were articulated in the late eighteenth and nineteenth centuries and formed part of the overall colonization of the non-Western world. Political implications should not be considered marginal in trying to understand them. Moreover, these narratives are extremely influential in all kinds of modernization theories (liberal, Marxist, Third Worldist), and yet still operate within the political context described above. Tacit within them are certain totalizing excesses and abuses of power which do not facilitate or encourage an open dialogue around the issue of modernity. These narratives need to be unearthed from their tacit burial, where from out of the darkness of time they extend their pernicious influence. This is therefore a calling to rethink the foundations of what we call modernity.

With regard to Islamism, social theorists who approach the issue through the particular "modernist" lens we have been describing tend to see merely the affirmation of their already existing precepts about the possibilities of the Other. Everything fits in advance to a preconceived model, and in this unconscious imposition there is a blindness to specificity, detail, ultimately to actuality, and hence the possibility of dialogue and understanding is foreclosed. But these precepts do not arise from the breath of the spirit; they are contained in a discourse and form an ingrained intellectual habit. As such, upon being identified, they can and should be transcended in favor of a more open and less totalizing horizon.

2   Reconciling with the West's Other

In the opinion of the writer of these lines that which is today in the highest degree necessary for Persia, which all patriotic Persians should exert themselves to promote, literally, with all their strength, and should place before everything else, is threefold:

First, the adaptation and promotion, without condition or reservation, of European civilization, absolute submission to Europe, and the assimilation of the culture, customs, practices, organization, sciences, arts, life, and the whole attitude of Europe, without any exception save language; and the putting aside of every kind of self-satisfaction, and such senseless objections as arise from a mistaken, or, as we prefer to call it, a false patriotism . . .   Hasan Taqizadeh[1]

Introduction

Much of the scholarship on the social history of modern Iran is modeled after a perceived European narrative of progress. Many Iranian historians have attempted to write a narrative of "progress" in the Iranian setting.[2] This genre of historiography renders the struggle between "tradition" and "modernity," positing the eventual victory of modern ideas, institutions, and personalities over local customs, outlooks, and cultural habits. A grand narrative of progress in this vein leaves little room for those ideas, institutions, intellectuals, and processes which function as a bridge between the local and the global, tradition and change.[3]

Ideas, institutions, and social tensions are often portrayed as sites of the struggle between traditional impulses and modern desires.[4] Intellectuals are equally subject to such "either/or" classification, and their ideas and dispositions too often defined in terms of traditional (Islamic, feudal, backward, local) or modern (cosmopolitan, Western-secular, progressive). Complexities and ambiguities are glossed over as traditional/modernist boundaries are constructed and installed.

Yet, a close reading of Iranian politics and culture in the twentieth century suggests that this imagined binary does not hold, and may function poorly as an analytical tool. If one is to select a single motif which has

54

continuously taken a fundamental position in the cultural dialogues, political discourses, and intellectual debates of modern Iranian society, it is perhaps the question of accommodating modernity and reconciling it with its geographical lineage in the West.[5] This may appear to be simply a testimony to the realities of contemporary intellectual life in Iran – but the multitude and complexity of responses to the challenge of modernity in the Middle East, and in Iran in particular, have not yet been adequately appreciated. The routine stereotyping and classification of intellectual currents under the "traditional/modern" or "Islamic/Western" dichotomies reduces the cultural complexities of Iran's encounter with modernity and the West, and provides an inadequate space for understanding the intellectual discourses which have evolved in Iran.[6]

While some recent scholarship, critical of modernization and "Orientalism," has begun to critique this rigidly ideological perspective on the history of modern Iran, still most analysis of Iran's modern intellectual history is grounded in the standard East/West split. In this and the following chapter, I argue that a more useful interpretation of Iranian history can be achieved by forgoing this binaristic formation and instead seeking to explore Iranian efforts at "localizing" (reflexive) modernity within their own contemporary cultural experiences and contexts. To do so, I focus on two particularly charged moments in twentieth-century Iran: the constitutionalist (Mashruteh) movement of the turn of the century, and the Islamic Revolution of the 1970s. Despite very distinct social and political visions, both of these revolutionary movements reveal a nation's efforts to embrace modernity, as well as the tensions, difficulties and dangers involved in embracing modernity for a non-Western society.

The Mashruteh movement marked the first large-scale attempt to reconcile the European idea of modernity with the Iranian social context. While introducing the important concepts of secularism and participatory politics into Iranian political discourse, the Mashruteh movement represents, in the end, a failed effort to "localize" the totalizing tendencies of modernity. For a variety of reasons, particularly the call for unconditional capitulation to European social norms, the Mashruteh movement was unable to lay the foundation for a viable and democratic modernity in Iran.

The Mashruteh movement: reconciliation through capitulation

The historical conditions leading to the Iranian Constitutional Revolution (1906–11) were more complex and diversely inspired than conventional historical writings on the subject have generally indicated.

Frequently, this event has been depicted in a causal manner as the effect of modern Western ideas being received by an ancient Eastern society. Even though the Mashruteh (constitution) movement ended up taking a secular political form along European lines, other critical and underlying issues are veiled by the conventional interpretations of its history. As we will see, the intellectual influences and impulses to construct an Iranian modernity came from a variety of sources and locations, including non-Western European places. Further, those ideas coming from the West were not confined to the dominant Western narrative of modernity. In order to sketch the conditions of the Mashruteh period, we must give full consideration to this more complex picture.

It may be interesting to note that the liberal Western model of modernity was not initially perceived as something totally and ontologically different from the historical or cultural contexts of the Iranian society. Many Shi'i clerics, for example, adopted aspects of modernity without thinking that it clashed fundamentally with their own cultural sensibilities. However, the conventional and extremely dogmatic intellectual version of modernity ultimately took hold among many Iranian intellectuals, establishing a paradigm open only to very limited roads to modernity, with predictable and deeply unfortunate consequences.

The period of time between Iranian society's encounter with the modern West and the Constitutional Revolution of 1906–11 is identified as the *Asre Bidari* (Period of Awakening) in modern Iranian history. This period marked Iran's encounter with European modernity on a larger scale than ever before, especially among the educated elite, and led to the formation of a new intellectual and political discourse among the Iranian intelligentsia. Iranian intellectuals became increasingly educated in modern ideas (particularly through translations of European texts) and tried adopting them to the political and cultural specificities of the Iranian context. There were also those who became involved in negating and rejecting the value of modernity, although during the Mashruteh era they remained a minority. In either case, the encounter with modernity transformed the entire landscape of political and intellectual culture in Iran. This was true not only of the more secular segment of the Iranian intelligentsia, but also of Shi'i Ulama. Shi'i clerics were faced with the Western encounter and the challenge of modernity, a fact evidenced by the growth of clerical devotion centered on the question of modernity, and by efforts to articulate a response to modernity.

The constitutionalist (Mashruteh) project intended to recast the existing Iranian political culture in the modern liberal tradition. To accomplish this goal, its leaders had to introduce modernity into Iranian culture and democratize the existing political institutions and processes. As political power was concentrated in the state structure, and the dominant culture heavily shaped by religion, these two centers of power became the object of critique and transformation for the intellectuals and social critics of the time. Many of the Mashruteh intellectuals came from the political elite (in the earlier period: Amir Kabir, Qa'immaqam Farahani, Mushir ud-Doleh, etc.) or from the ranks of religious clerics (Jamal al-Din Asad-abadi, Mohamad-Husayn Na'ini, Malek al-Mutakalemin, etc.).

Many Iranian historians have offered various explanations concerning the history of the constitutionalist movement in Iran. Morteza Ravandi, author of the multi-volume *Social History of Iran*, provides the following point of view: "[F]rom the time of Nasser al-din Shah, some Iranian thinkers, who were already familiar with European civilization and culture, were active in Iran and abroad in awakening the Iranian people to the struggle against oppression and dictatorship."[7]

Ravandi's analyses offer a causal relationship between what is called the awakening (*bidari*) of the Iranian people and their introduction to European culture: "[T]hose Iranians who were educated in Europe, after witnessing the advantages of Western civilization, ventured by all means at their disposal to awaken the Iranian people from ignorance by showing them the value of nationalist government and the evil of an absolutist state upon their return home."[8] The implication here is that the movement against the Qajar absolutist state originated with those who had the opportunity to experience European life and culture. Ravandi continues: "In the middle of Fath Ali Shah's reign the movement of Europeans to Iran started and with it the introduction of principles of modern civilization, which in the Safavid, Nader Shah, and Karim Khan Zand periods began to accelerate."[9] Ravandi also describes the national context for the movement:

Consecutive defeats of Fath Ali Shah by Czarist Russia, excessive expenditures by the Shah and the courtiers, economic mismanagement, oppression of the masses by local rulers and governors, collaboration of some of the Ulama with reactionary and oppressive officials, visits by Iran's diplomatic and military delegations to France, England, and Russia, and travels to Europe by groups of Iranian elites, little by little introduced Iranian society to the benefits of Western civilization and brought awareness of the corruption of the ruling circles, the state bureaucracy, and the social and political system of Iran.[10]

We can see from this account that the corruption of the court and the general poverty of the country's social and political situation played an important role in making the benefits of Western civilization more attractive to Iranians.

Fereydoun Adami'yat, who has contributed more than any other contemporary Iranian historian to studies of the constitutional movement, offers a different narrative about the intellectual roots of the constitutional movement. His chronology is more systematic and broadly articulated: "[The] transformation of the horizon of Iranian thought in the 13th century [19th century AD], of which the constitutionalist movement was only one civic manifestation, was a chapter in the history of the encounter of ancient societies of the East with the new civilization of the West."[11] He further lays out the following chronological account of the constitutional movement:

In her quest for a modern social and intellectual transformation in the constitutional movement, Iran underwent numerous historical ruptures: the inauguration of reforms in the period of Abbas Mirza; the period of comprehensive reform in the times of Mirza Taghi Khan; the pursuit of progress or historical development; the time of *tajadud* (modernity) and the movement or time of Sepahsalar, these experiences formed the genesis of the ideology of the constitutional movement.[12]

This account successfully charts the history of the reform movement that gave rise to the ideas of the Constitutional Revolution, and the many intellectual currents formed in this process. Yet even though Adami'yat points out some very critical elements in the emergence of modern ideas and intellectual discourses in the second part of the nineteenth century, this historical narrative of the movement lacks complexity.

One should examine the historical context for reforms in Iran along with its corresponding regional and more global interactions and influences in order to explain adequately the content of the "Constitutional Revolution." This broader preview illuminates several important aspects of the situation which the preceding accounts, though basically correct within their limits, fail to consider. Within the Iranian context the role of the clergy was decidedly ambiguous with regard to the constitutional movement, and there is no simple way to categorize their participation along modern or anti-modern lines. Second, the stimulus for the constitutional movement came from a broader basis than the preceding accounts indicate, and it was not simply exposure to Western Europe that instigated a national drive for social transformation. Both local and global circumstances contributed to the form of the constitutional movement.

As I have suggested above, modern ideas were not imported solely from Western Europe. Geographically speaking, the new ideas came to Iran from several locations including Russia, Western Europe (particularly France and England), the Ottoman Empire and India. Mehdi Malik Zadeh, author of *History of the Constitutional Revolution in Iran*, cites the French Revolution and Iranian travels to Europe as major influences. He also notes the social democratic movement of 1901–05 in Czarist Russia and the Revolution in Japan for being critical factors in encouraging Iranians in their quest for freedom and the rule of law:

The inauguration of the short-lived Doma Assembly was a blessed surprise [*migdeh*] for the Iranians. The participation of the Russian people in their own self determination gave inspiration to Iranian Intellectuals and all freedom loving men in Iran, and encouraged them to prepare and instigate a movement for change.[13]

Political events in Japan, particularly the constitutional movement and the defeat of Czarist Russia by a nationalist Japan, had a notable impact in encouraging Iranians to strive against absolutism and for constitutional government:

Because Japan is one of the nations of Asia and in those times all Asian countries were living in darkness and oblivion, the coming of the shining star of a nationalist government in a far away Asian country had momentous influence in all countries including Iran. Iranian intellectuals looked at this great transformation and unanticipated progress in Japan, which was the fruit of a sacred tree of liberty, with amazement and exaltation and they hoped for a day when they themselves would be free from enslavement and proceed by the same course . . .[14]

Malik Zadeh gives evidence that the news of Japan's constitutional movement reached Iran through different sources and from different countries:

Habl al-matin, the constitutionalists' largest Persian language newspaper, published in Calcutta but banned in Iran, was secretly smuggled into Iran and obtained by nationalist circles. There was also the *Hekmat* newspaper and Egyptian journals and newspapers, which were published in Egypt by Zaim al-dowleh and dispatched to some progressive Iranians who knew Arabic. These were printing detailed accounts of the progress and achievements in Japan and were encouraging other Asian nations to pursue the principles and the route of this ancient state.[15]

Well-known leaders of the constitutional movement such as Malik al-Mutakalimin and Seyed Jamal al-din, the acclaimed orator, talked about the situation in Japan and the country's great advancements. Malik Zadeh goes as far as to suggest that "the constitution in Japan was an important factor in the making of the national government in Iran."[16] Yahya Dowlat Abadi, leader of the constitutional movement, also indicates that the news of Japanese victories over Russia were received with immense pleasure by Iranian intellectuals and students, who were encouraged in their movement against the Iranian government.[17] Another internal factor encouraging the movement was ethnic and particularly religious minorities, including "Jews, Armenians, Zoroastrians, and Babis," who are recognized as having been vital forces in favor of the movement for constitutionalism.[18]

In general, the Iranian intellectuals of this period were heavily and somewhat uncritically influenced by the ideas of the eighteenth-century

European Enlightenment, and to a lesser extent by the intellectual trends of nineteenth-century Europe. Cultural relations with France and England were very apparent and significant. Amongst the European intellectuals, French thinkers had the most influence and were the most widely read. France served as the Mecca of modern intellectual and political thought, and also enjoyed popularity because of its oppositional relation to Britain. Although Iranian intellectuals were attracted to English culture and political systems, as is clearly demonstrated in Iranian writing of the time, the British alliance with the Iranian ruling class, and their semi-colonial rule throughout the country, created, especially among the more radical thinkers, a love-hate attitude toward the English. In general, the French influence could be more readily used in critiques of religious, cultural and historical matters, while English liberal thought influenced economic and, more importantly, political ideas. There is no question that the Iranian intellectuals of the mid-nineteenth and early twentieth centuries were very much interested in and affected by the experience of the French Revolution, and that reformers felt a great deal of sympathy for its principles and aims. Mokhber-adowleh Hedayat, a historian of Qajar Iran, made the following observation about young Iranian nationalists: "[E]ach has a book about the French Revolution and yearns to play the role of Dante, and they are hot with fiery words."[19] Among the European thinkers who shaped the Enlightenment, the German philosophers enjoyed the least popularity and seemingly did not appeal to the Iranian intelligentsia. There were several possible reasons for this: it may have been due to the time lag in the Enlightenment movement in Germany, the more philosophical nature of the German intellectual debates, or because of Iran's closer relations with England and France at the time. It is definitely an interesting issue for further elaboration and investigation, particularly in light of the subsequent influence of German intellectuals in later periods of Iranian history.

The more radical segment of the constitutionalist movement was clearly attracted to radical versions of modern ideas. Adami'yat gives the following account of two radical thinkers of the period: "Mirza Aha Khan Kirmani was directly influenced by the ideas of western socialism; and we knew that Aburrahim Talibuf Tabrizi, having spent his life in the Caucasus, had knowledge of liberation movements and the ideas of social Democrats."[20] Akhund Zadeh was under the direct intellectual influence of Russian thinkers, having lived in Russia and participated in intellectual circles there. In fact, many Iranians acquired European ideas through Russian books they obtained while living in or visiting Russia or the Caucasus. Yahya Arian Poor, the author of a famous literary history of modern Iran, pointed out that:

Akhund Zadeh, who was familiar with the history and literature of Iran, studied the languages, literature, and philosophy of the West, and studied the writings of 18th century European authors like Hollbackh, Diderot, Hlosious, Voltaire, etc. He also became acquainted with scientists and freedom fighters of his time like Khajate Asodian, an Armenian writer, Malinsky the Russian Decaprist and others who were exiled to the Caucasus.[21]

In contrast, Mirza Aha Khan Kirmani adopted a more critical and radical attitude towards social and political issues: "[F]rom the ideas which were expressed in his writings, one can judge that he has read works of Descartes, Rousseau, Voltaire, Montesquieu, Spencer, and Darwin. His work also shows his knowledge of socialist and utopian movements of the 19th century."[22] Interestingly, intellectuals like Kirmani were introduced to Western ideas and writing through journals and writings from the Ottoman Empire.

We see here that the movement for reform and constitution was represented by a plurality of voices and visions about Iranian modernity. It is hard to try to explain the diversity of modernities among various Iranian intellectuals at this time. It may be that different geographical influences led to hybrid versions of modernities which were circulating in Iran at this time. Those who were influenced by Ottoman and Russian ideas imagined a more radical and critical modern project for the Iranian. In contrast, those Iranian intellectuals, such as Melkum Khan or Taghizadeh, who were directly influenced by the colonial British idea of modernity, offered a more rigid and totalistic vision of modernity for Iran.

But for all the richness, the diversity of visions and voices, the dominant trend in this movement called for the imposition of the Western narrative of modernity in Iran. This resulted in a cultural capitulation and a concession of inferiority to European ideas. It would be mistaken to view this as an accidental side-effect of accepting modernity. Rather, the cultural capitulation to the West was proclaimed with intellectual and political pride, and the liberal modernists of the time who theorized it eagerly claimed credit for the proclamation. The inability of the Mashruteh movement to be critical of Western ideas was problematic and came to be known as "the paradox of the Mashruteh discourse." The real practical implication of such a Western-centrist attitude came to light during the rule of Reza Shah. The Pahlavi state offered a brutal iron cage of modernity to Iran. It was the reaction against this vision of modernity which later led to an anti-Western movement towards a different kind of modern Iran in the 1960s–70s.

Most Mashruteh intellectuals perceived themselves as modernist and universalist, and therefore citing the writings of Ernest Renan, John Stuart Mill, or any other Western thinker or Orientalist was seen as an expression of the universalism of their world view. Moreover, it was interpreted as an alternative mode of thinking to more traditionalist and loyalist cultural modes of thought in Iran. The problem with this version of intellectual universalism (in fact closer to Eurocentrism) was its superficiality and intellectual pacifism, and its non-interventionism. Modernism meant imitating and surrendering to the West, and thus even for its progressive goals, the modernist project of this time lacked the intellectual vigor and spontaneity that a truly modernist movement should bring about and carry within itself. To think of Europe as one's mirror image and to capitulate to its views and contribution is less modernism than it is a crude form of worship. The outcome of this approach was a simplistic mode of thinking, making the Mashruteh intellectual less a producer of culture and value than a medium to express European ideas.

The central theme of the Constitutional discourse was the concept of a new science, perceived as the only genuine form of human knowledge, by nature both objective and progressive. The constitutionalists believed science to be chiefly responsible for the social, economic and moral superiority of the West. They viewed modern science as existing in opposition to the old science (religious knowledge) and as the only valid means of reasoning and human judgment. At the same time this positivist interpretation of social realities led to other problems – in particular, to the articulation of a critique of Iranian socio-political and cultural values and their historical significance. A dogmatic rationalism blossomed from the positivistic foundation, creating a mechanical and non-historical ideology which launched a clumsy and unnuanced critique of Iranian society and history. Some went so far as to repudiate and reject poets like Mowlavi and Hafez, because they did not correspond to the laws of science and scientific truth. Akhund Zadeh's critique of Mowlavi was done along the same lines. In fact, Newton's laws of physics provided the cornerstone for this statistical judgment.

Taking this background into consideration, it should not be surprising that some of the most prominent Constitutional reformers (or modernists as they called themselves) proposed "unconditional capitulation of Iran to European civilization."[23] They not only voiced their desire for this, but some of them even volunteered to advance it. Fereydoun Adamiy'at suggests that it was Malkum who proposed "Iran's capitulation to the Western values," and initiated the call for the "acquisition of Western civilization without Iranian intervention."[24] In fact, his political philosophy called for nothing less than an unconditional Iranian capitulation to European civilization. Another Iranian liberal intellectual and politician of the time claims a pioneering role for himself, saying: "I have been an initiator in promoting and instigating the acquisition of western civilization; and as everybody knows, I was the one who forty years ago insisted upon the capitulation to European civilization, which under the circumstances and milieu of that time may have been extreme."[25] He also observes that Taghi Zadeh, as an intellectual and politician, failed to communicate to the Iranian people that the only way for them to escape existing social ills was the "unconditional acceptance and promotion of European civilization and absolute capitulation to European customs, education, sciences, industry and ways of life without any exception."[26] This glaringly depicts the naive mind state of such intellectuals and seems closer to the words of a colonial administrator than a progressive (even radical) Iranian intellectual who wants to lead his country out of corruption and poverty.

Yet for all its internal contradictions and simplicity, it was precisely this political discourse that informed Reza Shah's reforms soon after the Constitutional Revolution. Surprisingly enough, most of the oppositional intellectuals of Mashruteh in some way participated in Reza Shah's rise to power and some of them became the state intellectuals under his reign, playing a significant role in the process which would later be called the "black dictatorship." It was this discourse that trumpeted for itself the role of ushering in the era of *Iran-e Noveen*, "modern Iran."

However, the culture and politics of the constitutionalist movement were not homogeneous or monolithic. Some of the more radical intellectuals of the time, like Kirmani, proved more realistic than the ones we have been describing. Yet in these times intellectual life remained generally dominated by the Mashruteh movement's critique of social and political ills in Iranian society and their emphasis on European values and ideas. That they were for the most part intellectually naive and simplistic should not make us lose sight of the reality within which their ideas were formed. The Mashruteh discourse was able to introduce some of the concepts and values of modernism into Iranian culture and politics and assisted future generations of Iranian intellectuals in articulating radical social critiques of a more realistic nature. At the same time, it is important to remember that the problems they created gave more traditionalist discourses a chance to discredit modernist discourses in Iran.

Today, any serious intellectual project whose objective is to accommodate modernity and secularism to the social and cultural context of Iranian society cannot afford to ignore this important experience in the quest for social change and political democratization. The constitutional movement gave rise to such secular intellectual figures as Malcom Khan, and to religious reformers who engaged in new interpretations of Islamic teachings and practices compatible with modernity. In the diversity of responses to the common theme of modernity, Iran witnessed the creation of a deep and enduring rupture in its political culture and intellectual discourses. The specter of modernity haunted the Iranian cultural environment, and there was no option of declining the issue or remaining detached. One can say with confidence that the central concern in Iranian intellectual and cultural discourses for the past 150 years has been the problem of reconciling modernity with Iranian culture. All of this forms a prelude and supplies the context for what is now known, and frequently decried, as the Islamic resurgence. The quest for Islamic identity is a continuation of the same national effort to accommodate modernity, only this time through Islamic reformation.

3   The crisis of secularism and the rise of political Islam

> People always quote Marx and the opium of the people. The sentence that immediately preceded that statement which is never quoted says that religion is the spirit of a world without spirit. Let's say, then, that Islam, in that year of 1978, was not the opium of the people precisely because it was the spirit of a world without a spirit.   Michel Foucault[1]

Introduction

We can only appreciate the perplexing meanings of the Iranian Revolution of 1978–79 by exploring such de-familiarizing statements. Building on my analysis of the Mashruteh movement, this chapter attempts to go beyond the prevailing interpretations that explain the Iranian Revolution as an extension of the historical tensions between "tradition" and "modernity."[2] I will look at the rise of Islamic politics as a new effort to come to terms with the challenge of modernity in Iran.

The Revolution was a historical turning point in the crisis of modern secular politics in Iran. Impeded by the autocratic rule of the Pahlavi state for more than two decades (the 1960s and 1970s), secular democratic politics were effectively contested in Iran and a new theocratic state power ascended to lead the Revolution in the absence of any other viable political alternative.[3]

The following analysis of contemporary Iranian political history will underscore three intertwining processes in contemporary Iranian socio-political life. The socio-historical processes that we will address in more detail are: (1) the formation of an autocratic state in post-1953 Iran, which successfully destroyed the already fragile democratic secular political institutions (political parties, unions, and Parliament) in Iranian society; (2) the social and psychological alienation experienced by Iranians as a reaction to the processes of "modernization" in the 1960s and 1970s. This led to the formation of a new type of ideology which utilized Islamic symbols and ideals to provide a new and yet familiar meaning to the subjectivity of Iranians. This new ideology had a very powerful populist

65

appeal, and associated itself with ideas of community, social justice, and involvement.[4] (3) The transformation of the Shi'i hierarchy and the construction of a new Islamic ideology which evolved into a viable political alternative to the ruling regime, and was able to allure a broad segment of Iranian society. These processes are treated as the critical factors in the accumulation of contradictions that in turn resulted in the political and discursive hegemony of political Islam in post-revolutionary Iran.

The articulation of these processes in the revolutionary conjuncture molded the character of the Revolution and helped the final outcome of political hegemony within it. Therefore, the dominance of political Islam in the course of the Revolution had little to do with the myth of a "return" to Islam. Many other mediums and forces were involved in generating an ambience where Islamic discourse could become dominant. For example, secular, liberal/nationalist and radical/leftist organizations provided intellectual, institutional, and other crucial resources for the making of the Revolution. They were critical in the mobilization of the revolutionary movement, they articulated a critique of the old regime, and they participated in the everyday revolutionary process.

The decline of democratic secularism (1941–53)

It has been argued that "Islamic revivalism can best be understood as a reaction to a crisis in the modern secular state. This crisis may be defined as 'state exhaustion.'"[5] Others have suggested that the current rise of the Islamic movement is largely due to "the fragile foundation of secularism" in Islamic societies.[6] In the case of Iran both of the above factors are present. The fragile secular-democratic institutions in Iran never enjoyed a firm and viable foundation, and could hardly withstand any serious challenge because they were routinely undermined by an autocratic state.[7] As M. Bayat, an Iranian historian, has acutely observed: "The 1978 Revolution has pointed out the most fundamental weakness of Iranian political life in modern times – namely, the absence of a secular, nationalist ideology strong enough to sustain a war on two fronts: both against the absolutist regime of the Pahlavis, and against the predominant clerical presence in politics."[8] In the following account I outline the rise and decline of secular democratic institutions.

The post-Reza Shah period (1941–53) provided Iran with a rare historical opportunity to construct the democratic political structure and secular pluralist culture that the country had strived for so long to achieve. During this interval, and in spite of its ups and downs, Iran witnessed political and cultural practices and intellectual achievements unprecedented in its entire modern history.

Soon after the fall of Reza Shah (1926–40), workers' unions were formed, new political parties were organized, and Parliament (which in the previous years had worked as the regime's rubber stamp) was restored to its proper role in the national state of affairs.[9] Iranian intellectuals initiated new forms of creative and artistic experimentation.[10] The print media was revitalized,[11] and the number of Iranian periodicals in publication increased from 41 to 582 after the fall of Reza Shah.[12] There was a progressive shift from family, clan, tribe, sect, ethnic group, and other forms of traditional (horizontal) social organization and solidarity to modern (vertical) forms of organization based on class, occupation, and other secular social stratifications.[13] People participated in a widespread renewal of political parties, unions, guilds, and many other associations and voluntary societies. The urban middle strata, workers, women, and intellectuals experienced a surge of collective participation. In summary, a very impressive social transformation of public life and culture evolved.

The unions

The popularity and activities of various forms of trade union and other professional associations and organizations played a very important role in molding secular institutions in this period. Workers, civil servants, professionals, and other social groups – including women, ethnic and religious minorities, artists, intellectuals, and students – organized themselves in numerous unions and other social, political or cultural associations. The whole phenomenon of unionization in this period mirrored the interests and aspirations of large segments of Iranian society to control their own fate and to voice their needs and goals through autonomous institutions.

The union movement surfaced immediately after Reza Shah's downfall. By the summer of 1942, several labor organizations united to form the Council of United Workers, representing over 26 industrial, craft, and white collar unions. In May 1944, the Central Council of Federated Trade Unions of Iranian Workers and Toilers (CCFTU) was formed. British foreign office documents record the number of union members at this time as 275,000, 75 per cent of the total industrial labor force in the country.[14] It is interesting to note that the rise of this relatively large union movement in Iran was not due to any massive structural changes in its economic development. The majority of the unions did not belong to advanced industries, as only a few industries existed in Iran at this time; however, the CCFTU had branches in all 346 modern industrial plants operating at the time. The rise of the union movement is primarily a result of the weakened authoritarian state, and the relatively democratic atmosphere of the period.[15]

Political parties

For the first time in the history of Iran, political parties and organizations were the dominant forms of political participation and citizen involvement in national affairs. The National Front, the Tudeh Party of Iran, the Democratic Party of Iran,[16] the Democratic Party of Azarbaijan, and the Democratic Party of Kurdestan were among the most prominent political parties. In a society with strong traditional bonds and institutions – ethnic, tribal, religious, etc. – political views, group association, occupational and other social attributes developed into important social units.[17] The mere fact that a new political ambience permitted such experimentation triggered a mass participation in the political process, despite the fact that there was no continuous tradition of modern political process in Iran. Political parties mushroomed throughout the country, and almost every form of political organization was represented. This in itself established a pluralist public space open to virtually every conceivable form of political ideology – radical, communist, liberal, conservative, ethnic, religious, regional and many other forms of political organization. This climate led to the formation of a political culture based on democratic politics and to a more open, communicative political discourse than Iran's traditionally authoritarian and non-participatory political system had ever allowed.

Among the active political parties, the Tudeh Party of Iran was the most well organized and was able to attract an important segment of the urban workers, modern petty bourgeoisie, and intellectuals. The liberal parties formed an umbrella organization, the National Front, which under the leadership of Mohammad Mosaddeq led the popular movement for the nationalization of the Iranian oil industry.[18]

The presence of these secular and democratic institutions should have provided Iranian society with a rare opportunity to enter a new phase in the political process. Given the relative invisibility of religious politics, there was every reason to be optimistic about the future of a modern, secular and democratic public life in the future of the country.[19] Inauspiciously, this did not happen and the process was terminated.[20] Several problems within the progressive movement led to agitation against Mosaddeq: the Tudeh Party's suspicion of his pro-American sentiment,[21] the Tudeh Party's unconditional following of Soviet foreign policies, the ambivalent nature of the National Front coalition, and the tensions between the radical-nationalist forces and the religious leaders.

Each of these factors contributed to the fall of the democratic move-ment.[22] The internal problems and strains within the secular radical-nationalist movement prevented it from acting effectively, and a coalition of conservative and reactionary forces (the court and the clerics, assisted by the British and the U.S.) was able to alter the course of events by staging a coup in August of 1953, overthrowing the nationalist govern-ment of Mosaddeq and establishing an autocratic state power.

The culture and politics of the pre-coup period, as charged and inter-esting as they were, suffered from several crucial weaknesses which made their historical continuity problematic. To critique the secular politics of this period we will focus on two major forces that virtually dominated the political activities of these years: the Tudeh Party of Iran and the National Front.

Immediately after Reza Shah's abdication and the collapse of despotic state power, different groups of radical intellectuals, the middle class, nationalist figures, long-time leftist activists, and other radical and secu-larist Iranians took advantage of the relatively democratic political atmos-phere and formed the Tudeh (Communist) Party of Iran in 1941. A glance at the makeup of its leadership and members in its earlier years reveals that the party was an umbrella organization where progressive Iranians with socialist tendencies organized themselves and participated in national political affairs. The party was initially committed to Iranian national independence, and applauded the Soviet Union as the champion of anti-fascist struggle and an ally of Third World and colonized coun-tries.

The party in its earlier years was a coalition of radical and progressive Iranians and perceived itself as such. However, during the course of its political activities a group of pro-Moscow individuals gained control over the leadership. As a result the party's initial orientation gradually changed, until it degenerated into a typical Stalinist party existing only to echo the politics of the Soviet Union in Iran.[23] For this and other reasons, the Tudeh Party made some tragic mistakes with grave consequences for the Iranian labor movement. For example, the party entered into "real-politik" on behalf of the Soviet Union, launching a campaign to help the Soviet Union acquire the oil concession of northern Iran. For this reason the party hesitated to support the popular mobilization to nationalize the British-controlled oil industry in Iran. In addition, the party used its influence in the labor movement to gain political advancement. These events led to feelings of disappointment and alienation from the party within the labor movement and among Iranian intellectuals.

Mosaddeq and the movement he incited represented a long and often difficult endeavor that the Iranian liberal bourgeoisie has historically been devoted to: the movement toward a civil society based on a legal system of government and a parliamentary democracy. The Constitutional Revolution of 1906–11 might have realized such a political system, but it was not long before the autocratic political power of Reza Shah destroyed it. Mosaddeq himself came from the liberal tradition of the Mashruteh era and was one of the most candid and ingenious politicians in that tradition that Iran ever had.[24] He was consistently clear about his goals and his ideas. He sought an independent and sovereign political system in which the autocratic rule of the state and the powerful individual is replaced by the rule of law.

Yet Mosaddeq underestimated the strength of his enemies, both domestic and foreign. The realization of the political system that he envisioned for Iran required much more than his sincerity. He also seems to have underestimated the complex processes that Iranian society had to undergo in its transition to a secular political system. Two areas in particular were problematic for Mosaddeq and both imply that he lacked an understanding of the complexity of his task.

The first is the fact that although he championed secularism and parliamentary democracy, he did not fully support the institutions that enable a democratic system to work and assure its continued existence. Secular institutions like trade unions, political parties, and other formal organizations never played a major role in Mosaddeq thought and politics. For example, while he tolerated the semi-legal activities of the trade unions as prime minister, he did not lift the ban on them. He recognized the role of Majlis (Parliament), but was forced to dissolve it.[25]

Secondly, he was involved with election campaigns, parliamentary debates, foreign policy affairs, and the role of political figures in politics, but not with the structure of the state. Although he planned to alter the autocratic structures of state power in Iran, he neither restructured the army and police nor helped to develop grass-roots organizations or other institutions to counterbalance them.

The political aftermath of the coup

The process of formation for secular politics and cultural pluralism endured a fatal blow with the successful coup d'état of August 1953. As will be shown, the events that followed the coup d'etat obliterated any possibility of real modern-secular politics in Iran. The returning Shah's most important political "contribution" was to successfully and effectively limit or destroy all forms of democratic and secular political organization and institutions.[26] The many secular institutions either outlawed or rendered functionally impotent included trade unions, student organizations, political parties and associations, and Parliament.[27] During the last two decades of the Shah's rule, no legal opposition political parties or organizations existed in the country. The state-run trade union only extended control of the state to the workplace. Parliament was reduced to a rubber-stamp institution. The regime was also very effective in crushing the underground opposition forces (i.e., guerrilla organizations) and other forms of non-legal dissent.[28]

The aforementioned changes in the political structures of society transformed the location and arrangement of political oppositional activities and protest. If in the pre-coup period, the oppositional groups and voices were located in such secular and democratic institutions as unions, parties, and the media, under the new autocratic state of the post-coup era (in the 1960s and 1970s), new political spaces for dissent emerged in the mosques, seminary schools, bazaars, universities, underground organizations, and groups organized outside of the country.[29]

The locational transformation of political activities in the post-coup period contributed to a process of desecularization of politics and public life in Iran. Let us examine the three important forms of political activity and their cultural effects on the formation of political culture in Iran during the 1960s and 1970s. The increasing leverage of traditional political spaces, i.e., mosques, hoseyniyyehs, seminary schools, and bazaars, on the political culture of these two decades radically altered the whole of secular and modern modes of political action. A more traditionalist (religious) and conservative political culture evolved and in the end dominated the national political scene. This transformation evolved through the introduction of Shi'i mythical symbolism into political discourse (the Karbala events),[30] and the adoption of Shi'i ideology and politics by secular opposition groups. Significantly, control of the social and cultural spaces was in the hands of the Shi'i hierarchy. It was within this context that new spaces of oppositional political activism sprouted and developed.

The second location of political dissent was inside the universities and other educational institutions. These were not religious spaces and in fact the leftist politics of the post-coup era dominated the student movement of the 1960s and 1970s.[31] However, during that time, when no other oppositional secular political institution existed, and there was therefore no interaction with outside political groups, the student movement remained an isolated political force with almost no relation to other sections of society. Consequently, a somewhat isolationist and particularly naive mode of political culture dominated the student movement and the leftist groups that sprang from it. The bazaar was perhaps the only other site of political dissent which did not exist under the direct institutional control of the Shi'i Ulama.[32]

The political activities of Iranians outside of the country (mostly in Western Europe and the U.S.) constituted the third source of oppositional politics in the 1960s and 1970s. The composition of politically active exiles consisted mainly of college students but also included some activists and political figures of the older generations. They were organized largely in different bodies of the Confederation of Iranian Students. The expatriate Iranian political activists were effective in starting a campaign against the dictatorial politics of the Shah's regime and in exposing the regime's repressive character to Western European and U.S. publics and governments. They were also successful in recruiting many young Iranians into the Confederation and oppositional activities.[33] Yet expatriate Iranian oppositional politics also suffered from the erosion of secular politics inside the country. There was no substantial continuity or organic link between the expatriate movement and the political culture of Iran. The expatriate movement was slowly and quietly absorbed into the politics of the Left in Western Europe and the U.S. and by the Third Worldist ideology of the 1960s and 1970s.[34] Even most of the National Front activists soon found themselves involved in leftist and Third Worldist politics.[35]

It was a good opportunity for the Iranians in exile to make themselves familiar with the political tendencies and movements of the larger world. This could have been a very positive cultural and political experience for them, but instead the politics of expatriate Iranians were transformed into sectarian politics marked by internal tensions, factionalism and unending intersectarian fighting. They paid little attention to the specificities of Iranian society and culture, and subscribed to one version or another of leftist or Third Worldist views. For this and other reasons, Iranian politics in exile created a political culture that could not contribute much to the enhancement of Iranian internal political transformation. The politics of exile in fact exported some of their characteristics from post-coup Iran. This was most clearly exemplified in the rigid and sectarian language and isolationist politics of the leftist movement in the 1980s.

These major spaces of oppositional politics could not offer a secular-democratic and modern political discourse and practice in the post-coup era. Most importantly, the Shah's policy inadvertently worked to the advantage of Islamic politics. The regime was very sensitive to any manifestation of oppositional secular political activity and brutally suppressed it, while the Shi'i clergy enjoyed a relative freedom of access to religious institutions and practices. In fact, there is some evidence that the Shah's secret police, SAVAK, never took the clerical threat seriously.[36] This does not mean that the regime worked to strengthen the clergy position. It indicates that the government was unable, or for reasons of their own delusion, unwilling, to destroy the Islamic institutions in which Islamic politics were most active. In sum, the secular opposition was always perceived as the real "danger" by the Shah's regime while the Islamic opposition was overlooked. In so far as this is true, political Islam benefited from the Shah's policies.[37]

Under the conditions that were instituted in post-coup Iran, no viable secular political forces were permitted to exist which might fill the void that would result if autocratic state power ceased to function. The Shah's attempts, at the end of his rule, to incorporate some liberal opposition groups into the government did not work precisely because the secular opposition was not politically relevant at that time and could not fill the power vacuum. Therefore, in this respect, the ascent of political Islam owes much to the fragile foundations of secular politics and to the political vacuum that the Shah's regime effectively created in the 1960s and 1970s.

Modernization and its discontent

Although Iran's encounter with modern ideas and institutions dates back to the mid-nineteenth century, the socio-economic relations in Iran remained predominantly pre-capitalist.[38] During the 1960s and 1970s, Iranian society underwent a state-sponsored modernization program that affected the economic relations, social institutions, and cultural patterns of the country.[39] The reforms of the 1960s and 1970s (in particular, the land reform program which changed the existing structure of rural Iran and spurred a huge migration of the rural population to the urban centers) profoundly transformed the urban way of life in Iran.[40] Traditional social structures, such as the guild system (Asnaf), family life, religious institutions and the spatial division in the urban center, all underwent a process of transformation and experienced severe tensions as a fallout of the modernization program.[41]

The modernization programs did not, however, encompass change in the political power structure, nor did they introduce cultural and political modernity.[42] On the contrary, through the modernization process, a more structured and powerful autocratic state power was built.[43] Thus, "modernization in some spheres of life occurred without resulting in 'modernity'."[44] The Pahlavi state's vision of social change neglected critical elements of modernity dealing with culture and politics: that is, the very complex process dealing with accommodation of social change in the context of the Iranian cultural and historical experience. Those, including oppositional intellectuals, concerned with questions of cultural diversity, local sensibilities, and individual and collective identities, found themselves unable to influence the direction of the modernization process. It seemed as if Iranians were trapped in an impasse. The future of modernization, in its blind and brutal rampage forward, appeared increasingly bewildering and confusing.

The economic and social relations of the society were changing without the participation of the people affected by these changes. In many cases, even the state elite did not have a say in policy making.[45] The Shah viewed the reform programs as "his" plan and "his" policy.[46] Thus, people who were affected by the modernization programs and policies were in large numbers alienated from the process, and in many respects an attitude of resistance to and even hostility toward modernization developed. Let us now explore two features of these changes that transpired in Iran in the 1960s and the 1970s: the crisis of urban life, and the shift in the Iranian intellectual paradigm from a secular modernist to an Islamic romanticist vision.

The social polarization of urban life

The most visible development experienced by Iranian society in the two decades leading up to the Revolution was the flourishing of urban centers and the new social stratification that emerged. Urbanization in the country provided glaring evidence of an uneven capitalist development and a corresponding unequal distribution of the society's wealth and resources among its population. The boom in oil revenues in the 1970s merely intensified an already existing gap between the poor and the rich. It has been reported that "Iran [was] one of the most inegalitarian societies in the whole world."[47]

The urbanization process introduced a new language to the culture of the period. New terms like *Shomal-e Shahri* (people who live North of the city, the rich) and *Jonub-e Shahri* (those who live South of the city, the poor) entered the Iranian language at this time. It was in the 1960s and 1970s that a new spatial division transformed the way in which Iranians lived in the cities. As an Iranian, from a very wealthy industrialist family, portrayed the metamorphosis of urban life in Tehran:

When I returned to Iran in 1967, my parents had moved to a new residence in an enclosed compound located at the foot of the Alborz mountains in Niavaran. In 1965, after another assassination attempt on his life, the Shah abandoned his administrative residential palace in the center of Tehran and moved to the north-eastern corner of Tehran near my parents' house. From 1963 to 1968, my daily drive from my house in Niavaran to my office on the edge of the Bazaar was a daily reminder of the great chasm developing between the northern and southern parts of Tehran – the one pseudo-modern, the other traditional.[48]

The urban population of Iran, which was 2,300,000 in 1940, increased to 15,710,000 in 1970. The ratio of urban to rural population, which was 21 per cent and 27 per cent in the 1940s and 1950s, increased to 46 per cent and 33 per cent in the 1960s and 1970s.[49] The massive rural migration to urban centers, and the changes in the urban structures of Iranian cities, affected the relations between people and their environment, their fellow citizens, and political power, reducing them to silent spectators of the whole process of modernization in the country. The few rich became more isolated from, and therefore less responsive to, the rest of the population. They lived, behaved, entertained, socialized and viewed society in a totally different manner from other Iranians.

New social groups were created.[50] The rural migrants who made up the majority of the urban poor were the unfortunate participants in the new urban social structure of the country. They faced multi-dimensional problems and experienced great anxiety and discomforts in their new environment. They could not comprehend new changes and could not cope with what was happening before their eyes. These newly uprooted migrants "experienced social isolation, and developed a sense of anomie."[51] They had to adapt to new and unfamiliar ways to make a living, a money economy, regular working hours, the absence of the warmth of family living, large numbers of impersonal contacts with other human beings, new forms of recreation, and a quite different physical setting, often involving new kinds of housing, sanitation, traffic congestion, and noise.[52] It seemed, to them, as if life had suddenly lost all of its meaning. The only exception to their feeling of estrangement from their new urban environment was their association with religious institutions. This is how a poor immigrant describes his relations to a religious institution in Tehran: "Nothing brings us together more than the love for Imam Husayn. My personal view is that these hay'ats [religious associations] have a positive aspect in uniting us and keeping us informed about each other's affairs."[53]

As the urban poor were enduring these conflicts in adjusting to the new urban environment, the state-sponsored modernization program did almost nothing to improve their difficult situation. In fact, state policies contributed additional problems to the existing complexity of life in the urban centers. This fostered a hostile attitude among the urban poor and other urban social groups toward modernization, and engendered their negative reaction to the imposition of Western-oriented culture which they correspondingly viewed as the root cause of their predicament. It is important to note, however, that the modernization program was, in large measure, blamed above all for not delivering on its promise of economic prosperity, social equality, and extravagant consumerism. In this respect, the Shah's modernization program was not criticized for being modern, but because it failed to achieve modernity in the fullest meaning of the term.

One of the reasons why the movement against the Shah and his modernization policies was translated into an Islamic discourse was that the only existing sub-culture to survive the political terror of the Pahlavi State were the institutions of Shi'i Islam. As we will discuss later in this chapter, Shi'i Islam at this time was going through a serious process of reform and "revitalization" which made it and its message very attractive to the disillusioned people of Iran.

Intellectuals and the romanticization of Shi'ism

The crisis of cultural identity and anomie were not confined to the urban poor and other urban social groups. Various sectors of the society – youth, women, the professional middle class, and the intellectuals – were all experiencing some kind of social or cultural alienation and displacement resulting from the changes that were increasingly transpiring in these years, and they too voiced their feelings of resentment and frustration with the political system. Moreover, Iranian intellectuals had every reason to be opposed to the regime. The Pahlavi regime was both arrogant and deeply conservative, and Iranian intellectuals had no compassion for either of these traits. "Thus in an age of republicanism, radicalism and nationalism, the Pahlavis appeared in the eyes of the intelligentsia to favor monarchism, conservatism, and Western imperialism."[54]

The post-coup period has been characterized by Iranian poets, novelists and other intellectuals as a period of "strangulation," "loneliness," "darkness," "fatigue," and "nothingness."[55] In the view of a literary historian of Iran,[56] "attention to the degeneration of culture and mode of life" – a revived consequence of the modernization process in this period – "compelled progressive intellectuals to espouse a critical attitude and to look for local answers" to their predicaments.[57] This shift of paradigm was reflected in different ways involving the turn to native cultures and solutions among influential Iranian intellectuals. Some, such as Al-e Ahmad and Shari'ati, turned their attention to Islamic traditions; others, including the Iranian poet Akhavan Sales, embraced the pre-Islamic Iranian heritage, and many others romanticized the rural life and created fictional and non-fictional works about life in rural Iran. In the words of one observer of Iranian politics:

The generation of the 1960s and 1970s had an ever-lengthening list of reasons for detesting the Shah. They included socio-economic grievances such as the failure of the land reform to raise production and bring prosperity to the rural masses;

the adaptation of conventional capitalist strategies for development and the subsequent widening of the gap between the rich and the poor; by the 1970s Iran's income distribution was one of the most distorted in the world.[58]

Two intellectual figures, Jalal Al-e Ahmad[59] and Ali Shari'ati,[60] best represent the feelings and the world views of the dominant intellectuals in the 1960s and 1970s. The anti-Western nostalgia among Iranian intellectuals was symbolized through the concept of Gharbzadegi (Westoxication). The romanticism of the Islamic and Iranian traditions induced a very hostile reaction against modernization as a Western-centered project. The romanticism of the Gharbzadegi discourse embodied an image of modernity that could only be realized in the context of Iranian national settings. However, such a critical attitude toward modernity is not a uniquely Iranian phenomenon. Ernest Gellner characterizes the same predicament in an eloquent way: "These societies are torn between 'westernization' and (in a broad sense) populism, that is, the idealization of the local folk tradition . . . the romanticization of the local tradition, real or imagined, is a consequence of the desire to maintain self-respect, to possess an identity *not* borrowed from abroad, to avoid being a mere imitation, second-rate, a reproduction of an alien model."[61]

This style of thinking laid the ground for a critique of "modernization" in Iran. Al-e Ahmad, for example, portrayed Iranian modernization (Westernization) as a disease that had infected Iranian society from the outside and debased Iranian life and cultural subjectivity. Al-e Ahmad, in another work, *Dar Khedmat va Khyanat-ye Rowshanfekran* (On the Service and the Treason of the Intellectuals), extends his critique of modernity in Iran to the entire modern intellectual tradition of secularism and social progress, condemning modern Iranian intellectuals for their critique of Islamic values and the Shi'i clerics. He traces the roots of Gharbzadegi to the mid nineteenth-century intellectual movement of secular ideas and Western oriented political systems.[62] Thus, the political culture of the period tended to romanticize Shi'i values and what was called the Iranian way of life and cultural practices. A second intellectual current, which dominated most of the 1970s, was led by a French-educated Shi'i ideologue, Ali Shari'ati. He, like Al-e Ahmad, came from a religious family with a clerical background. In a sense, Shari'ati can be seen as continuing Al-e Ahmad's critique of secular-political ignorance of the Islamic culture of Iran. But while the former concentrated on the critique of secularism and modernism in Iranian culture and politics, Shari'ati made every attempt to construct and popularize a "modern" Shi'i ideology as a response to the existing secular ideologies.

Both Al-e Ahmad and Shari'ati were concerned with the destructive effects of colonialism and imperialism on their societies and they perceived themselves as the defenders of local values and the people from what they perceived as Western-dominated Iran. Interestingly enough, the Gharbzadegi discourse had a very broad and populist appeal. The popular view is that the discourse of Gharbzadegi was a "traditionalist" critique of modernity and that it therefore set an agenda for the "return" to Islamic traditions and mode of life. I would like to stress that the apparent "anti-modernization" movement of the 1960s and 1970s in Iran was an attempt to reconcile with modernity in the context of the "Iranian" and "Islamic" context. More importantly, this was not a monolithical movement. Different social classes and groups participated in the movement for different and even sometimes contradictory agendas and outlooks. Only if we believe that this movement was an extension of "tradition" vs "modern" dichotomies may we ignore the diversities and differences within the movement which led to the Iranian Revolution. Moreover, as Reinhard Bendix has pointed out, tradition and modernity are not mutually exclusive and even the two revolutions of the eighteenth century are best understood as culminations of specific European continuities, i.e. that "modern elements were evident long before the modern era."[63]

The popularity of anti-Westernization and Iranian–Islamic romanticism became the focus of cultural discourse among almost all of the oppositional intellectuals.[64] It was even popular for the intellectuals who participated in the government to make anti-Western rhetoric and remarks.[65] The radical intellectuals, too, engaged in similar political discourse and under the banner of anti-imperialism paid lip service to Shi'ism and clerical politics.[66]

This movement, like many other populist movements, was full of ambiguities and inconsistencies. It was traditional but reformist, religious but blessed by secular intellectuals and the modern middle class. The anti-modernization project of Gharbzadegi attracted a broad but heterogenous coalition of the Iranian people who in one way or another were dissatisfied with the state of affairs in the country. The reasons behind the secular intellectuals' participation in the anti-modernism movement were different from those of the Shi'i clerics. Even among the religious activists within the clergy one could find a diversity of currents and views. Intellectual figures such as Al-e Ahmad and Shari'ati, who espoused the appreciation of Islamic values and ideals, were seen as Western-type intellectuals or Gharbzadeh in the eyes of the conservative Ulama. This was a tension within the movement which was carried over to the post-revolutionary period and even today it is a source of struggle and conflict within the different fractions of the Islamic Republic.

The Iranian poor and the intellectuals came to the same conclusion: the simultaneous rejection of modernization and the romanticism of local cultures, although the two groups may have had different motivations. The poor were frustrated with the uneven process of urbanization and economic changes, and the intellectuals were undergoing an identity crisis. This confluence of attitudes constituted a populist oppositional political culture with a very strong anti-modernization orientation and a shift toward religious culture and politics. On the one hand there was the isolation of secular politics and on the other the ascendancy of religious culture, values, and practices. Ironically then, the secular intellectuals contributed much to the rationalizing, popularizing, and even legitimizing of Shi'ism and the Shi'i clergy in the decades before the Revolution of 1978–79.

The politicization of Shi'ism

Having laid out the political and cultural setting of the last two decades of Iranian society, we now turn to an analysis of Islamic politicization. Political Islam, like any other form of politics, evolved over a period of time. But Khomeini's populist Islam did not evolve as an extension of the history of Islamic politics. A historical analysis of political Islam provides us with the opportunity to observe the continuity, but more importantly, a break in the development of Shi'i politics and the political role of Shi'i clerics in contemporary Iranian history.[67]

At approximately the same time that secular politics were in crisis, and the modernization program of the Pahlavi state was generating a backlash in the society, there was a debate under way within the ranks of the Shi'i clerical hierarchy and among religious intellectuals on the nature of political authority in Shi'ism and its relevance to the contemporary realities of the state and society in Iran.

Shi'ism arose from a controversy over the selection of a leader for the Islamic community after the death of the Prophet Mohammad in 632 AD. The majority favored the election of a close companion of the Prophet, Abu Bakr, as the Caliph, or leader, of the Muslim community. A small group of Muslims, however, opposed the selection of Abu Bakr and rallied around the Prophet's cousin and son-in-law, Ali ibn Abu-Taleb. The basis for Ali's leadership was what his supporters viewed as his hereditary right.[68] From this minority view emerged the various branches of Shi'ism (Zaidi, Ismaili, and Imami). This is why the concept of political authority is crucial to Shi'ism.

It is noteworthy that there is no distinction between secular politics and religious authority in Islam. "All political theories in Islam start from the assumption that Islamic government existed by virtue of a divine contract based on the Shari'a. None, therefore, asks the question of why the state exists. Political science was thus not an independent discipline aspiring to the utmost heights of intellectual speculation, but a department of theology. There was no distinction between state and society, or between church and state."[69] Although from its inception Shi'ism stressed the importance of its doctrine on the nature of authority and leadership, in practice Shi'ism was a minority current within the Islamic community throughout most of its history and did not claim temporal power. This led to structural tension between Shi'i doctrinal authority and its actual practices. This tension is also the source of two seemingly contradictory aspects of Shi'ism, a quietist side and an activist side.[70]

The concept of authority and temporal leadership of the community became increasingly problematic and prompted further internal controversies and conflict after the " 'great occultation of the Twelfth Imam.' Ever since the disappearance of the Twelfth Imam in 874, the transfer of his authority to the 'ulama' has remained a subject of controversy. For over a century, the prevailing attitude was staunchly traditionalist: no jurist or rather, no human authority, could use any legal norms other than those explicitly transmitted through the Traditions (*Akhbar*) of the Imams."[71]

It was under the Qajars (1796–1926) that a new development in the doctrine of authority in Shi'ism transpired, and more complex relations between the Shi'i establishment and political power evolved. Under the Qajars the Shi'i clerics were given the opportunity to rise to high levels of prominence in the nation's political affairs.[72] The focal point in the political development of Shi'ism of this period was the controversy between the Akhbaris and the Usulis on the nature of authority in Shi'ism and the role of Shi'i Ulama in it.[73] The controversy was an extension of the aforementioned perpetual and inherent tension between Shi'i doctrine and its practice. The Akhbari school represented a more quietistic and purely doctrinal interpretation of Shi'i Islam. It was traditionalist, holding that no jurist, nor human authority, could derive legal norms other than those explicitly transmitted through the Traditions and/or the Imams.

Under the Qajar dynasty, the Shi'i clerics' influence transcended their religious duties and moral leadership. The Shi'i Ulama, who enjoyed institutional and financial independence and religious prestige, became a powerful political mediator between the state (the king and the court) and the rest of society. For that reason, and because of their "neutral" position in the politics of the society, the Shi'i clerics were viewed by the Qajar rulers as the protectors of their kingship, while ordinary Iranians looked to them as political sources of power against the arbitrary rule and political oppression of the state. There are many indications that according to Iran's folk culture, Iranians were cynical about the Shi'i Ulama and their role in the power structure of society. However, traditionally Iranians do not perceive the clerics as the principal oppressor and in most cases they supported them and sought their aid.

It was not until the rise of the Constitutional Revolution of 1906–11 that the Shi'i hierarchy became involved in Iranian national politics to any large extent. The role of the Shi'i clerics in the constitutional movement is surrounded by controversy, as they intervened on both sides of the issue. What is clear is the fact that many Shi'i clerics participated in the movement and were instrumental in mobilizing the people for the cause of the constitutional government. It is also clear that an important faction of the Shi'i clerics, led by Sheik Fazlallah Nuri, vehemently opposed the movement and fought it.

The constitutional movement was a coalition of secularist and pro-constitutionalist religious forces. The first group of constitutionalists consisted primarily of liberal secularists who were to a large extent swayed by European ideas of progress and the secular constitutional government. The other group were the reformist clerics, who believed that the Mashruteh (constitutional) government was in keeping with Islamic traditions and practices and claimed that Islamic values were in fact compatible with democratic ideas.[74] The mere fact that these two groups supported the constitutional movement with different and socially contradictory motives injected a kind of eclectic tension into the constitutional movement, which later was transformed into the secular discourse in Iran. The motives of the Shi'i clerics in participating in the constitutional movement as a means of demonstrating the leading role of Islamic values in the process of social and political change were not consistent with those of secular intellectuals and politicians who believed in the European model of government, and its potential to reverse the backwardness of Iranian society. The involvement of Shi'i clerics in the political struggle that led to the Constitutional Revolution (both in support of it and in opposition to it) shows the activism and political intervention of the clerics in the "non-religious" affairs of society. However, post-constitutional politics in Iran developed into a more secular and non-religious trend. This was particularly true during the reign of Reza Shah.

During the first half of the twentieth century, the overall role of the Shi'i clerics in the politics of the country was at a low ebb. The first Pahlavi monarch effected some major structural changes in the political, legal, educational and administrative systems, which in practice had the effect of undermining the active role of the Shi'i clerics in legal and educational matters. In this period, a very powerful autocratic state structure controlled almost all aspects of political life in the country, with little or no space for clerical intervention in this sphere.

The post-coup era marked the transformation of the political and cultural life of Iran. Now that the radical and liberal parties and their secular politics were reduced to virtual invisibility, the only viable political force was a huge autocratic state headed by the Shah. During the transitional period of 1941–53, the Shi'i conservative leadership chose to stay out of the daily political affairs of the country and concentrated instead on building the structures and institutions of Shi'ism. Ayatollah Boroujerdi, the grand Mojtahed, did not show a great interest in politics and enjoyed a good relationship with the Shah's regime. At the same time, he made a great contribution to the advancement of Shi'ism by expanding the number of religious instructors and institutions that would later be used by the Shi'i clerics to mobilize the people and form a network for their political activities against the regime.

The returning Shah did not seek the assistance of the Shi'i Ulama in formulating and implementing his modernization programs, instead devoting his energy and the country's resources to building a strong army and a powerful secret police. The Shah did not take the clerics seriously as a political threat. He initiated several programs that conflicted with their views and even went so far as to clearly undermine their position in society. With the death of Ayatollah Boroujerdi, which occurred at this time (1961), the clerics lacked the leadership of a strong central figure who might unite them and present their case to the regime. At this conjuncture state–cleric relations were severely damaged by the Shah's insensitivity towards the clerics' demands. The Shi'i clerical leader who eventually prevailed changed the political course of the country. Ayatollah Khomeini organized a clerical movement against the Shah, and in doing so filled the gap that existed in the leadership of the Shi'i hierarchy. Khomeini took advantage of Boroujerdi's death and, in protest against the increasingly powerful influence of the United States in Iran, led a movement that was quickly defeated by the regime's forces. Although Khomeini was subsequently sent into exile, the clerical opposition achieved its goal of politicizing the Shi'i clerics and pushed political Islam in opposition to the regime.

With the growing discontent among the Iranian population with the regime's policies and the elimination of the secular oppositional forces by the regime's police forces, the emergence of a religious oppositional movement around Khomeini became possible. During the 1960s and the 1970s, this initially small group of clerical and religious intellectuals laid the organizational, political, and ideological ground for a movement that initiated the most important mass uprising against the Shah and his pseudo-modernist state structure.

The Islamic political movement waged its campaign against the regime and for the Islamic state from two different but critically important fronts. At the political level, the emergence of Khomeini as a prominent Shi'i militant voice granted political Islam a viable and determinant leadership and a cardinal figure to organize a political network of clerics who would congregate around him and his ideals of Islamic government.[75] It is interesting to note that when the Shi'i clerics proved to be the most organized group in the pre-revolutionary process many, including some Iranian observers of the anti-Shah movement, were caught by surprise. The clerics had spent almost two decades preparing themselves for such a development. Mixing political ambitions with religious traditions, the Shi'i clerics took advantage of their institutional position in the society and organized a movement at a point when there was no other viable oppositional force active in Iran:

Khomaini loyalists found their way into a network of Mosques in Tehran and other cities. After Khomaini's arrival in Iraq, substantial amounts of money were contributed in the form of charitable dues (the Sahm-e Imam) in Khomaini's name. Religious figures in towns and villages across the country collected these contributions as Khomaini's representatives and transmitted them to Khomaini's brother Morteza Pasandideh, in Qom. The funds constituted a source of considerable influence and were used not only to support clerics, Mosques, seminary students, and Islamic cultural activities, but also to fund opposition political movement.[76]

Khomeini's role was not confined to his personal leadership; he also provided an innovative political doctrine for the political Islamic movement. He thought of himself as the heir of the Usuli movement within Shi'ism and formulated a political theory justifying his political endeavors against the Shah's regime and for the Islamic state. He expressed these views in a series of lectures delivered while he was in exile in Najaf, Iraq. The lectures, given in 1969, were published as a book under the title of *Velayat-e Faghih*.[77] The book presented the essential ideas about the concept of state and society according to political Shi'i Islam. It included Khomeini's critique of modernization and secularism in Iran under the Pahlavi, constructed a Shi'i concept of an Islamic state, and finally, justified the leading role of the clerical class in an Islamic community.[78]

At the same time that Khomeini and his clerical associates were actively organizing their movement, a second front molded by other Shi'i scholars and intellectuals waged a "war of position" against the regime and formulated a Shi'i ideology that they believed corresponded to the reality of contemporary Iran. The effects of this second movement in the development of the political Islam in Iran may have been less visible than the first one, but it was crucially important in terms of popularizing the politics of Shi'ism and attracting youth and the middle class. There were several highlights within the Islamic intellectual movement of this period. One was the publication of *An Inquiry into Marja'yyat and Religious Institutions*, the other was the three volumes of *Guftar-e Mah* (monthly discourse), and yet another notable event was the publication of the *Maktab-e Tashayo* (the School of Shi'ism).[79] Still another turning point in Shi'i intellectual activity was the opening of a new Islamic Center, the *Hoseyniyyeh-ye Ershad* in northern Tehran. All of these developments deserve careful attention and analysis if one is to evade simplistic generalization and naive conclusions about the rise of Islamic politics and the Iranian Revolution.

Reform in Shi'i institutions

Although here we emphasize the unity of the Islamic political movement, it should be noted that this was not an absolutely coherent movement. Many of the tensions and differences of political conviction which surfaced in public after the Revolution can be detected in the discussions and reform programs of this period. Three specific currents of Islamic thought can be observed: the more conservative and theocratically oriented currents (Motahhari, Beheshti, and other Shi'i clerics), a liberal tendency (Bazargan, Taleghani, Zanjani, Shabastri), and a more radical current (Shariati, and the Mojahedin).

Immediately after the death of Ayatollah Boroujerdi in the spring of 1961, a group of politically minded Shi'i clerics and lay intellectuals took advantage of the vacuum created as a result of the absence of a *sole marja'-i taglid* (source of emulation), and initiated a series of discussions on the nature of clerical leadership and the Shi'i religious institution in lieu of the modernization of Iranian society. These lectures were later published in a book entitled *An Inquiry into Marja'yyat and Religious Institutions*, in the winter of 1962.[80] An introductory essay to the book by the Islamic Association of Iran,[81] which organized these discussions, stated that: "It is perhaps unprecedented in the Shi'i world that such systematic attention, collective analysis and elaboration has been applied to the past, and that investigation of the present situation and the future development of the issue of Marja'iyat has been given such forceful attention."[82] This book has also been pictured as the most important work published in Iran in the past fifty years.[83]

With the death of Ayatollah Boroujerdi, the clerical activists and politically oriented religious intellectuals perceived the lack of internal resistance to their political program. They were prepared to launch a campaign to politicize the Shi'i clerics and to formulate a political theory compatible with Iranian society in accordance with their political objectives.

The composition of the participants in the discussions is in itself very significant. They were Morteza Motahhari, the most prominent ideologue of the Islamic Republic; Allameh Tabataba'i, the prominent Shi'i theologian and Motahhari's mentor; Mohamad Beheshti, the second most important political figure of the Islamic Republic in post-revolutionary Iran; Mohamad Taleghani, a prominent nationalist clerical figure in Shi'i politics of Iran in the 1960s–70s; Mehdi Bazargan, a long-time nationalist religious activist and the first prime minister of the Islamic Republic; Abu al-Fazl Zanjani, a liberal clerical activist; and Morteza Jaza'iri, a member of the Shi'i clergy, active in the movement of Islamic politics. The fact that these figures later constituted the most important leaders of the Islamic Republic should not be viewed as coincidental.

An analysis of the contents of the lectures' proceedings indicates a deliberate endeavor focussed on the problem of reforming and modernizing the structure of the Shi'i clerical hierarchy and associated religious institutions and practices, and more importantly, the construction of a new theory of politics and political leadership by the Shi'i Faghih (jurisconsult). While the more conservative figures such as Tabataba'i and Motahhari were more preoccupied with articulating a coherent Shi'i theory of politics, the liberal participants, Bazargan and Zanjani, concerned themselves with reconciling Shi'i theory and practice with contemporary Iranian life. A glance at the topics of discussion in the book suggests that the following issues were most pivotal in furthering the course of political Islam.

The meaning of political leadership

There is a very deliberate endeavor to rejuvenate Shi'ism and politics. In this regard they underscore the importance of Marja'yyat (source of emulation) and valayat (deputyship). There are two essays on the issue of the legitimacy of clerical involvement in politics that are particularly noteworthy. Morteza Motahhari, in an essay titled "Ijtihad Dar Islam" ("Making Independent Judgment in the Interpretation of Islamic Law"), makes a polemical critique of the Akhbari School, using a very reformist and non-traditionalist language. He contends that Akhbarism was a movement against reason and that a very peculiar fanaticism and dogmatism dominated this school of thought. He even goes so far as to draw a parallel between the rise of Akhbaris in Iran and the sensationalist philosophy of the West.[84] Motahhari here is setting the stage for a more unconventional interpretation of Shi'ism and the concept of religious leadership. Tabataba'i's discussion of "Valayat Va Za'amat" ("Deputyship and Leadership"), however, is a far more articulated philosophical argument on the nature of political theory and the rule of clerical leadership in Shi'ism.[85] In this regard, Tabataba'i was the most prominent contemporary Shi'i cleric to introduce the concept of Islamic government and the leadership of the *faghih* (jurisconsult).[86]

Tabataba'i's discussion on "Valayat Va Za'amat" is based on his belief in the natural and intrinsic need (*niyaz Fetri va Tabi'i*) of every human being for guidance and supervision:

Each society, in order to endure, relies on a person or an official whose intelligence and will-power is superior to those who are ruled and who can control the will and mind of others and will safeguard and preserve the system that exists in the society . . . in a manner that a guardian is responsible for an orphan and the head of the family is responsible for the minor children of that family and the ministry of endowment administers the public endowment and the king or the president is presumed to rule among the people . . . this position according to which a person is appointed to take care of the affairs of others, as a real person administers his life, we call valayat.[87]

The intervention of the Shi'i clerics in politics is rationalized on the basis of the belief that Islamic teaching is a comprehensive system of beliefs covering all aspects of life, promoting the spiritual and material well-being of the individual and society. Hence, there cannot be a separation of religion from other aspects of life in Islam.

The principal dilemma of the Shi'i institution

Almost all of the participants urge a program of reform in the practices of the Shi'i institution and propose suggestions on such issues as financial conduct, leadership organization, intervention in the country's social and economic affairs, and the reorganization of its political practices. Motahhari presents an extended analysis of the problems facing the Shi'i institution and offers a plan to reform it.[88] His essay entitled "Moshkele Asasi Dar Sazemane Rowhaniyat" ("The Principal Dilemma of the Religious Institution") declares the conservative populism of the high-ranking clerics to be the central impediment to any reform program. Motahhari is confronted with a paradox. On the one hand he acknowledges that the Shi'i hierarchy is conservative and is cautious not to alienate the masses of believers by advocating major changes in the practices of religious affairs. On the other hand he cannot conceive of any reform movement in the Shi'i hierarchy without the blessing of the clerical establishment: "If we envision a reform movement being initiated by some individual or a group of people which the religious hierarchy is not prepared for and will not cooperate with, it is most unlikely that this movement will be successful."[89]

Thus, Motahhari makes an attempt to analyze and understand the root causes of clerical conservatism and to deal with it from within. The central issue for him is how the religious leaders and believers conduct their affairs, particularly on the financial level. Motahhari introduces the concept of *afate avam zadegi* (plague of populism):

Our religious leaders cannot render a leading role because of the plague of populism. They cannot lead the crowd from the front of the caravan and lead it in the proper sense, hence they are compelled to follow the crowd. It is intrinsic to the character of the lay people to adhere to the past and the ways they are accustomed to; they do not distinguish between right and wrong. Common people usually label any new phenomenon as heresy or carnal desire; they do not understand the principal law of creation and the circumstances of nature and therefore they object to any new ideas and merely endorse the status quo.[90]

Motahhari states the root cause of the clerical *avam zadegi*: "The root cause of all problems is the practice of sahme immam [the share of immam]."[91] Here Motahhari presents an argument that stands in sharp contrast to the common belief that simply because people voluntarily make financial contributions to their religious leaders, it symbolizes their submission and obedience to the religious institution and the will of its leader. Motahhari challenges this view:

The practice of sahme immam as it is conducted today has its advantages and disadvantages. Its positive aspect is the fact that its sole target is the people's convictions and beliefs. The Shi'i Mojtahed do not collect their budget from the state and therefore the officials of the government have no control over their hiring and firing. . . . On the other hand, this is precisely the weakness of the Shi'i clerical institution. The Shi'i clerics are not obliged to obey the state, but they are bound to submit to the taste and opinion of the faithful and must be attentive to their favorable opinion. Most of the corruption in the Shi'i clerical hierarchy stems from this fact.[92]

One cannot overlook the fiercely elitist and authoritarian logic that is implicit in this line of reasoning. Nothing which limits the arbitrary power of the Shi'i clerics is tolerated. In fact, views similar to this were later translated into practice in the Islamic Republic of Iran and contributed to its enormous authoritarian state power.

In summary, the goal of the participants of these lectures was to construct a Shi'i theory of Islamic government in the context of changing Iranian society and in the global context. On the one hand there was an attempt to present Islam as a total way of life, and on the other hand it was established that unless the Shi'i clerical leadership initiated a reform movement to make Shi'ism more compatible with the new realities of the modern world which were reshaping Iran, the chance of an Islamic government would be dim.

It is explicitly apparent that the lecture participants were more concerned with reforming Shi'ism than making it conform to the values and practices of early Islamic history or the Prophet's tradition. Thus, it is more pertinent to describe the movement as a political reformist movement which was trying to come to terms with modernity than a "traditionalist" movement to restore Islamic values in Iranian society.

Maktab-e Tashayo (School of Shi'ism)

A group of religious political activists formed this circle (*Mahfel*) to address the problem of "the revitalization of religious thought" and the "true path of Shi'ism."[93] A three-volume account of the proceedings of these lectures is the product of this religious circle's activities, published under the title of *Maktab-e Tashayo* from 1959 to 1965.[94] Almost all of the participants of these lecture series were prominent figures in the Islamic political movement, many of them future leaders of different fractions of the Islamic Republic.

The first volume of *Maktab-e Tashayo* was published in the spring of 1959. A partial list of participants and their topics of discussion includes: Allameh Tabataba'i, "Woman and Islam"; Musa Sadr, "Islam and the Problem of Class Difference"; Mohammad Falsafi, "Islam and the Contemporary Modern World." The most important essay in this volume is the introductory editorial, a manifesto of the group and entitled "Our Problems and the Causes of Their Existence."[95] The editorial opens with a brief historical remark on the great "scientific" and "material" transformation of the Western world, and the inability of the church and Christianity to make a suitable response and adjustment to the new situation, in turn precipitating a significant gap between "the religious leaders and modern scientists and therefore between religion and the new civilization." The essay then contends that when the Islamic world was confronted with Western civilization, "they [Islamic clerics] discreetly welcomed the scientific achievement of the West, as long as the aliens would not damage the independence and the integrity of the Muslims." It became critical to confront the West only after it betrayed its own intentions and assaulted the Islamic clerical establishment, and endangered it.[96]

In its conclusion the editorial attempts to present an answer to the crucial problem of what should be done. "Now that we live in a world where there are many different kinds of misgivings, deviations, moral decadence, class and institutional contentions, a huge gap between the clerical institution and the other classes and a thousand other misfortunes, what is to be done?" The answer is a very straightforward one: "A very powerful propaganda organization which is based on the sacred law of God."[97] They developed this masterfully and successfully over the next two decades.

The entire second volume of *Maktab-e Tashayo* (April 1960) is devoted to Tabataba'i's discussion on Shi'ism.[98] This in itself symbolizes the pivotal role of Tabataba'i as the mentor and the high-ranking Shi'i cleric who actively participated in almost all of the circles of the political Islamic reform movement. The book is actually a discussion that Tabataba'i had with the eminent French Orientalist Henri Corbon.[99]

The third and the final volume of *Maktab-e Tashayo* was published five years after the second one (April 1965). A look at the topics and the content of the discussion in this volume reveals that they were influenced by the changing climate of the 1960s modernization program in the country. Topics are more concrete, dealing with the everyday problems of Iranian society, and the analyses are more focussed and better articulated. Some of the essays and participants include: "An Inquiry into the Religious Affairs in Iran," the editorial possibly written by Mohamad Beheshti; "Koran and our Constitution," by Hadi Khosrow Shahi; "In the Path of a Propaganda Reform," by Mohamad Javad Hojati Kermani; and "Jahad the Ultimate Measure of the Development of National Struggle," by Jalale din Farsi.

The editorial essay in this volume is perhaps the most representative of the new level of analytical articulation by this group of Shi'i ideologues and political activists. Opening with an analysis of what religion is, the essay argues that:

Religious affairs are those issues which have the color of religion and as religion, in the form of faith, tradition or practices, endure among the population, whether or not they are in fact religion. They are habits and customs that evolved out of a specific predicament and have survived and/or ideas and opinions which have emerged because of particular misgivings; these apprehensions are the outcomes of historical, political, social, or philosophical factors or conflicts. These are tensions within thought which have gradually taken root on the deepest level of thought and morality in society, where subsidiary nature and instinct are at rest.[100]

This is conspicuously an attempt to treat the issue of religion and its social base in an objective and sociological manner. The editorial then goes on to make some methodological suggestions on how to gather information about religious affairs in Iran:

Questions should be made or personal interviews may be conducted. For example, five thousand people from different classes: urban, rural, inhabitants of the capital, civil servants, workers, bazaaris, poor people, middle income individuals, Vaez (preachers), clerics, educated, illiterates, old, young, male and female, people from the shore coast, people from the tropical areas and Kurds, Baluchis, Bakhtiaris, Turks, Fars, and Arabs.[101]

Ironically, at a time when Iranian secular intellectuals were abandoning secular values and modern methodology, and paying lip service to religion and tradition, the Shi'i clerics were making every effort to incorporate modern sociological methodology into their understanding of Iranian culture and traditions.

The monthly religious society

This "society" was a more formal version of *Maktab-e Tashayo* which concerned itself more with the daily political affairs of the country. In an introduction to the first volume of the society's lecture series, the goal of the society is expressed in the following manner:

There is an effort to cover subjects for discussion which do not deal exclusively with theoretical discussions, but with practical aspects of general problems of daily life; in particular, contemporary problems of religion are the main focus of attention. We have done our best to help solve the problems that Muslims are facing today, something which unfortunately has not been paid the attention that it deserves.[102]

The editors of the society conclude that: "[I]t can be said that all of the lectures have a common point, and that is the 'revitalization' of religious thought."[103] The revitalization of Shi'i thought has a very new meaning, that is, the transformation of Shi'i religious values and practices in such a way as to answer the problems facing the Iranian individual and society at this time. In other words, the decisive point in reforming and revitalizing Shi'ism in Iran is bound to its potential practicality in dealing with social and political problems within society. This is a depiction of religious thought closer to the concept of "ideology" in a secular sense than to a religious promise of human eternal salvation.

A look at the substance of these lectures reveals that the founding agenda of the society was to construct a "political ideology." The topics of the lectures are important evidence of the politics within Iranian society at this time. In volume one there are such discussions as: "A New Social Stratum in Our Society" by Mohamad Beheshti; "The Revitalization of Religious Thought" by Morteza Motahhari; "The Causes of the Decline of Muslims" by Morteza Jaza'iri; and "The First Step Toward Success" by Morteza Shabastri. Volume two (Lectures of 1961–62) includes: "The World is Ready to Hear the Islamic Appeal" by Imam Musa Sadr; "Ownership in Islam" by Mohamad Taleghani; "Islam and Social Relationships" by Mohamad Beheshti; "Method of Propaganda" by

Hossein Mazini. The third volume (Lectures of 1961) is the most explicit evidence of the group's attempt to attract Iranian youth to their political program and Shi'i ideology. In an introduction to this volume the editors emphasize the initial program of monthly religious lectures: "With the efforts of a group of faithful and benevolent youth, this society has been established for this sacred goal [revitalization of religious thought], and has been a very effective vehicle in illuminating and educating the young generation and introducing the true path of the faith, the traditions of the Prophet and those of his household."[104]

Yet despite this claim, it is interesting to note that the clerics and lay intellectuals of the monthly religious society paid little attention to the Koran and the Prophet's tradition. They were evidently more concerned with increasing the attractiveness of Shi'ism for youth and in making a political impact rather than merely spreading religious propaganda. Titles of some of the lectures in the third volume include: "The Leadership of the Young Generations" by Morteza Motahhari; "The Law of Causality in Human Science and Religion" by Mohamad Beheshti; "The Need for Candidness in Religious Leadership" by Morteza Jaza'iri; and "Islam and the Proclamation of Human Rights" by Ali Ghafari.

Shi'ism as a radical ideology

A very important development in the process of forming and popularizing the "political ideology of Islam" in Iran was the establishment of the Hoseyniyyeh-ye Ershad and the lectures of its central figure, Ali Shari'ati (1933–77). Although many participants of the previous religious discussion groups and societies had participated in the activities of Hoseyniyyeh-ye Ershad, this institution was in many respects different from all previous intellectual and cultural institutions of reform Shi'ism in Iran. The version of Shi'ism propagated by Shari'ati had a huge success in attracting a much wider audience than any previously established religious institute. Most importantly, Hoseyniyyeh-ye Ershad was able to attract youth – high school and college students – and the modern petty bourgeoisie, segments of the Iranian population which were, for the most part, newcomers to religious lectures and politics.

Previously, ideological/political debate and discussions had been confined to either small groups of individuals or to exclusive settings. The establishment of the Hoseyniyyeh-ye Ershad was supremely important for it enabled the movement to expansively encompass more people and to enchant those segments of the population which had heretofore remained outside of religious institutions and practices. The central figure in the activities of the Hoseyniyyeh-ye Ershad, Ali Shari'ati, came from a family with a clerical background and had spent a few years in France. Ayatollah Motahhari, who helped to establish the center, said this about the Hoseyniyyeh-ye Ershad and its goals:

In recent years our educated youth, after passing through a period of being astonished and even repulsed [by religion], are paying a renewed attention to and showing a concern for it that defies description. . . . The Husuyniya Irshad, a new institution in existence for less than three years, has made its task to answer, to the fullest extent possible, these needs [of youth today] and to introduce Islamic ideology [to them] such as it is. This institution deems it sufficient to unveil the beautiful face of the beloved martyr of Islam [Iman Hossein] in order to transform the true seekers into restless lovers [of Shi'ism].[105]

Shari'ati did his best to perform this task. His lectures in Hoseyniyyeh-ye Ershad attracted a large segment of Iranian educated youth. He was able to attract many people to Shi'i politics and ideology who probably would not have been swayed by a Shi'i clergyman. He was a passionate speaker who utilized rhetorical language and mixed it with religious emotions and radical politics. This made him without a doubt the most conspicuous intellectual personality of Iran in the 1970s.

Shari'ati articulated a brand of Islamic discourse which was most desired by the educated middle class of Iran. Shari'ati, as a personality, represented many of the qualities that the Iranian middle class could identify with. This was evinced in the way he dressed, always in a Western style business suit with a tie; in his language – he used a more secular and modernist Persian; and in his lifestyle – he grew up in a traditional religious family and went to Paris to study at the Sorbonne. While in Paris he was attracted to existentialism and Marxism, as well as to Third Worldist politics.

More importantly, Shari'ati's version of Islamic ideology had an anti-clergy tune, and he rationalized a kind of Islamic humanism in which there was no need for the Ulama to mediate between the believers and God. It was a more secularized Islam situated in individual preferences and choices. Shari'ati's Islamic reformism granted a sense of self-respect combined with a collective and national identity based on cultural authenticity.

This overall situation in Iran, the general dissatisfaction of the population with the Shah's regime and its pseudo-modernist programs, the isolation of other oppositional forces, and a construction of a Shi'i ideology and culture combined to the advantage of the politically militant Shi'i clergy under the charismatic leadership of Khomeini. The disenchanted masses of Iran were mobilized by the only viable political alternative and became members of Khomeini's Islamic movement.

During the 1970s, the popularity of religious activities became increasingly more visible and attracted Iranians from a broad spectrum of social and class bases. This was particularly true of the Islamic cultural activities at the beginning of the decade, and their organization and political presence in the latter years. During the 1960s and 1970s, Shi'i literature was published and read in increasing amounts. "Religious periodicals gained progressively wider circulation and religious books became more and more popular. A survey in 1976 found 48 publishers of religious books in Tehran alone, of whom 26 had begun their activities during the 1965–1975 decade."[106] The Islamic movement did not limit itself to traditional forms of religious activities and modes of propaganda. By the mid-1970s, a survey reported some 13 centers for the recording and distribution of tapes.[107] In fact, the demand created for religious tapes and cassettes in these years was so great that they became religious institutions in themselves.

These "cultural activities" had other advantages and were of crucial importance to the success of the Islamic political movement. The organizers distributed Khomeini's taped messages and planned massive demonstrations during the winter of 1978.[108] There was thus already a network of clerics and Shi'i activists based in various traditional religious centers and institutions which served as huge organizational resources for the Shi'i clergy. By 1974 there were 322 Hoseyniyyeh-ye type centers to commemorate the martyrdom of Iman Hossein and other religious events in Tehran, 305 in Khuzestan, and 731 in Azerbaijan. In addition, there were over 12,300 religious associations in Tehran alone, most of which were formed after 1965.[109] There are no reliable statistics available on the numbers of religious institutions and those who worked in them. One estimate is that, "The number of mosques and holy shrines in Iran are estimated to be 80,000 and the mullahs about 180,000."[110] Although these may be inflated figures, it nevertheless shows the institutional strength of the Shi'i political movement in a country like Iran. Therefore, it should not have come as an astonishment that:

[W]hen the first protest against the Shah's regime broke out in January 1978, there existed the nucleus of a Khomeini organization, a more elaborate network of mosques, Islamic associations and clerics sympathetic to Khomeini, large numbers of young men who had learned at Islamic discussion groups to regard Islam as a dynamic force for social change and opposition, and a vast reservoir of dissatisfaction with the regime which the opposition could tap.[111]

It is clear that the constellation of events and the political context of the Iranian situation, already in crisis, worked to the advantage of political Islam. The Shi'i clerics were destined, partly because of their previous activities and partly by force of "accident," to act as the dominant players in the contest of Iranian politics.

Conclusion

The most striking factor behind the rise and popularity of Islamic politics in Iran was that it articulated an alternative discourse to overcome Western-centric projects of modernization, enabling Iran to try and accommodate modernity within the context of her own historical and cultural experiences and specificities. This was an ideal, real or imagined, that no other modern movements were able to achieve (or even offer). Therefore, the hegemony of political Islam was made possible through capturing the "imaginary" of the Iranians in a way that presented itself as the only desirable answer to the country's dilemmas.

The hegemony of political Islam in the course of the Iranian Revolution was not a historically pre-determined phenomenon, nor an accident.[112] The appraisal of developments in the social, cultural, and political structure of Iranian history and society should render the proper perspective from which to view the Iranian Revolution; that is, in the context of political Islam's ascendance as a hegemonic force and the extension of its power over Iran. The crisis and decline of secular and democratic institutions resulted in a political vacuum in the country, and provided an ideal opportunity for the forces of political Islam to organize themselves and mobilize the population on their own behalf. In the absence of any formal institution or organization of political dissent, the Islamicists took advantage of the existing religio-traditional institutions to organize themselves and promote their political agenda, and mobilized the disenchanted Iranians against the regime. The Iranians, who could hardly identify themselves with the ideals of the Pahlavi state, embraced the populist Shi'i ideology as a source of self-empowerment and national identity. The Shi'i clergy became the leaders of the movement by offering a religious populist ideology as a safe haven to the masses.[113] Shi'ism, in this setting, offered a sense of social solidarity and individual identity to a population who felt alienated from the existing social processes and agonized from disadjustment to the emerging state of affairs in Iran.

In this context one can say that the anti-Shah movement was actually delivered to Khomeini and his political movement. There was no contesting force or opposition to challenge political Islam or to avail itself to the people. In addition, the Shi'i clergy was both organizationally prepared and anxiously waiting to clutch the historical movement and establish the Islamic State.

One of the most ironic lessons of the Iranian experience is the extent to which the autocratic state power of the Shah on the one hand, and the secular opposition forces on the other, contributed to the political and cultural formation of the Islamic movement. The Pahlavi state contributed by suppressing all forms of the secular democratic politics, and secular opposition contributed to the hegemony of the Islamic movement by romanticizing it, obscuring the nature of Shi'ism and supporting the clergy. Therefore, in the political and cultural context of the 1960s and 1970s, the Islamic state in Iran is a contemporary social phenomenon whose rise and dominance can best be understood in the context of the present crisis of secularism.[114] At the same time, one should not underestimate the fact that the Shi'i clergy made an invariable effort to construct a political ideology and organize a viable movement congruent to the realities of modern life in Iran.

4   Islam as a modernizing ideology: Al-e Ahmad and Shari'ati

Introduction

In this chapter I will discuss the discourse of authenticity through close examination of the works of Jalal Al-e Ahmad and Ali Shari'ati, two of the most influential intellectuals in the Iranian politics of the last half century. Both Al-e Ahmad and Shari'ati played major roles in the effort to articulate a local, Islamic modernity as a blueprint for revolutionary social change.

For Al-e Ahmad, this effort is sparked by disillusionment with the socialist Tudeh Party's capitulation to Soviet demands. Al-e Ahmad articulates a powerful critique of the hegemonic power of the West centered around the concept of "Westoxication" (*Gharbzadegi*). This critique attacks Iranian secular intellectuals as complicit in Western power, and incapable of effectively constructing an authentically Iranian modernity. Al-e Ahmad argues that a "return" to an "authentic" Islamic culture is necessary if Iran is to avoid the homogenizing and alienating forces of socio-technological modernization. Yet, the "return" advocated by Al-e Ahmad was a rather complicated political discourse. Ahmad's populist Islam would not reject modernization as such, but would seek to reimagine modernity in accordance with Iranian–Islamic tradition, symbolism, and identities.

Ali Shari'ati continues and extends Al-e Ahmad's critique by articulating a positive theory of Islamic ideology as a modernizing force. Convinced of the necessity of an ideological basis in the struggle for Iranian national liberation, Shari'ati draws liberally from Marxism to construct a populist and activist Islam. Shari'ati urges "good" Muslims to overthrow the corrupt social order, an idea which resonated with Iranian students and youth. Shari'ati's discourse does not seek to uphold binaries between East/West, but to foster a dialogue between the two in order to articulate a viable modernity.

Through these readings, the discourse of authenticity emerges as a dialogic mode of reconciling local cultures with modernity, rather than a stubborn determination to avoid modernity at all costs. Their calls for a revitalized and politicized Islam represent attempts to negotiate with the universalizing tendencies of modernity, rather than the gathering storm clouds of a clash of civilizations.

The ultimate contradiction

How does one reconcile the tension between the universalist claims and practices of modernity with the longing of modernizing societies to construct their own national modernities? Jeffrey Herf, in his study of German "reactionary modernism," points out that "[t]here is no such thing as modernity in general. There are only national societies, each of which becomes modern in its own fashion."[1] Even in the age of global modernity, the boundaries of national communities define, to a large extent, individual and collective identities. It is often assumed that the desire to modernize embodies a willingness to go beyond parochial bounds of native communities and identities. In practice modernization is often a preferable way to emphasize the uniqueness of national identities. Nationalist rhetoric exerts such a powerful mobilizing force because it communicates with people in a language that celebrates communal and national traditions, morality, and qualities at the same time that it promises future prosperity.

The authenticity discourse represents a cultural attempt to reconfigure modernity to make it more inclusive and diverse, and less homogenizing and totalizing. Here, the discourse of authenticity is presented as an attempt in reconciling the "universal" culture of modernity with the Iranian's local cultural context. The rise of the modern and autocratic Pahlavi state, modernization from above, and the cultural alienation of the urban and migrant population, composed important socio-political conditions of the "return" to a "nativist" ideology.

The focus of this chapter is the presentation of a narrative of authenticity in the works of two Iranian intellectuals who dominated the Iranian political culture in the 1960s and 1970s, Jalal Al-e Ahmad and Ali Shari'ati. Jalal Al-e Ahmad, a radical intellectual, was the central figure in the construction of the Islamic authenticity discourse in Iran. Al-e Ahmad builds this discourse around a critique of Iranian modernity. Ali Shari'ati takes up this critique, and builds upon it a positive and "practical" ideology based on Islamic and Iranian identity.

Al-e Ahmad: "return" to the "roots"

...Albert Camus, Eugene Ionesco, Ingmar Bergman and many other artists, all of them from the West ... all regard the end of human affairs with despair. Sartre's

Erostratus fires a revolver at the people in the street blindfolded; Nabakov's pro-
tagonist drives his car into the crowd; and the stranger, Mersault, kills someone in
reaction to a serious case of sunburn. These fictional endings all represent where
humanity is really ending up. A humanity that, if it does not want to be crushed
under the machine, must go about in a rhinoceros skin.[2]

Jalal Al-e Ahmad (1923–69) represents a generation of Iranian intellectuals who in the earlier part of their lives enthusiastically embraced radical
universalism as a solution to the ills of their country, only to abandon universal modernity and embrace a "local" and "authentic" solution. Al-e
Ahmad was a short-story writer and a novelist, an essayist and social
critic, a translator of French literature, and a political activist. His works
embodied the tensions between traditional Shi'i Iran and the secular
modernizing programs of the Pahlavi regime. His earlier writings, mainly
fiction, challenged the ignorance of blindly following Iranian and Islamic
values and habits. His latter works, as a social critic, focussed on developing a discourse extremely critical of Western secularism. Although the
political urgency of this task prevented him from becoming a sophisticated scholar or a deliberate thinker, he nevertheless was the most powerful social critic of the last two decades of the Shah's regime. In many ways,
his fiction was an autobiographical sketch of a man ripped between these
opposing tensions within himself. Some personal musings over his social
vocation reveal the split he felt between religious tradition and modern
intellectualism:

There is a difference between a teacher and a preacher. A preacher usually
touches the emotions of large crowds, while a teacher emphasizes the intelligence
of a small group. The other difference is that a preacher begins with certitude and
preaches with conviction. But a teacher begins with skepticism and speaks with
doubt . . . And I am professionally a teacher. Yet I am not completely devoid of
preaching either. I don't know what I am.[3]

Throughout his life, he tried to identify the inner struggle he felt with
various organized political movements, from communism to nationalism to existentialism, and finally to a resolute yet ambiguous Islamic
populism. The inner struggle, in his own terms, was a sickness –
"Westoxication" – and he once called his writing a "cry for help." But
many others heard in his writing the secret to revolutionizing Iranian
society along authentic and non-Western lines. His work produced the
basic vocabulary of the Islamic ideology, and his concept of
Gharbzadegi (Westoxication) represented a "secular" contribution to
the prominence of Islamic populism in the Revolution of 1978–79 and
in later years.

Al-e Ahmad came from a long line of respected clerics, and his family upheld a strong religious tradition.[4] As a child in the twenties, he experienced Reza Shah's consolidation of power over public life and his "determination to give his Iranian subjects a European look."[5] Al-e Ahmad's young life was split between the "ethical absolutism" of his father's religious household and the aggressively secular transformation of society at large. The family was reasonably prosperous until 1932, when the government deprived the clerical class of their notorial function and eliminated their income.[6] His father tried to resist these changes, and as a result lost his "official" religious position. Al-e Ahmad had to go out to work after elementary school, fixing watches and electrical wire in the bazaar. But he secretly attended night school throughout this time, hoping to complete his high school education.[7]

At twenty, his father sent him to religious school in Iraq so he could become a cleric, but after three months he returned to Iran to finish in secular school. This open defiance of his father was the first sign of what soon would separate them for nearly a lifetime.

In 1943, Al-e Ahmad encountered Ahmad Kasravi at Dar al-Fonun high school. Kasravi, a historian of the Constitutional Revolution, social critic and a radical anti-clerical reformer, acted as a midway for young Iranian Muslims who felt disgusted by the political weakness of Islam, but who weren't ready to join the Tudeh Party.[8] In the same year (1943) he translated a pamphlet from Arabic entitled, "Illegal Mourning." Years later he wrote about this work: "Would you believe it that religious minded merchants of the bazaar bought them on credit and then burned them."[9] Earlier, he had written a number of works on the reformation of Islamic ideas, which he never published.[10] Within the same year, he joined the Tudeh Party, thereby completely breaking all ties with his religious background.

The Tudeh Party had been established in 1941 when Allied occupation forced Reza Shah to abdicate his throne, and political repression was subsequently relaxed. At that time, Al-e Ahmad recalled, "political parties were spreading like mushrooms." He also remembers it was a time of deep national humiliation. There was no "killing and destruction and bombs," but there was "famine and typhus and chaos, and the painful presence of occupation forces."[11] The Tudeh Party emerged as the most effective organized political group in modern Iranian history and went on to preside over the political Left for more than a decade. It offered an ideology of "universal struggle" which appealed to many young Iranians. Al-e Ahmad was quickly recognized for his talent within the Party, and in 1945 he was sent to Abadan to organize industrial workers and promote the socialist cause. There he learned important tactics of political organization. By 1946, he had risen to membership of the Party's Tehran

Provincial Committee, and had the job of supervising Party publications. These positions allowed him great power, and he used the Party press to publish his own book, *Our Suffering*, which featured "socialist realist" stories depicting political battles of the time.[12]

In 1947, a crisis in Party leadership occurred over events developing in Azerbaijan. The Democratic Party of Azerbaijan seized power in the region in 1945, and set up an "autonomous state" under the protection of the Soviet Red Army. The Tudeh headquarters in Tehran officially issued support, but the event produced dissension within the leadership. Al-e Ahmad and another important member, Maleki, had been pushing for more democracy in the choice of Party leadership, and less blind obedience to the Soviet Union. The event provided the focus for this struggle. When the Soviet army remained in Azerbaijan, and Stalin began to demand oil concessions from the Iranian government, this split the Party between pro-Moscow and nationalist factions. Maleki led a small group of intellectuals, including Al-e Ahmad, to break from the Tudeh Party in 1948.

Al-e Ahmad's break from the Tudeh was prompted by a confusion about the relation between national and "universal" interests. He later criticized the Tudeh Party for failing to give itself a native and national identity.[13] At a time when the leader of the National Front, Mosaddeq, was promoting the nationalization of oil to help build the Iranian infrastructure, and profits from Iranian natural resources were being appropriated by Western oil firms, the Soviet demand seemed like merely another instance of foreign exploitation. For Al-e Ahmad, this made the Tudeh Party a traitorous puppet to foreign interests. This experience disillusioned him profoundly, and he later wrote:

There was a time when there was the Tudeh Party and it had something to say for itself. It had launched a revolution. It talked about anti-colonialism and it defended the workers and the peasants. And what other objectives it had and what excitement it generated! And we were young and members of the Tudeh Party, not having the slightest idea who was pulling the strings.[14]

Immediately after the split, the group lead by Maleki organized their own Socialist Tudeh League of Iran and tried to receive Soviet recognition. But recognition was not granted, and when Radio Moscow denounced them as traitors, the new party self-destructed rather than daring to oppose (what they considered) the "world's most progressive nation."

After this experience, Al-e Ahmad withdrew from organized politics for several years to consider new approaches to Iran's problems. In his own words, he endured "a period of silence"[15] and during this time he made translations of European literature. He considered his translations as political work, introducing key documents and concepts into Iranian national discourse. His choice of books reflects a need for affirmation in a time of solitude: Camus's *The Outsider*, Sartre's *Dirty Hands*, Dostoyevski's *The Gambler*, and Ionesco's *Rhinoceros*. All of these works contain existentialist themes of individual resistance to modern mass society. He also translated André Gide's *Return from the Soviet Union* as an indictment of the Tudeh Party,[16] and embraced Sartre's theories of a non-Soviet socialism. Later, in his seminal *Occidentosis: A Plague From the West*, he cited these "authorities" on the West as proof of humanity's future should the "Western way" prevail in Iran.

Al-e Ahmad's critique of the "West" is inspired by three different influences: (1) the encounter of Iran with the West and the history of Western domination and humiliation of this country by the British empire and by the 1953 U.S.-led coup which overthrew the popularly elected prime minister of Iran, Mohammad Mosaddeq; (2) Al-e Ahmad's personal involvement with radical and nationalist movements and ideas and his disillusionment with secular political culture. To him the Iranian secular intellectuals had no "roots" in the country's culture and were inordinately influenced by ideas and politics that were foreign and even irrelevant to the problems of Iran; (3) finally, his own reading of European literature and critical intellectuals such as Camus, Ionesco, Sartre, Junger, Heidegger, Kafka, Beckett, and their critiques of Western nihilism.

Al-e Ahmad's critique of the West (*Gharbzadegi*) is a complex and contradictory concept that cannot simply be reduced to an anti-Western polemic. Although his writings lack scholarly style or even historical accuracy, he nevertheless writes with personal passion, intellectual sharpness and anger, and as a victim with a "cry for help."

Al-e Ahmad's return to Islam was a quest to realize a national modernity in Iran. Simin Daneshvar gives an interesting biographical description of her husband Al-e Ahmad's intellectual conversion:

If he turned to religion, it was the result of his wisdom and insight because he had previously experimented with Marxism, socialism and to some extent, existentialism, and his relative return to religion and the Hidden Imam was toward deliverance from the evil of imperialism and toward the preservation of national identity, a way toward human dignity, compassion, justice, reason, and virtue. Jalal had need of such a religion.[17]

Al-e Ahmad's attitude toward secularism and religion underwent a number of changes, but remained fundamentally consistent all along. In his early writings, he was preoccupied with the ignorance and defenselessness perpetuated by religion upon the common people. This is made possible, in his scheme, by a lack of education. For example, a short story,

"Untimely Breaking of the Fast" (1946), shows that the religious fast of Ramadan is experienced completely according to one's social class. While the "prosperous brokers at the heart of the bazaar secure several years' income with a single transaction [and then] crawl into a cool corner of the columned hall" to relax for the remainder of the fast, the impoverished hero must slave in the dust and hot sun from morning until night. Eventually, deranged by thirst and the pounding sun, the hero leaves town to break his fast. When he returns, his wife and child have still not eaten, and then his wife's fasting becomes her bitter instrument of resentment and rage as she heaps religious insults upon her husband.[18] The fast, then, while designed to engender religious unity and moral discipline, becomes a source of petty strife and resentment among the poor, while the rich barely experience a change from their normal routine. If Al-e Ahmad's fiction says anything about religion, it asserts that truly religious society is incompatible with the class system. Class privilege turns religion into hypocrisy and annihilates any possibility of brotherhood.

In a 1949 story, *The Seh'tar*, Al-e Ahmad repeats this theme but also evokes spirituality as a state of human fulfillment, a connection to personal creativity and human community. Again, he asserts that such fulfillment is impossible in class society. But the presence of a "humanist religion" of fulfilled potential and brotherhood gives an indication of what Al-e Ahmad considered important about religion: much less the soul, the afterlife, the existence of God, and much more the realization of religious ethical ideals here on earth. As we will explore in more detail below, Al-e Ahmad's "return" to Islam in his 1964 pilgrimage to Mecca, as expressed in *Lost in the Crowd*, further indicates such an understanding of religion.[19]

In *The Seh'tar*, a poor musician plays seh'tar at rich people's houses. Although he gives them joy, he must "pay [them] an arm and a leg to rent" the instrument, and can never feel relaxed enough in their domain to enjoy himself.[20] Thus, although the hero has been naturally inclined to music since a young age, he could never bring himself joy from his own artistry. Most importantly, he repeatedly emphasizes, he has not "been able to cry as a result of his own music."[21] In Shi'i Iran, crying is associated with the weekly *rowzeh*, a ceremony where the faithful cry out of devotion to their faith. The musician in the story is denied access to the spiritual ecstasy which his instrument offers him. But eventually, through "backbreaking" work and at the point of starvation, the musician saves enough money to buy his own seh'tar. At this point, despite his physical illness, he undergoes a miraculous transformation. Although his "cheeks were sunken and his complexion sallow," he was "ecstatic and strode along blissfully" with "reddened cheeks" and a "hot" forehead. Now he can affect everyone with "his own inner and hidden joy," and most of all he can now "produce such excitement out of [his music] that he himself wouldn't be able to stand it and would suddenly start crying."[22] But in the next moment, as he carries his seh'tar into a mosque, a nearby perfume seller "wants to take out his slack trade" on the musician, and starts a fight with him for taking a musical instrument inside a mosque. In the fray, which is joined by a mass of equally angry people, the seh'tar is destroyed and with it the musician's "inner warmth" and hope.

This simple narrative contains a complex message concerning religious society and the class system. The hero's music is his happiness, his spirituality, and his connection to others (which might be seen as three terms for the same thing). But because he is poor, he can only prostitute his musical talent to make the rich happy. The work remains external to him, denies him, and makes him miserable. When eventually, near the point of starvation, he buys a seh'tar of his own, the ownership of this seh'tar fills his heart with warmth and ignites his religious soul. But because he had to buy spiritual fulfillment, it can easily be taken away from him, especially in a society of deprivation. Thus, another pauper (the perfume seller), frustrated by his failing business, resentfully attacks the musician and destroys his seh'tar. He does so under the pretext of upholding religious law, but in actuality with only resentment and anger in his heart. Thus, Al-e Ahmad lets us know how in a class system religious law is used as an instrument of petty anger, destroying true spirituality. Class society makes religion produce the very opposite of its intended effect, thereby nullifying its laws. In addition to becoming an instrument of resentment among the poor, it also becomes a commodity purchased by the rich at the expense of others' suffering. In such a society, the rich attain spiritual fulfillment, but only at the cost of others' pain. Thus, the foundation is evil, and the spirituality not truly real. Finally, the story implies the possibility of spiritual fulfillment for everyone beyond the system of property: only classless society could let everyone share in spirituality, and thus be a truly religious society.

In the period that he described as his "period of silence," Al-e Ahmad apparently decided to avoid politics. At this time he married Simin Daneshvar, a prominent writer, art historian, and translator, and moved to the northern part of Tehran to build a house. He later described the period by saying, "[W]hen one comes up short in the big world, you build a smaller one with the four walls of a house."[23] However, in the early fifties he was jolted back into politics for, in his words, "three more years of struggle."[24] The National Front, a coalition of liberal parties, was trying to nationalize Iranian oil. Al-e Ahmad felt his political hopes revived, and with Maleki, he organized the Toilers Party to support the effort. When that party split, he and Maleki formed the Third Force, a nationalist-leftist group with social democratic and Third Worldist tendencies. But in 1953 the CIA-backed coup overthrew Mosaddeq's nationalist government and the Shah was restored to power. After this Al-e Ahmad returned to political isolation, feeling disgust at the impotence of organized politics.

Al-e Ahmad used his second "period of silence" (1952–62) to perform his "ethnographic works," travelling through the Iranian countryside seeking to acquaint himself with the true masses, their culture, and his own true roots. His projects were amateur, but appealed to urban activists in Tehran who felt out of touch with the rural majority they were allegedly fighting for. When he recommended other intellectuals do the same, many heeded the call and performed their own ethnographic visits. For his first study, Al-e Ahmad visited Owrazan, the village where his ancestors had lived before urban migration. In these villages, Al-e Ahmad found a supposed "purity" which was lacking in the urban centers.

In his works Al-e Ahmad implicitly relates the city to the disease of Westoxication and equates the rural with the pure wisdom of the common people. Repeating this theme throughout his works, he creates a mood of nostalgia for a lost yet superior world, which newly urbanized and oppressed people eagerly embraced. The same year his visits began, Al-e Ahmad wrote his "Tale of the Beehives," in which the bees decide to return to their ancestral home.[25] This complemented his ethnography, which was explicitly soul searching. His investigation of the "onslaught of machine and machine civilization" produced this dismal anticipation: "The entire local and cultural identity and existence will be swept away. And why? So that a factory can operate in the West, or that workers in Iceland and Newfoundland are not jobless."[26]

The ethnographic labors prompted the university of Tehran to invite Al-e Ahmad to supervise their ethnographic publications. After a short period he resigned, stating that his aim was not "objective science" but self-realization for the Iranian people. Later, he wrote:

I saw that they wanted to make a commodity out of those monographs for European consumption and only with European criteria. But I wasn't cut out for this sort of thing. Because my aim in such an endeavor was a renewal of self-awareness and a new assessment of the local environment with our own criteria.[27]

This remark, of course, begs the question, what are authentically Iranian "criteria" as opposed to European? After all, ethnography is supposed to produce an "objective" representation of its subject of studies. These questions were answered in the culmination of Al-e Ahmad's self-discovery, his rhetorical masterpiece *Gharbzadegi* (1962). This is how Al-e Ahmad explains the discourse of Gharbzadegi:

I speak of "Occidentosis" [Gharbzadegi] as of tuberculosis. But perhaps it more closely resembles an infestation of weevils. Have you seen how they attack wheat? From inside. The bran remains intact, but it is just a shell, like a cocoon left behind on a tree. At any rate, I am speaking of a disease: an accident from without, spreading in an environment rendered susceptible to it.[28]

This laid the ground for a critique of "modernization" in Iran. Al-e-Ahmad portrayed Iranian modernization (Westernization) as a disease that had infected the Iranian society from outside and debased Iranian life and cultural subjectivity. In his other critical work, *Dar Khedmat va Khyanat-ye Rowshanfekran* (On the Service and the Treason of the Intellectuals), he extends his critique of modernity in Iran to the entire modern intellectual tradition of secularism and social progress, and condemns modern Iranian intellectuals for their critical attitudes toward Islamic culture and the Shi'i clerics. He traces the roots of Gharbzadegi to the mid nineteenth-century intellectual movement of secular ideas and Western-oriented political systems.[29] He goes so far as to defend the anti-constitutionalist clergyman Shaik Fazllulah Nouri, and calls him a martyr.

Jeffrey Herf, in his study of "reactionary modernism," points out that "Romanticism took different forms in different national contexts but everywhere it was part of modernity."[30] More specifically, "There was much in the German romantic tradition and its modern Nietzschean variants that denigrated the role of reason in politics and/or saw in politics above all opportunities for self-realization, authentic experiences, or new identities."[31] The anti-modernization romanticism of the Gharbzadegi discourse was similar to the German "reactionary modernist" movement's longing for the preservation of unique German qualities. Al-e Ahmad himself points out the affinity between his ideas and the German "romanticism." In the Preface to *Occidentosis*, he wrote:

I would like to thank Dr. Mahamud Human, who urged me to see one of the works of the German, Ernest Junger, a work on nihilism entitled *Uber Die Linie*. As Dr. Human pointed out, Junger and I were both exploring more or less the same subject, but from two view points. We were addressing the same question, but in two languages.[32]

For Al-e Ahmad too, the critique of Gharbzadegi was an answer to a yearning for an "authentic" (Islamic) identity. Therefore, the Shi'i romanticism was more an embodiment of the self-realization of a modern intellectual lost in the plight of modern life than a return to traditional Islam where concepts such as the self do not play a focal role.

The deepest revelations of Al-e Ahmad's life were expressed in *Occidentosis*. Having considered all the intellectual ideas which had moved his life – Marxism, nationalism, existentialism – he saw that their political value was thin compared to the organic power of culturally authentic Shi'i Islam.[33] Furthermore, he realized that every successful uprising in twentieth-century Iran had included the participation and support of the clergy – the Tobacco Revolt, the 1905 Constitutional Revolution, and Mosaddeq's nationalization of oil.[34] Only alliance with the religious authorities gave an uprising symbolic justification in the eyes of the Iranian masses. With this claim, Al-e Ahmad encouraged a belief that the "good era" of democracy under Mosaddeq depended on an alliance of religious and secular politics. Ultimately, he hoped to bring the religious and leftist opponents of the government into an alliance. In 1964, he visited Khomeini and gave him a copy of *Gharbzadegi*. At the end of the meeting, they shook hands and Al-e Ahmad supposedly said, "[I]f we continue to join hands we will defeat the government."[35]

Gharbzadegi opens with a dismissal of formal ("Western") learning. After proclaiming the world a division between East and West, the author claims "it is beyond the scope of this book to define these two poles in terms of economy, politics, sociology, or as civilizations." Instead, he evokes the superior peasant instinct with a clever metaphor: "Although one must secure exact data on an earthquake from the university's seismograph, the peasant's horse (however far from thoroughbred) will have bolted to the safety of open land before the seismograph has recorded anything."[36]

In our age, he begins, every ideal has perished to make way for blind mechanization. The ideological adversaries, Russia and America, have joined in a common drive to expand industry and secure commerce: "now all of these 'isms' and ideologies are roads leading to the sublime realm of mechanization." Soviet industry is as greedy as capitalist industry, and "Soviet Russia is no longer the vanguard of world revolution."[37] This union of superpowers has left the world divided in two parts – "the beat of progress is in that ascending part of the world, and the pulse of stagnation is in this moribund part of the world."[38] Thus, he sets up nihilistic expansionism as the determining force in world politics, preying upon the Third World and Iran at the center. His own word for such nihilism is "mechanosis." One effect of mechanosis is the destruction of local cultures, and "we [Iranians] have been unable to preserve our own historico-cultural character in the face of the machine and its fateful onslaught." Mechanosis is the "murderer of beauty and poetry, spirit and humanity."[39]

Only one defense exists – the authentic culture of Islam.[40] But, he explains, Islam has been turned into a harmless relic among many educated ("Westoxic") Iranians, who try to adopt European modes. He deplores a historically sealed Islam as a device of Western domination: "I, as an Asian or African, am supposed to preserve my manners, culture, music, religion, and so forth untouched, like an unearthed relic, so that the gentlemen can find and excavate them, so they can display them in a museum and say, 'Yes, another example of primitive life'."[41]

This is rootless, nihilistic Islam – true Islam must adapt to the times and battle against social evils. Al-e Ahmad argues that the clerics have historically been the "last citadel of resistance against the Europeans," but "since the onslaught of the first wave of the machine, [they] drew into their shell and so shut out the outside world"[42]

In fact, since the institution of the Pahlavi autocracy, the clerics had been relatively subdued. But in 1961, the clerical leader Ayatollah Boroujerdi died, and the radical Ayatollah Khomeini moved to fill the vacuum. The publication of *Gharbzadegi* coincided with Khomeini's mobilization of the clergy and politicization of the Shi'i establishment. The book contains many hints of the Islamic Republic to come, such as Al-e Ahmad's celebration of Sheikh Nouri, the "great martyr" who was hung for advocating rule by Islamic law. At the time of the Constitutional Revolution, "Westoxicated" liberals killed him to eliminate Islam as a political force:

I look on that great man's body on the gallows as a flag raised over our nation proclaiming the triumph of Gharbzadegi after two hundred years of struggle. Under this flag we are like strangers to ourselves, in our food and dress, our homes, our manners, our publications, and most dangerous, our culture . . . If in the beginning of the Constitutional era the danger brushed up against us, it has now touched our souls – from the peasant who has fled to the city and never returns to his village [to] the minister who seems allergic to the dust of our country and spends the year knocking about the world.[43]

The generation tainted by these developments believes that modernization and Westernization are identical concepts, and that Islam must be abandoned in the name of progress. Al-e Ahmad then issues a stark prophecy for these "Westoxicated" youths – the very same secular mechanization has already caused nihilism to triumph in the West: "They failed to see that the god technology had for years exercised absolute rule over Europe mounted on the throne of its banks and stock exchanges, and it no longer tolerated any other god, laughing in the face of every tradition and ideology."[44]

This is followed by a lamentation over the passivity of the Shi'i clerics, and a recommendation for them as the last power capable of resisting nihilistic mechanization:

[T]he clergy could and should have armed itself with the weapons of its enemy and countered the occidentosis of governmental and quasi-governmental broadcasting by installing its own transmitters in Qum and Mashad . . . If the clergy knew what a precious seed for rebellion against every government of the oppressors it had implanted in the hearts of the people with its doctrine of "the non-necessity of obeying the holders of rule . . ."[45]

The clerical establishment, Al-e Ahmad says, are a "government within a government," or a "secret government." They have authority over the nation, but have yet to awaken and realize that the most potent political force in Iran lies dormant in the Shi'i culture of the common people. Al-e Ahmad aims to make this politically mute everyday cultural power into a political ideology of revolution:

90% of the people of this country still live according to religious criteria, including the whole rural population, some of the urban tradesman, bazaaris, some civil servants, and those making up the country's third and fourth classes . . . they're all waiting for the Imam of the Age. Well, we're all waiting for him, each in our own way; and we have a right to because none of our ephemeral governments has lived up to the least of its promises, because oppression, injustice, repression, and discrimination are pandemic . . . It is by reference to this belief that 90% of Iran's population look upon the state as the agent of oppression and the usurper of the rightful role of the Imam of the Age.[46]

Islam, under these circumstances, is the only possible and authentic means to revolution. But what is the goal of the revolution? Al-e Ahmad outlines two undesirable options for the future, and then implies the unrealized revolutionary existence of a third:

[W]e, as a developing nation, have come face to face with the machine and technology, and without our volition . . . Must we remain the mere consumers we are today or are we to shut our doors to the machine and technology and retreat into the depths of our ancient ways, our national and religious traditions? Or is there a third possibility?[47]

The third option, and the only one for liberation, is the reconciling of Islamic tradition with industrial and technological modernity. Al-e Ahmad is never in doubt about the need for the "machine":

I am not speaking of rejecting the machine or of banishing it, as the utopians of the early nineteenth century sought to do. History has fated the world to fall prey to the machine. It is a question of how to encounter the machine and technology . . . Although the [West] who created the machine now cries out that it is stifling him, we not only fail to repudiate the garb of machine tenders, we pride ourselves on it.[48]

The "garb of machine tenders," of course, is Western culture and ideology. The problem for Iran, he contends, is how to build the machine without following the same nihilistic path as the West, which allows "technology and the machine to have stampeded out of control."[49] The "third road" beyond romantic primitivism and consumer subordination – the "road from which there is no recourse" – is:

... to put the jinn back in the bottle. It is to get it under control, to break it into harness like a draft animal ... One must have the machine, one must build it ... the machine is a means, not an end. The end is to abolish poverty and to put material and spiritual welfare within the reach of all ... Thus first we need an economy consistent with the manufacture of machines, that is, an independent economy. Then we need an educational system, then a furnace to melt and impress it with the human will.[50]

Just as in Al-e Ahmad's story of the Seh'tar, his political aim is to build an independent socialist economy which fulfills people's collective spiritual needs. Clearly, he believes Islamic society is capable of managing and using the machine in a superior way to the West, and of avoiding the Western crisis of the soul. The machine must not, as in the West, be an autonomous mover beyond human ideals, ideology and tradition (i.e., nihilism). Instead, it must be subordinated to the human ideal, ideology, and tradition of Islam. Although the ideals he purports may differ from those of Ernst Junger, there is implied here a similar adherence to a philosophy of will. In the West, nihilism grew organically from the culture. But in Iran, and most of the Third World, the nihilistic nature of the machine is an imposition of the West. Colonialism and imperialism imposed the nihilist culture along with the machine, as though the two were inseparable. Al-e Ahmad argues that Iran must Islamicize the machine by rooting it in Iranian culture.

Gharbzadegi (Westoxication) met with massive success. Gharbzadegi as a concept became the most popular concept that the oppositional intellectuals and critical public used to show their resentment of the Pahlavi society in Iran during the 1960s and 1970s. When, in 1963, Khomeini's politically mobilized clergy mounted the first nationwide rebellion against the Shah since the clampdown of 1953, it seemed to confirm for many the message of Al-e Ahmad's book.[51] Afterwards, Al-e Ahmad accused the secular intellectuals of causing the uprising to fail with their "imported ideas." He expressed this in *On the Service and Treason of the Intellectuals*, in which he condemns secular intellectuals as unauthentic: "That is how the Iranian intellectual has gradually turned into a root which is not planted in the soil of this land. And he always has his eyes on Europe, and always dreams of escaping there."[52]

Both books articulate a theory of "authentic modernity," as a critique of the West and a revitalization of tradition. Additionally, he defined politics as an issue of authenticity:

Even if politics is a science, it is one of those very loosely defined [branches of the] humanities, with its foundations on the latent collective consciousness from religion to superstitious behaviors, from language to codes of etiquette.[53]

In a strange way Al-e Ahmad appears to have constructed a pure mass consciousness and raises it as a banner of revolution. In evoking a mass consciousness, of course, Al-e Ahmad is also evoking a tacit "mass unconscious," which he can freely construct at his behest. The development of this ideology let him burst into his most important phase of collective action (and what better way to conceive of unified, collective will and action than by positing an unseen yet revolutionary and unifying mass unconscious?) since the Tudeh Party (whose unity was structured along class lines). But a dilemma persisted – although he had unquestionably recognized the power of Shi'i Islam for mass uprising, there still remained the issue of his personal faith. While he had brought public attention to the latent political power of Shi'ism, he was not the man qualified to lead those politics. Instead, he was caught between the hostility of the secular intellectuals and the mistrust of the religious opposition movement.

In 1964 Al-e Ahmad made a pilgrimage to Mecca, the test of his commitment to authentic Iranian culture and the opportunity to live out his convictions. It was a type of political participation beyond parties, strategies, and goals, a loaning of his body, instead, to a temporal ritual of the masses which has reproduced itself for centuries. Perhaps he hoped to fuse into the whole, and discover the higher truth in self-abandonment. He may have been affirming his belief that the Islamic community offers the best possible future for humanity (and Iran in particular). Certainly, his deed inspired many other intellectuals to perform the same ritual and write about it. But his written account, *Lost in the Crowd* (1966), shows that his predisposition as a writer forced him to retain his subjective individuality, and that he views the Hajj in almost completely human (non-religious) terms.[54] Ultimately, he went on the Hajj as a thinker, and looked at it in terms of possibilities for human society. In 1962, he had visited Israel and had been very interested in the Kibbutz system as an alternative form of socialist society. It is apparent that he searched for the realization of his political dream in diverse places. This is not to say, however, that he lacked a spiritual concern, or a special identification with Islam. It is to say that he appeared to understand spirituality as limited to the human world, that is in a "secular" mode.

Lost in the Crowd is a revealing "travel diary" as far as Al-e Ahmad's attitude toward Islam and religion in general is concerned. Al-e Ahmad decided before embarking on the Hajj to write about the "experience," thereby ensuring a self-conscious separation between himself and the other pilgrims. Michael Hillmann gives an interesting reading of this text:

In *Lost in the Crowd,* Al-e Ahmad presents himself as an unlikely and almost unwilling hajj pilgrim. At the outset, he admits that he is unclear as to why he is going. It is a question he repeats again and again through some fifty-seven entries in the diary covering the period from Friday, 10 April 1964 through Sunday, 3 May 1964. Not having prayed for the previous twenty-or-so years, he is self conscious about performing ritual prayers and being on the pilgrimage. In addition, he reveals in several places his recognition that secular intellectual confreres in Tehran will think his going on the pilgrimage foolish . . . Al-e Ahmad hardly contemplates or mentions Allah, sin, heaven, human soul, or the like.[55]

He refers to himself, at one point, as the "only observer" at the Hajj. By writing in a notebook that others cannot see, he makes visible the barrier of private and public. Plainly, as a result, he does not transcend his private self to join the others, and throughout the pilgrimage he (and others) are self-conscious of this. As he writes about his time at the Holy Shrine:

(I'm now sitting on the second level of the new outer corridor, and writing) . . . (A tall, fat, dark, swarthy man carrying an umbrella just passed, saying "Haji sir, mention me in your journal too – Qundahari of Mashad." "Sit down," I said, though there was hint of mockery in his voice. It seems that this sort of activity is distastefully ostentatious in this setting, though I've so far seen two or three others writing on paper, notepads, or what-have-you . . . From now on I must be more careful. Out in public writing?).[56]

Al-e Ahmad is simultaneously hungry for human experience in general and hungry to identify strongly with some group in particular, but he cannot have both. His dilemma is the classic peril of modern writers and intellectuals at "liberty" in their alienation from mass society, yet yearning to belong. The Hajj, as a piece of writing, became part of a "collection" of experiences from Al-e Ahmad's entire life, marking perhaps the paramount one.

Throughout the Hajj, Al-e Ahmad is burdened by the nagging of a radical conscience, which points out the unjust economic relations behind every holy shrine. He never loses the self-conscious political perspective which marks his individuality.

When it pleases God to have a house built on the surface of this land, he should have realized that land would one day fall into the hands of the Saudi government, and that its doors and walls would be covered with neon because of the exigencies of oil exportation . . . [As a result] even the House of God [has] become a common consumer for Pennsylvania. That means tainting even the world of the unseen for company profits.[57]

At another point, he uses the Hajj as an opportunity to muse over questions of European philosophy: "I was quenching my thirst with one of these 'colas' thinking of something I'd read by a European on the question of the 'individual' and society. And that the greater the society that envelops the 'self', the closer the self comes to being nothing."[58]

He launches from here into a long meditation on the "ultimate individualism of seclusion" and its parallels with the "Eastern 'ego' that forgets itself and its troubles . . . in the presence of the world of the unseen." Ultimately, he concludes that the "ego is sacrificed in isolation just as much as it sacrifices itself in society," and then raises a new intellectual issue: "[W]hat is the difference between existentialism and socialism?" His experience is conveyed in terms of Western secular philosophy. Once having descended from these speculations, Al-e Ahmad almost instantly launches into an attack upon the political contradictions of the Hajj:

God save us from the police, who are everywhere. With their hats, badges, and pistols . . . What would it be like if you didn't see the trademarks, emblems, and weapons at the mouth of the Zamzam well and you forgot that there too you're under government control? Even on the Hajj there's not a moment's opportunity to evade this ugly unavoidable reality. Oh yes. Unless the Hajj rites were to be brought under international Islamic control, and so on.[59]

The final sentence hints at Al-e Ahmad's concealed political agenda: to investigate the subversive possibilities of a mass politicized Hajj. Building subversive purpose into traditional structures of Islamic ritual was a successful tactic of the Iranian Revolution.

The final point about *Lost in the Crowd* is that he views the journey in terms of its secular human possibilities as a culture which provides collective meaning, as a hope of uniting Muslim peoples across international boundaries, and as an instrument for resisting the West. Throughout his narrative, he makes an argument for an international Islamic government and the abolition of monarchies.

In sum, Al-e Ahmad's account suggests that he goes as a writer, as a political thinker, and for the sake of mankind rather than God. It is possible that what Al-e Ahmad saw with the most excitement was the promise of a strong Muslim cultural identity. Al-e Ahmad's journey to Israel in 1962 had impressed him with the might of Jewish cultural solidarity – a solidarity not engendered in Muslim peoples by secular systems. While critical of the state of Israel for its abuses against the Arabs, Al-e Ahmad could not help feeling that a strong connection to authentic roots provided this modern nation with its power. He wrote: "In the eyes of an Easterner such as myself . . ., Israel despite all its flaws and notwithstanding all contradictions it harbors, is the basis of a power. And it is the first step in the promise of a future which is not that far."[60]

Al-e Ahmad's diary of his visit to Israel shows in a revealing way that his "authentic" theory of an Islamic Iran is very similar to a secularized Jewish society:

In any event, I as an Easterner [prefer] an Israeli model over all other models of how to deal with the West. How to extract from its industries by the spiritual power of mass martyrdom, how to take restitution from it and spend the capital thus obtained to advance the country, and how with the price of a short interval of political dependency give permanence to our newly established enterprise.[61]

Could it be, then, that the model political power for the great Islamic theorist of authenticity is Israel? He derived this message from Israel: by turning ancient religious structures into modern political weapons, industry, capital, and political independence can be achieved without the sacrifice of cultural identity. Indeed, Al-e Ahmad contrasts Israeli strength to secular Turkey, which he regards as having been robbed of its authenticity: "Let's stick to something, perhaps we can hold onto our identity. Not the way Turkey ended up."[62]

In *Lost in the Crowd*, Al-e Ahmad arrives at a revelation about individuals that proclaims them fodder for the power of mass faith and cultural identification. The manner in which he describes this, though he refers to Asia, implies that any cultural base might be as adequate as another, whether it be Christian, Islamic, or even Marxist:

This self, if it doesn't exist as a particle working to build a society, is absolutely nothing. It is not even a "self." It is that piece of rubbish or particle of dust, except (and a thousand exceptions) when it exists in the context of a great faith, or a great fear. Then it becomes the builder of everything from pyramids to the Great Wall of China, and even China itself. This goes for the entire Orient, from the fall of man until today.[63]

The equation of "faith" and "fear" as ontological movers for all mankind could easily spring from the pages of Heidegger. Initially, it blends the sublime (faith) with the mundane (fear) as though they were, on some level, the same thing. And then, across cultures (Egypt to China), the ontological impulse is presumed to derive from a common basis. The socialist understanding is mixed with religious faith, i.e., was it really faith, or fear, that made thousands of European workers spend lifetimes building the ornate cathedrals of medieval times? And does such a distinction matter, if we are considering (as an ideologue of authenticity) the raw totality of human labor power applied to a goal?

Whether Al-e Ahmad truly "rediscovered" Islam as a faith or as a cultural identity, his reason for reclaiming either seems clear: a conviction that Iranian politics is impossible without the symbolic power of Islam. Around the time of these experiences, he wrote:

One can be effective in politics, or in the affairs of a society, when you have weighed the degree of acceptability or resistance of that society vis-à-vis your ideas. And in order to achieve this measure, you should have known that society, its traditions, its history, and those factors that are essential in shaping its collective belief, forces that mobilize its masses in the streets, and then its silence and its sitting quietly at home.[64]

At the end of his life, Al-e Ahmad prepared an account of his travels to the "West" (Western Europe and the U.S.A.), the Soviet Union, Israel, and Mecca. He called it "Four Ka'bahs" – or "Four Directions of Prayer" – and gave an account of each place, its merits and flaws.[65] Mecca symbolized the possibility of Muslim renewal in the modern world, the final commitment of Al-e Ahmad's unsettled life. Despite his checkered past as a Muslim, the Islamic Republic praised his contribution to the revolution. In the early 1980s, the government named a boulevard, high school, and neighborhood in Tehran in his honor. On the thirteenth anniversary of Al-e Ahmad's death, the Tehran magazine *E'tesam* wrote that:

He was a Marxist, then [he found] socialism in the National Front organization, but eventually he realized that his lost soul belonged in righteous Islam, period. He tried to become alienated from himself and drown himself in the abyss of intellectualism. Motivated by confrontation with his pure Islamic mentality and his authentic Islamic nature, he returned to his true self.[66]

Ali Shari'ati: Islamic ideology as an authentic discourse

Now I want to address a fundamental question raised by intellectuals in Africa, Latin America, and Asia: the question of "return to one's roots" . . . Since the Second World War, many intellectuals in the Third World, whether religious or non-religious, have stressed that their societies must return to their roots and rediscover their history, culture, and popular language. (Ali Shari'ati)

Ali Shari'ati (1933–77) took up from where Al-e Ahmad had left off when he died of a sudden heart attack at the age of forty-six. In a sense, Shari'ati can be seen as continuing Al-e Ahmad's critique of the secular political culture of the time for ignoring the Islamic culture of Iran. But while Al-e Ahmad concentrated on the critique of secularism and modernism in Iranian culture and politics, Shari'ati made every attempt to construct and popularize a modern Shi'i ideology as a more authentically grounded alternative to the existing secular ideologies. If Al-e Ahmad's works focussed on the critique of Iranian modernity, Shari'ati's writings and lectures offered a positive theory of Islamic ideology.[67] He was by far the most influential Shi'i oppositional intellectual of the 1970s. Although Shari'ati died just before the Revolution in June of 1977 from a massive heart attack in London, he became one of its most celebrated figures. The

People's Mojahedin of Iran, the main oppositional movement in post-revolutionary Iran, adopted him as their ideological mentor. Shari'ati's ideas continue to be the subject of an important debate and controversy between two intellectual circles within the Islamic republic.

Raised as a political Muslim by his father, Shari'ati was involved in pro-Mosaddeq demonstrations and other nationalist political activities.[68] In 1959 he won a scholarship to study philosophy in France. This was a very political period in France, with the Algerian national liberation movement at its height. Shari'ati soon joined the Iranian Students' Confederation in Paris and helped with the publication of *Nameh-e Parsi* (the theoretical journal of the anti-Shah students in exile), and *Iran-e Azad*, a publication of the National Front abroad. He also helped to organize demonstrations in support of Third World liberation, wrote for the Algerian FLN (in English, National Liberation Front), and translated Frantz Fanon's *Wretched of the Earth* into Persian.[69] On one occasion he was hospitalized after receiving wounds from the police during a pitched political battle in the street. In Paris he belonged to the exiled Iranian National Front, a secular–religious coalition for democratizing Iran. He also closely studied efforts to synthesize Marxism and Christianity, including Liberation Theology, and he read the radical Catholic journal *Esprit*. This journal featured a Christian–Marxist dialogue, with writings by such prominent thinkers as Lukacs, Foucault, Fanon, and various radical Catholic thinkers. The journal introduced Shari'ati to Jaure's religious socialism and essays on Christ as a revolutionary egalitarian, almost certainly influencing his lifelong ambition to fuse religion with radical politics.[70]

While at the Sorbonne, Shari'ati attended lectures by Louis Massignon and Henri Corbin (two prominent Orientalists), Raymand Aron, Roger Garaudy, Georges Politzer (the orthodox Marxist philosopher), Michel Foucault, and Georges Guirvitch. He later wrote a chapter of his auto-biography on Massignon and his other teachers in Paris and titled that chapter "My Idols."[71]

His studies and encounters convinced him of the necessity for a single ideological basis if Iranian national liberation was to succeed. Rejecting Marxism, the alien ideology, he determined to create a full-fledged Islamic alternative, generously utilizing Marxist categories and concepts.

When Shari'ati returned to Iran in 1964 he was immediately arrested at the border and was imprisoned. He was released in 1965 and began teaching at the Mashhad University. He was soon dismissed for the radical content of his lectures, and then went to Tehran where he began lecturing at Hoseyniyyeh-ye Ershad. Although many others participated in the activities of Hoseyniyyeh-ye Ershad, this institution was in many respects different from all previous intellectual and cultural institutions of reform Shi'ism in Iran. What made it unique was the version of Shi'ism propagated by Shari'ati, and its huge success in attracting a much wider audience than any previously established religious study circles. Most importantly, Hoseyniyyeh-ye Ershad was able to attract youth, high school and college students, and the modern petty bourgeoisie, segments of the Iranian population who were for the most part newcomers to religious lectures and politics.

Shari'ati articulated a brand of Islamic discourse which was most appealing to the educated middle class of Iran. Shari'ati, as a personality, represented most of the qualities that the Iranian middle class could identify with. He always dressed in a Western-style business suit and tie and lectured in secular and modernist Persian.

Shari'ati's version of Islamic ideology had an anti-clergy tone. He articulated a kind of Islamic humanism in which there was no need for a professional clerical class to mediate between the believers and God. It was a more secularized Islam, based more on individual preferences and choices. Shari'ati's Islamic reformism granted a sense of self-respect, collective and national identity, and cultural authenticity.

Shari'ati's work spoke to the Iranian youth, particularly the underprivileged university students, those from the traditional middle classes, and educated young women from a more traditional background. Many of these students felt compelled to fight for social change and perhaps a revolution, but their religious and cultural background made such a commitment problematic. There was no explicit precedent for a Muslim social revolutionary in the modern context which would speak to the needs of Iranian youth, and the prevailing ideology, namely Marxism, was secular and openly atheist.

Shari'ati's Islamic ideology offered a theory of radical change which insisted, on religious grounds, that to be a good Muslim one must fight to overthrow the existing social order. Revolutionary strength, he asserted, could be mustered only by deriving ideology from indigenous roots, and not from alien Western ideologies. With this mix of authenticity discourse and revolutionary ideology, he bridged the inner contradictions for a generation of Muslim youths. But his project in effect amounted less to a categorical split between "Western ideology" and Shi'i Islam and more to a dialogue between the two, creating a modern revolutionary ideology for the Iranian context.

This achievement should be understood in the context of Shari'ati's larger project of reconciling the experience of modernization with Iranian traditional life. He wanted to give Islam a dynamic quality to let it survive – and triumph – in modern times. Because of this, he was openly critical of conservative clerics and Islamic doctrines, which he considered "backwards looking."[72] In his lecture "Modern Calamities," he vividly depicts the failures of prevalent forms of modernity as he understands them:

The modern calamities that are leading to the deformation and decline of humanity may be placed under two main headings: (1) Social systems and (2) Intellectual systems. Within the two outwardly opposed social systems that have embraced the new man, or that invite him into their embrace, what is plainly felt is the tragic way that man, a primary and supra-material essence, has been forgotten . . . Both these social systems, capitalism and communism, though they differ in outward configuration, regard man as an economic animal . . . [as a result] modern technological prodigies, who ought to have freed mankind from servitude to manual labor and increased people's leisure time, cannot do even that much . . . Humanity is every day more condemned to alienation, more drowned in this mad maelstrom of compulsive speed. Not only is there no longer leisure for growth in human values, moral greatness, and spiritual aptitudes [but it has also] caused traditional moral values to decline and disappear as well.[73]

This passage shows Shari'ati's central concern with the human (and particularly the Iranian) "soul" within modernity, and his conviction that Western materialist ideologies and culture are destroying it. It is interesting that there is little separation between cultural and ideological infestations from the West. Shari'ati intends to emphasize that the intellectual and social systems are fundamentally conjoined. Ideology is the vanguard of culture, and both communism and capitalism are ideologies which defend a materialist-atheist cultural base. As in Heidegger, the superpowers are externally opposed, but ontologically equivalent. This ontological dimension is important, because although Shari'ati sees modernity as characterized by warring ideologies, he will also raise the Islamic ideology from a mere intellectual option to the ontological necessity for mankind. The ontological dimension provides the criteria for authenticity, from which Islamic ideology derives an ultimate legitimacy beyond intellect and reason. The ontological validation of an ideology comes from a claim to authentic roots in the culture. The result is a collapsing of "culture" (i.e., the masses), "ideology," and "God" into one unified force. "God" – or the Heideggarian substitute "Being" – is extremely important for granting singular and ultimate authority to the mass movement. Ideology is the voice of this authority. In his lecture on the "Ideal Society," Shari'ati described such a mass movement as "a society in which a number of individuals, possessing a common faith and goal, come together in harmony with the intention of advancing and moving toward their common goal (of Islamic classless society)." He notes that the basis for unity is unlike fascism ("unity of blood or soil"), unlike communism ("sharing of material benefit"), and unlike "irresponsible and directionless liberalism," the "plaything of contesting social forces."[74] In another lecture,

"Humanity Between Marxism and Religion," he describes the emergence of the Islamic solution for modernity:

We are clearly standing on the frontier between two eras, one where both Western civilization and Communist ideology have failed to liberate humanity, drawing it instead into disaster and causing the new spirit to recoil in disillusionment; and where humanity in search of deliverance will try a new road and take a new direction, and will liberate its essential nature. Over this dark and dispirited world, it will set a holy lamp like a new sun; by its light, the man alienated from himself will perceive anew his primordial nature, rediscover himself, and clearly see the path of salvation. Islam will play a major role in this new life and movement.[75]

Despite the apparent dichotomizing of Islam and the West, Shari'ati took what he considered "most revolutionary" from both Western ideologies and Shi'i tradition. However, he was always certain to anchor the "Western" elements in Shi'i symbolism, as if that was their true origin and the West had merely produced an inferior copy. Marxism, for example, stole its revolutionary ideas from Islam: "It is the Marxists who have just learnt it from Islam."[76] Hence, Shari'ati's work was a type of revivalism: out of the dialogue he produced between Shi'ism and Western ideology, he "revived" Islamic tendencies which perhaps never existed, but spoke to people's contemporary needs in a traditional-symbolic language. He considered himself a modern Shi'i ideologue of the future, fighting for technological advancement and national independence. The major critique of modernity in his work is the attack on secularism, or what he called "the materialist cosmos," where "man turns out to be an object." In contrast, Islam shows "a fundamental bond, an existential relation [between man and the world], in regarding the two as arising from 'a single [sublime] origin.'"[77] His purpose is to bring this bond explicitly into the everyday political lives of Iranians, as a recovery of the ideal and unified Islamic society. Like Heidegger, he felt a pervading religious background had slipped away and left people atomized from the ontological bond to their community.

His lectures often did not depict Iran's domination by the West as primarily political or economic (as the passages quoted above show), but as a suffering from Western infestations within Iranian society. To be sure, he uses the specter of the West to target many elements within Iranian society, accusing them of succumbing to false Western ideologies and lifestyles. Extending the 'Gharbzadeh' discourse, he conveyed a historical vision of Iranian spiritual decline, with Western infestations destroying a society already in deterioration after centuries of deviation from the true path of Islam. The Western intrusion represents an ideology as false as the corrupted Islam which led Iran (and all Muslim peoples) astray to begin with, and both signal the need for a return to the "true Islam." Corrupted

Islam and Western infection merge into one with the Pahlavi regime, Western ideologies in Iran, and the conservative strains of the clergy. In this manner, Shari'ati helped to structure the political discourse of the 1970s around a binary of authenticity/inauthenticity within Iranian society. What was most ironic about Shari'ati was how he was perceived by others. He was regarded by the Shi'i establishment as too eclectic and careless in his interpretation of Islamic texts and history; the secular radical intellectuals viewed him as too religious and anti-Marxist to be a radical and enlightened intellectual; the Iranian regime labeled him an Islamic Marxist.

In his *Red Shi'sm*, Shari'ati presented the "true Islam" as a modern construction of the faith designed to bring out its most radical political tendencies. He crafted it in relation to a revolutionary predecessor, Imam Hossein, who died in Karbala in 680 trying to overcome the "degenerate and tyrannical" rulers of the time. On this basis he declared the dual threads of Islamic tradition: "the war of religion against religion," or "*tauhid* [religion of revolution] versus *shirk* [religion of the status quo]."[78] The historical struggle between these two Islams pits "justice and human unity" (the mass revolution) against "social and racial discrimination" (the state and its clerical supporters), but the "inevitable revolution of the future [will culminate in] the triumph of justice, equity, and truth." Furthermore, "it is the responsibility of every individual in every age to determine his stance in the constant struggle between the two wings we have described, and not to remain a spectator."[79] Thus, Shari'ati "created" a perennial yet historically repressed tradition which gave young Muslims the moral mandate to fight for the overthrow of existing society.

In the promise of renewal for Shi'i identity, Shari'ati found the most visceral axis for the politicization of urban Iranian youth. His highly inventive conception of history served this purpose. Yann Richard has pointed out that Shari'ati "disliked (studying) history" and "refers very little to it," preferring to evoke "an ideal original Islam, not its historic compromises."[80] Shari'ati freely blended his conception of history with an explicit ideological agenda. In effect, Shari'ati's historical work rejects the amassing of so-called "one-dimensional facts" (as with Western social science) and constructs a revolutionary purpose to bring the most radical elements of "self" to the surface. It is history which interweaves cultural self-realization and radical political commitment. In his scheme, "ideology" has an especially powerful role, and control of the ideological superstructure can even transform the socio-economic infrastructure. Ideology has this power because it derives its roots from the living culture of the people's history which is cast in the shape of "geography" (the desert),[81] and in the "symbolic language" of religion, "the clear and explicit language that expresses meaning directly."[82] In sum, the Islamic ideology transcends existence as a mere intellectual property, and thrives in the domain of ontological legitimacy.

Shari'ati's work also employed the axis of class very effectively. In his *Islamology* (1972), for example, he prioritizes the economy as the determinant of class formations, political dynamics, and cultural features, and names class struggle as the "motor of history." He elaborates a religious basis for this class interpretation, citing the story of Cain and Abel as the symbol of class struggle throughout history.[83] Class struggle, as its symbolic expression in the Koran demonstrates, is perennial, but its formation differs across history. Accordingly, he insists that the essence of class struggle for our time is the conflict between developed and underdeveloped nations, probably drawing this insight from his exposure to Third Worldist political ideologies in Paris. The positing of the "Third World revolutionary subject" in place of the "Western proletariat" as the class of historical liberation is one of his chief disputes with Marxism. Western regimes, he contends, have eliminated the revolutionary potential in their countries by letting the workers "buy into" the bourgeois lifestyle at the expense of the Third World.[84] This new global class dynamic calls for a redefinition of the "revolutionary class." In the context of Third World peoples, revolutionary consciousness must be defined along different axes than merely class-conscious classes which are formed by "religious beliefs, symbols, mores, customs, traditions, cultures, and popular notions of justice" as well as economic rank.[85] The progressive potential of religion is a crucial ingredient for successful class revolution in this context. It is this revelation that allows Shari'ati to center a mystical religious "identity" at the heart of any class politics in Iran.

The issue of class struggle is integral to Shari'ati's thinking, and he employs what he considers the most sophisticated system for analyzing it: Marxism. But for Shari'ati, Marxism is like technology or industry: an objective phenomenon to be taken by Iran and "Islamicized" from its Western roots. In his Marxist lectures of 1972, he broke Marx's life into three parts to extract the most useful elements: (1) the young Marx as an irrelevant atheist philosopher, attacking religion out of personal bitterness; (2) the middle Marx, a genius sociologist who uncovered the objective laws of capitalist economy, and revealed the solutions to social oppression; (3) the aged Marx, as leader of the First International, a compromised politician overshadowed in his failings by the brilliance of his earlier career.[86] According to Shari'ati, this third trend was intensified by Engels, Kautsky, and Stalin, who turned Marxism into a crude and narrow dogma of economic determinism. He accused Soviet and Eastern

European Communism of lapsing into the "iron law of oligarchy," and "vulgarizing" and "bureaucratizing" Marxism.[87] He accused the Iranian Tudeh Party of employing incorrect tactics in dealing with the people:

Not surprisingly, the public has formed the distinct impression that [the Tudeh Party] are enemies of God, country, religion, decency, spirituality, morality, honor, truth, and tradition. In other words, the public has come to the conclusion that these gentlemen have one aim: to destroy our religion and replace it with foreign atheism. The reader is now probably smirking and muttering, "these criticisms are cheap, vulgar, and common." Yes they are. But then the common people are exactly the kind of audience we are trying to reach. And most of our common people are peasants, not industrial workers . . . they are highly religious, not secular as in capitalist Europe . . .[88]

Marx's scientific contribution, then, must be provided with an authentic Islamic substratum to be effective in the Iranian context. Atheism, this passage reveals, is not simply the absence of religion, but a foreign presence and imposition. It is over the issue of secularism that Shari'ati is most hostile to Marxism, and the closest to Heidegger and existentialism. In "Humanity Between Marxism and Religion," he acknowledges this kinship to Heidegger, and expresses sympathy for the wave of Western intellectuals who search in vain for a lost God:

Today, in philosophy, Heidegger does not speak in the (atheistic) terms of Hegel or Feuerbach. In science, Max Planck, the outstanding exponent of the new physics, opposes the ideas of Claud Bernard. Heidegger is searching for Christ in humanity, and Planck is searching for God in the world of physics . . . Today, in contrast to Marx, who felt human liberation depended upon the denial of God, and Nietzsche, who boasted, "God is dead," even an atheistic philosopher like Sartre speaks of God's absence from the universe "with painful regret," seeing in this a source of the futility of man and existence, the loss of values.[89]

The politicization of religion as an anti-secular movement is what brings Shari'ati's work into the camp of authenticity. His discourse of authenticity reaches obscure metaphysical depths as a "total ideology," but its most practical ramifications are evident in his correspondence with Frantz Fanon.[90] In his letter, Shari'ati disagreed with Fanon over the necessity for abandoning religion before national progress can be made. Instead, he insists, a nation must regain its cultural and religious heritage before it can fight imperialism and borrow Western technology without losing its unique identity and self-esteem. Religion is the strongest practical force for bonding masses and directing them toward progressive goals. Religion, as an ideology, is associated with the idea of "roots," and roots are a conceptualized public ontology (which is very similar to Heidegger's intellectualization of religious experience). The concept of public ontology becomes a theory of authenticity, with implicit limits as to what a human may be and still remain a true Muslim. Here we arrive at the heart of Shari'ati's dilemma, one not unlike Heidegger's: how can a unique cultural identity be preserved under the onslaught of modernization? Or, how can we as a people adopt modernity in accordance with our society and history, rather than allow it to master us as a Western tool of subjugation? In this sense, authenticity is a modern prescription for adopting modernity without sacrificing cultural or political autonomy.

In one of his major works, *Return to Self*, Shari'ati discusses the issue of "roots" in relation to Islam:

I want to stress that non-religious intellectuals, as well as religious ones, have reached this conclusion. In fact, the main advocates of "return to roots" have not been religious – Fanon in Algeria, Julius Nyerere in Tanzania, Jomo Kenyatta in Kenya, Leopold Senghor in Senegal . . . When we say "return to one's roots," we are really saying one's cultural roots . . . some of you may conclude that we Iranians must return to our racial [Aryan] roots. I categorically reject this conclusion. I oppose racism, fascism, and reactionary returns . . . [Our people] do not find their roots in [pre-Islamic] civilizations. They are left unmoved by the heroes, myths, and monuments of these ancient empires. Consequently, for us to return to our roots [means rediscovery of] our Islamic roots.[91]

This passage expresses Shari'ati's conviction that only with religion can a revolutionary ideology mobilize the masses to fight for social change and a new society. But his Islamic ideology is concerned with religion on a deeper level than just its political utility. He is also concerned with the meaning and purpose of human life and society. He gives the name "worldliness" (zendegi-ye donyavi) to the culture of Western nihilism.[92] In the secular West "all human beings must become consumer animals and all nations must get stripped of their authenticity."[93] "Worldliness" is a social philosophy which promotes individual hedonism and disregards any higher purpose to life. It "exclusively defines the purpose of man's life as pleasure and enjoyment."[94] "Worldliness" has tainted Iranian society, including the clerical establishment. Meanwhile, "true Islam," the revolutionary sort, has been "forgotten." "Worldliness" has produced "alienation, or even in some instances, hatred for self" in the Iranian people, and instilled a "deep, obsessive, or even boastful pretension to attachment to the West, and rootless and vulgar modernism." Shari'ati locates a class basis for this "plague" in Iranian society: it embodies all the most detestable attributes of the "bourgeoisie," a "dirty, stinking, money-grabbing class."[95] The corruption of the Iranian clerical establishment is a result of its organic ties to the national bourgeoisie:

Do you know what the source of misery is for Islam? It is the formation of, and the dependency of the religion on, this [petty bourgeois] class, establishing a connection between the seminary and the bazaar. Should Islam be able one day to get rid of this dirty connection, it will, forever, assume the leadership of humanity; and should this relationship continue, Islam has been lost forever.[96]

The worldliness grown from this relation has produced a hypocritical clergy, which passively supports a system which produces poverty, and then admonishes the rich to give handouts to the poor. As the dominant spirit of modernity, "worldliness" has enslaved humanity to modern technology, rather than making technology a servant to human need. Shari'ati describes this condition as "the idiocy of the contemporary philosophy of man, the result of purpose-free technology," where "the whole meaning of civilization has been robbed of any ideal." In a different passage, Shari'ati describes technology (and science) as the liberator of humanity from the prisons of "nature," "heredity," and "history" – but this is possible only in a society which has achieved union with God.[97] Thus, Shari'ati clearly perceives a necessary connection between "ideals" (i.e., religious roots) and a just ordering of material society. Without being explicit about what the purpose behind technology will be, he codes the idea of technology in Islamic language, as if this alone will improve its moral character. It seems that the triumph he envisions over technology is a psychological one, to create new associations for it, beyond rapid modernization and Westernization, in a realm more acceptable and familiar to the mass of Iranian people. Yet Shari'ati's revolution is not merely psychological in character. He is interested in more than merely changing the concepts in people's minds associated with technology, industry, and modernity in general. He explicitly states that his aim is a classless society, and openly attacks the vested interests of pre-revolutionary Iran. In the intermingling of socialist and authenticity diatribe, however, there is a tacit hierarchy which locates his ideological priorities. This hierarchy shows itself in his conception of truth on the level of knowledge and the level of practice. For Shari'ati, scientific method is universal: the correct cognitive method "is of far reaching importance in determining progress or decline," more so than "genius," "philosophy" or "mere talent." But at the same time, "each society has a fixed basis, or in the words of the Qur'an, it has a road, a path, a particular character."[98] The first is universal truth, the second is the particular ontological character of each society. The forces of timing and temporality stemming from the ontological basis are mightier than truth. Any formal knowledge is preceded with organic knowledge of context, i.e., social context, feeling, timing, etc. This is comparable to Heidegger's concept of mood as a basic structure of Being. Abstract understanding – such as Marxist economics – can only be effective in mobilizing the masses if the conveyor also has a strong familiarity with social and historical circumstances on the pre-thematic level of popular understanding. Thus, authentic knowledge is more primary than objective knowledge. Shari'ati cites this to explain the failed attempts by secular intellectuals to communicate with the Iranian masses. Although they possess the formal, "universal" truth, they lack the deeper and broader everyday truth which opens up space for communication. This space is not accessed by a knowledge of Islamic principles – anyone could learn these from a book in any part of the world – but by familiarity with the facticity and practice of Islam in Iranian culture. Such facticity is all but impossible to articulate objectively, but a familiarity with popular meanings of Islamic stories and myths enables one to speak in the "authentic" language of the people. It is coded slang, popular imagery, and secret language in the everyday world.

Authentic knowing, Shari'ati tells us in no uncertain terms, is a spiritual phenomenon: "Spiritual knowledge alone can raise the existential value of man to a degree that protects him against feelings of inferiority toward occidental greatness." Spiritual life is anchored in the past, and "it is absolutely impossible for an individual without a past to have a future."[99] From this we may surmise that the "soul" for which Shari'ati fights is, of course, tradition. The understanding of this tradition, or soul, is beyond scientific verification – "beyond the scope of examination, observation, and experiment (and hence knowledge)."[100] It unites man and God in "the whole universe as a unity, into this world and the hereafter, instead of dividing it into the natural and the supernatural," and this "whole existence [is] a single form, a single living and conscious organism, possessing will, intelligence, feeling, and purpose." Thus, while science deals with the "manifest and observable,"[101] which is to say the superficial, there is another essential, hidden level to knowing, which is authentic knowing. The ultimate truth of this cosmic knowing is Islam. On this basis, Shari'ati can claim with justification that although the West has made better use of scientific truth, Shi'i Islam is still in possession of the only ontological truth, and therefore remains in a superior position.[102]

For Shari'ati, then, objective knowledge is crucial but superficial in relation to authentic knowledge. The reality to which these two forms of knowledge refer is located in objective action itself, which has a will and intelligence of its own beyond human belief. Authentic knowing stems from this action, which is conditioned by everyday traditional structures. This outlook is a serious reversal of received Islamic doctrine, which normally places scholastic learning before correct action. With this bewildering reversal, Shari'ati is able to transform Islam into a nihilist-populist doctrine of revolution. Nihilist because it grounds its truth in action rather than intellect, populist because it raises the activity of the mass to a sacred and uncorrupted level, and revolutionary because with the correct ideology, this mass power can be motivated to destroy existing society to make way for a new one. In one passage, Shari'ati tells the story of a well digger to evoke his conception of the sanctity and revolutionary nature of everyday action:

I was deeply entrenched in . . . the awesome [artistry] of the Master [well digger], and the miracle he did with his axe, the beauty of labor, the striving in the dark, and the majesty of courage to plunge into the depth of the earth; and then meaning – so meaningful a meaning – of searching for water, and the superlative sanctity of digging in the heart of darkness, far from [the surface of] the earth, far from life, to open wells which have been closed down. Suddenly I felt a delicate caressing in between the [toes] of my bare feet. Gradually murmurs, intensifying and expanding every moment, came from everywhere, joining together, becoming one cry, and the cries were raised from all over, joining together, and now turning angry, rebellious, aggressive: water.[103]

In light of this prioritization of action over formal knowledge, Shari'ati's *Shi'ism: A Complete Political Party* outlined the difference between traditional "knowledge-Islam" and revolutionary "action-Islam." He cites the Koran to insist that one's beliefs do not make a Muslim, but one's practices: "Examine carefully how the Koran uses the term 'Kafer'. It uses that term to describe those who refuse to take action for the truth. It never applies that term to those who deny existence of God and the soul."[104] Thus, it is not subjective belief, but objective action that primarily defines a Muslim. Accordingly, Shari'ati relocates truth in a field of human action and not formal learning:

[In the midst of] life [we] cannot be in the course of understanding and comprehending the truth through intellectual genius, or inner illumination, or scientific thinking and subjective ratiocination. Just as one can only "understand" a fiery bullet when a fiery bullet hits him, so he can understand a concept precisely when he stands in the current course of application of that concept. It is in action that truth manifests itself.[105]

This conception of action in the everyday life of the people amounts to a central pillar of Shari'ati's ideology of True Islam, the legitimacy of populist Islam. Populist Islam is the pure form of Islam, while scholastic Islam can be corrupted to oppress the people:

Islam has two separate Islams. The first can be considered a revolutionary "ideology." By this, I mean beliefs, critical programs and aspirations whose goal is human development. This is true religion. The second can be considered scholastic "knowledge." By this I mean philosophy, oratory, legal training, and scriptural learning. The second can be grasped by academic specialists, even reactionary ones. The first can be grasped by uneducated believers. This is why sometimes true believers understand Islam better than *faqih* (religious jurists), and *'alem* (scholars), and the philosophers.[106]

Thus, there is an idealization of the religious wisdom of the common man, as opposed to the received learning of the religious establishment. It was this feature that allowed Shari'ati to introduce the most innovative currents into Islam and then bypass the religious authorities to go directly to the people for legitimacy. Shari'ati's claim to be attuned to popular Islamic wisdom allowed him at times to invent streams with only the loosest precedent in theological doctrine, but to claim that they were always in the hearts and minds of the people.

Shari'ati realizes the mass energy he has tapped, and at times speaks almost like an anarchist about the political role of the people:

Islam is the first school of social thought that recognizes the masses as the basis, the fundamental and conscious factor in determining history and society – not the elect as Nietzsche thought, not the aristocracy and nobility as Plato claimed, not the great personalities as Carlyle and Emerson believed, not those of pure blood as Alexis Carrel imagined, not the priests or the intellectuals, but the masses.[107]

Yet once having conceived this mass base of popular power, how does Shari'ati recommend it be harnessed? For the central pillar of his system is authenticity, a mass force which, while useful for political mobilization, is difficult to truly control or even define. There is a silent core to Shari'ati's philosophy which subordinates reason to will, intellect to "Being," and for these reasons (again) embraces a form of nihilism. Here he comes very close to the Nietzschean tradition of German Romanticism.

The concept of *Ummah* (religious community) shows where Shari'ati stands on the question of harnessing the popular will. He redefines Ummah as a "society on the move, a society not in place but on the way, towards an objective, having a direction."[108] Based on the majority support for Islam, a vanguard party must mobilize society for revolutionary action, and then lead society in restructuring the class system and resisting the imperialist world. In light of the betrayal of Islam by the clerics, this party must be led by revolutionary Muslim intellectuals. This, he calls the "Total Party of Shi'ism":

"Party," in the general vocabulary of modern intellectuals, with a "world-view," is basically a unified social organization, an "ideology," a "philosophy of history," an "ideal social order," a "class foundation," a "social leadership," a "political philosophy," a "political orientation," a "tradition," a "slogan," a "strategy," a "tactic of struggle," and ... a "hope" that wants to change the "status quo" in man, society, people, or a particular class, and establish the "desired status" in its stead.[109]

It is quite likely that this political party would be authoritarian in nature, considering that Shari'ati believes the masses are bound by "superstition" and would therefore elect reactionary representatives. In *Community and Leadership,* Shari'ati argues that only the intelligentsia has the authority to govern post-revolutionary society.[110] Their task would be to build a classless society in which religious devotion and industrial might could flourish side by side. Thus, in the economic sphere there would be no rich and poor, with individual greed a thing of the past. In the cultural sphere, there would be "religious collectivism" instead of "religious individualism" (i.e., secularism). This uniform religious culture must be mystical and ascetic, producing individuals who find satisfaction beyond material gain; but society at large must be productive and materialistic, employing the most modern techniques to serve people's needs and defend the nation.[111]

Shari'ati died just before the Iranian Revolution. The Islamic Republic named a city street after Shari'ati and put his portrait on postage stamps. He has been recognized as the thinker who "did the most to prepare the Iranian youth for revolutionary upheaval," and his work is studied widely in Iran as the "Islamic answer to Marxism and the West."[112] We need to ask, however: is the post-revolutionary Iran the society that he envisioned for his country?

Conclusion

This chapter has tried to explore the emerging face of modernity in our time. In the context of the disillusionment with so-called universalist alternatives (Marxism and liberalism), radical mass movements are likely to emerge in modernizing nations based on ideologies of cultural authenticity. These movements promote social and cultural institutions which are modern but "authentically local." These "local" forms of resistance confront a global problem – the universalizing and homogenizing tendencies of "Western" modernity – and thus they have a distinctly universal character. The politics of authenticity is therefore neither local nor authentic. What matters is that it is grounded in some construction of the "local."

Other studies on the politics of authenticity, such as the German romanticism of the early twentieth century, suggest that ideologies of cultural authenticity – whether cast in religious or national terms – are likely to hold great appeal for the publics of societies in crisis. This is not because of any popular attachment to the "roots," but because the banner of "culture" is such a unifying cover for confronting economic and political grievances.

The politics of authenticity have a strong intellectual history stemming back to some of Europe's "great philosophers," and the ideologues of the Iranian Revolution did not lose any time in exploiting the rich German intellectual legacy left to them.

Mass movements based on the discourse of authenticity tend to stem from the same conditions as most twentieth-century revolutions: rapid modernization from above, urbanization and destruction of traditional modes of life, domination by powerful foreign interests. However, the narrative of these movements is often presented in the language of cultural identity. We must look at these "cultural" movements as significant faces of modernity for our time. We should try to understand them and their causes without recourse to any simplistic distortions about the "resurgence of ancient impulses" or "religious fanaticism."

5 German intellectuals and the culture of modernity

Introduction

This chapter lays out a comparative analysis of intellectual discourses in Germany between the World Wars as a means to further explore, and strengthen, the argument that social movements based on discourses of authenticity are internal to modernity, and in fact represent a common means through which "cultures" attempt to localize the course of modernization. Detailed examinations of the work of Junger and Heidegger show how they constructed versions of modernity rooted in German traditions. By exploring their claims, we can further understand the centrality of discourses of authenticity as a cultural, intellectual, and political response to modernization.

The works we have examined so far make abundantly clear that by defining modern experience as lacking in "soul," "substance," or "meaning," particularly on the "collective" level, intellectuals like Shari'ati and Al-e Ahmad were not envisioning a new form of protest within the modernist discourse; on the contrary, they echo a constant, reappearing, and troubling aspect of modernity which is anything but unfamiliar to Western intellectuals. The situation of alienation they describe is evoked in nearly every major narrative representing the modern situation. This dilemma is made much of, not only in the mystical or religious-inspired works of, for example, Heidegger and Kierkegaard, but also in the self-proclaimed scientific narratives of modernity by writers such as Weber and Marx. For Weber, the experience of modernity is an "iron cage," a rootless world without any meaning. Indeed, he viewed modernity as an endless search for meaning by its very nature. In the early Marx, where social alienation from the self is a key concept, religion is presented as "the spirit of a world without spirit." This confrontation with nihilism occurred over and over in Western Marxism. We see it in the messianic yearnings of Benjamin, and his preoccupation with the destruction of the past. We see it also in the writings of the Frankfurt School, in Horkheimer's grim depiction of a world in which "none of the categories of rationalism has survived." The entire "community" of existentialist thinkers and writers, in their wide diversity, could be defined as a community largely on account of this obsessive preoccupation.

In this chapter we will call attention to the interesting points of comparison between the social conditions and resulting intellectual movements for Germany in the 1920s and Iran in the 1960s–70s. Yet while these points of comparison occur on the level of specificities, we also want to make clear the larger, overarching reflection of modernity provided by this comparison. Current debates frequently overlook the long-standing existence of a murkier, spiritually troublesome stream in modern discourse – the voicing of a profound and emotional experience of cultural emptiness.

By making this observation, we can show how decidedly inappropriate it is to interpret the Islamic discourse as a part of the "old war" between modernity and tradition. The types of spiritual concerns voiced by Iranian Islamic intellectuals represent a debate which exists, and has existed, very much within modernity itself.

One of the earliest and most brilliant expositors of this spiritual crisis was Friedrich Nietzsche. His work unleashed a vigorous and deeply damaging challenge to modernity on these very grounds. It would be inappropriate to label Nietzsche a "traditionalist" – yet there is a very definite appeal to the past in his work. His writing voices an obsession with the lack of an overarching tradition that would give life a higher meaning and purpose:

In order that there may be [great] institutions, there must be a kind of will, instinct, or imperative, which is anti-liberal to the point of malice: the will to tradition, to authority, to responsibility for centuries to come, to the solidarity of chains of generations, forward and backward ad infinitum . . . The whole of the West no longer possesses the instincts out of which institutions grow, out of which a future grows: perhaps nothing antagonizes its "modern spirit" so much. One lives for the day, one lives very fast, one lives very irresponsibly: precisely this is called freedom.[1]

This is no daydreaming notion of a "return" to any past; Nietzsche evoked a reconfiguration of the present, drawing off suppressed (and hence seemingly historically distant) yet profoundly alive elements within the culture itself, to construct a transformative vision for the future. He performed this task in a particularly spectacular and notable manner, not least of all given the remorseless cruelty and iconoclastic spirit embedded in his entire vision. Yet if he was the first explicitly to articulate and beget this titanic mode of intellectual insurgence, to demonstrate its sheer power and darkly enchanting aura, he was only foreshadowing a fundamental pattern of thought and practice which has surfaced in virtually all demonstrations of protest against modernity from within modernity itself.

This intellectual pattern of subversion most surely found an echoing in the ideological writings of Iranian Islamists of the 1960s and 1970s. It is no accident that translations of Nietzsche's writings – particularly *Thus Spoke Zarathustra* – became very fashionable in Iranian intellectual circles in the 1970s. The writings of Jean-Paul Sartre also gained considerable currency, and informed ideas about commitment, the relation of literature and politics, and the social role of intellectuals. But the defining idea of authenticity as a revolt against the rationalism and universalism of modernity most certainly drew inspiration from the likes of Nietzsche, Ernst Junger, and Martin Heidegger. To invoke a notion of authenticity – which is to say, to breathe life into a cultural configuration from the past and give it new life in the imagination – is to construct an experience of continuity in the face of the atomizing and empty form of modern society.

This chapter will show that what we are calling the "discourse of authenticity," and insurrection based on this discourse, should not be perceived as isolated or freak aberrations, nor should they be simplified as a spontaneous upsurge of fanaticism. Rather, it is a political mode with strong intellectual roots that lead back to some of the greatest thinkers of the modern world, as we will show in our examination of Nietzsche. And though varied in form, authenticity discourse and movements arise from specific conditions, and fit logically among the possibilities of modernizing nations.

The German context

Germany's defeat in World War I was interpreted by many Germans as a national humiliation which called for redemption and revenge. This was so largely because the outsider's victory compounded Germany's long internal history of political disunity and uneven development. Jeffrey Herf called the Weimar years (1920–33) the time-span where Germany's confrontation between technology and culture came to a head. It was a unique decade in German history – the first full-fledged experiment with democracy, constructed upon harsh military defeat and a crumbling authoritarian legacy. Modernization had occurred late, rapidly, and "from above," creating new social classes and interests which lacked political structures for exerting influence. With the relaxation of authoritarian government, then, much of the public confronted the structures of modernity as alien impositions. The growing middle class in urban centers "lived in the cities and worked in modern industry, but the memories of small-town life and less rationalized forms of production were still vivid in the Germany of the 1920s."[2]

The twenties included an unprecedented diversity of political opinion, a flowering of culture and the arts, an excitement for innovation and utopia; also a deep mood of pessimism and despair, a nostalgia for the "lost world of the past," and a yearning for vengeance upon those who had destroyed it. All of these factors came to bear on the confrontation between technology and culture, which Herf describes as "embracing aspects of the modern world in accordance with German national traditions."[3] Within the competition among varieties of such cosmopolitan ideologies as socialism and liberalism, a uniquely German discourse of authenticity arose and finally carried the day. The writers of the radical right who did the most to champion this ideology are sometimes called the "nihilist movement." The success of their visions fed off the public's nihilism after failed socialist revolution, humiliating military occupation, and unprecedented social change coupled with hopeless economic stagnation. These experiences disillusioned the German masses with the promises of both socialist liberation, from the "East," and liberal capitalism, from the "West." The divided German Left, the fragile foundations of Weimar democracy, and economic disaster ultimately allowed the authoritarian populism of National Socialism to prevail. A plethora of books promoting authenticity discourse throughout the twenties, and the movements inspired by these ideas, created the ideological atmosphere which made this outcome possible. However, the "nihilists" must be distinguished from Nazism, for many of them rejected the movement both before and after it came to power.

The twenties were preceded by an era of rapid modernization from above. Gilbert and Large point out that German unification was Bismarck's creation, "tailored to his forceful but prudent personality."[4] The rapid success of German development which began under Bismarck "intoxicated the upper and middle classes," who had long resented Germany's backward position in Europe, and they demanded the nation attain its rightful "place in the sun."[5]

When Bismarck was dismissed in 1890, his uniquely tailored and unprecedented position fell to an incompetent and corrupt man – Wilhelm II (ruled 1890–1918). As development produced increased conflict between rural and urban interests, and the divided core of the nation showed itself, he had no ability to cope. Moreover, he was an arrogant ruler, considering himself an "instrument of God," and he spoke to his people as an officer speaks to his soldiers.[6] Although he considered it his duty to uphold authoritarian Prussian military tradition, he also wanted to be a modern monarch who would lead Germany to technolog-

ical superiority as a "world power."[7] While this combination appealed to
the aspirations of the German bourgeoisie, the Emperor's aggressive anti-
socialism produced resentment among the working classes. However, the
Emperor refused to share power even with bourgeois representatives in
parliament – the National Liberals and the Progressives – who clashed
with his aversion to a democratic Germany. The Emperor set up his
government to bypass the influence of parliament, which remained
limited, and he gradually alienated himself from all but his most loyal con-
stituents.[8] In 1913, Wilhelm II's military authorities placed the Alsatian
town of Zabern under martial law and crushed demonstrations taking
place there. This flagrant abuse of power incited a parliamentary coalition
among socialists (Social Democrats), liberal progressives, and the
Catholic Center Party, which had traditionally represented different con-
stituencies. The coalition aimed to replace the existing authoritarian
system with a parliamentary one, but the outbreak of war in 1914 demol-
ished any chance of success.

In Germany, as elsewhere in Europe, the First World War was generally
met with wild enthusiasm. Even socialist parties ignored the decree of the
Second International to oppose war with a general strike, and supported
their governments in mobilization. Gilbert and Large suggest that war
provided a release from a divided and unbearable political situation, "a
restoration of common purpose after parliamentarism and authoritarianism had failed to resolve the hostile camps within modernizing nations."[9]
The German public, in particular, was disappointed that the election of a
socialist majority to the Reichstag in 1912 had proven barely effective in
influencing the government.

With the war's end, Germany faced more terrible conditions than those
preceding the war. Six million Germans were dead or wounded, and the
home situation was verging on collapse. Stefan Zweig, a writer, describes
the disillusionment of the German people at the end of World War I:

A bitter distrust gradually began to grip the population – a distrust of money,
which was losing more and more of its value, distrust of the Generals, the officers,
the diplomats, distrust of every public statement by the government and General
Staff, distrust of the newspapers and their news, distrust of the very war itself and
its necessity.[10]

News of the revolution in Russia spread to the impoverished German
masses. As the war grew more hopeless for Germany in 1918, soldiers
began to desert the front and revolution began to sweep across Germany
at home. Led by the Spartacus group and the USPD, within ten days the
revolution had forced every German prince, including Wilhelm II, to
abdicate. Communist republics and workers-soldiers councils were set up
throughout the country. But right-wing military opposition sprang up,

and after three months of civil war the Communist revolutionary movement had been crushed throughout Germany. In the wake of this defeat – which had been actively promoted by the conservative allied powers – many radicals became profoundly disillusioned with politics.

In June of 1919, representatives of the German government signed the peace conditions imposed by the Versailles treaty. The German delegation at Versailles was kept behind barbed wire. The conditions forced Germany to accept total blame for the war, denied them national self-determination, and brought economic devastation to the country. Considered "peace with shame," these conditions intensified the German public's sense of alienation from its Western neighbors. As Germany's suffering intensified in the following years, right-wing intellectuals declared the Weimar Republic an infestation of alien Western "Zivilization" and a symbol of national humiliation. They counterpoised this with a conception of authentic German "Kultur," which coded modern experience with familiarizing words and metaphors. This ideology borrowed much from the tradition of German Romanticism. However, Herf points out that it stands apart from that tradition by explicitly embracing and championing technology, rather than promoting a return to pastoralism.[11] In this way, the intellectuals who shaped it created a viable ideology for the modern political context: a modern nation-state, buttressed with a powerful industrial-technological infrastructure, with the purpose of defending the uniqueness of "German Kultur" against "externally imposed Western Zivilization."

The success of any ideology depends upon the social and economic context within which it flourishes. The discourse of authenticity was powerful for several important reasons. (1) It fed off the German public's disillusionment with Communism as a revolutionary alternative. (2) It manipulated a fear of foreigners already implicit in German culture and expanded beyond measure by World War I. (3) It succeeded in portraying the Weimar Republic as an instance of foreign domination. After a short period of economic recovery (1927–29), the sudden prospect of returning to economic ruin frightened many into trusting the supposed bearer of "order" and justice for the "little man" after years of "chaos."[12]

In the early 1920s, Germany was suffering from inflation, unemployment and hunger. In a debate among elites about whether to cooperate with or obstruct Western policy, the obstructionists won and the nation paid for its defiance with severe depression. The streets of cities were filled with war-wounded beggars and pedlars selling old textiles, chocolate, fish and books. Books became enormously popular at this time, and in 1920 Ernst Junger's *Storm of Steel* initiated a whole series of war memoirs which helped promote a nationalist vogue. A poll conducted in

1922 by *Das literarische Echo* magazine found the most widely read writers
to be Ludwig Ganghofer, Herman Lons, Rudolf Herzog and Gustav
Frenssen – all writers in this tradition.[13] Ludwig Ganghofer, a veteran,
wrote that Germany symbolized the three Magi guided by the star to
Bethlehem, and acted as the instrument of salvation for the world.[14]
Herman Lons, another veteran, wrote that only war can bring the genuine
nature of culture to the surface of the world, beyond the artificial constraints of everyday life. Amidst the misery of the depression, these books
evoked the comradeship of trench warfare, and implied that such unity
might be extended to the nation should Germany recover its dignity and
assume mastery of its destiny in the world. Oswald Spengler's *Decline of
the West* – a tormented and unwilling concession of a loss of faith in the
"Universal History" once evoked confidently by the likes of Hegel – was
also a bestseller in the early 1920s.[15]

At this time, nostalgic "Prussian" films were also achieving great popularity. This cinematic trend continued throughout the twenties, and often
featured glorifications of German soldiers in the First World War – *Emden*
(1927), and *U9 Weddingen* (1927) are examples.[16] Thus, aspects of the
discourse of authenticity extended to the most popular form of recreation
– in 1919, there were 2,280 cinemas in Germany, and by 1930 there were
3,500 selling a million tickets a day. [17]

Technology in general was blossoming in Germany, and its innovative
influence aroused great wonder in the people. The impact on society,
according to Schrader and Schebera, is comparable only with the first
industrial revolution in the nineteenth century.[18] A 1930 book on *Kunst
und Technik* (Art and Technology) began with this introduction:

Technology is the driving force of the era. It exerts a decisive influence on the
profile of the times. Most of the phenomena which occur in the economic, social
and political process are derived from consequences of technological development . . . we should also note that technology has invaded art. It is an invasion
which has taken place over recent years with primitive force.[19]

The tone in this passage is ambiguous because technology, as well as
inspiring wonder, also symbolized a decade of helpless national disintegration, change, and subservience. This mistrust of technology is
expressed by members of the German Youth Movement, who abandoned
the cities to roam in the "unchanging" countryside. They sought "spiritual renewal" by visiting small rural villages, communing with peasants,
and celebrating their part in the "primeval nation."[20] The German Youth
Movement enjoyed great popularity in the twenties, and clearly contributed to the atmosphere where "authenticity" carried great symbolic
weight in people's minds. But, as Herf has shown, the crucial reconcilia-
tion of German "Kultur" and technology occurred in the works of Hans

Freyer, Ernst Junger, Carl Schmitt, Werner Sombart, Oswald Spengler, and to a lesser degree, Martin Heidegger.

The appeal of military works, aiming at "German renewal," continued throughout the decade. The books were advertised in a tone which suggested a national call to arms: "Heroes of the World War Front. Clear a path for truth! Every stockist can serve the nation by selling this book! We are now distributing the fiftieth thousand [copy]."[21] These books, many of them now forgotten as rubbish, easily outsold such great modern classics as Robert Musil's *The Man Without Qualities* and Arnold Zweig's *The Case of Sergeant Grischa*. For example, Werner Beumelburg's *Germany Under Barrage*, a romanticization of the war, sold almost 200,000 copies in the twenties, and Hans Grimm's expansionist ideology, *Nation Without Space*, sold 260,000 by 1932. *The Case of Sergeant Grischa* had sold 40,000 copies by 1932.[22]

Foreign loans and investments helped to bring Germany back to prewar levels of industrial output by 1927. For several years, many in the middle classes felt confident that Germany was nearing its goal of liberal democracy. But when the world economic crisis hit in 1929, Germany's dependence on foreign capital triggered severe economic collapse. Many in the middle classes, who recalled the decades of prosperity under monarchical authoritarianism, lost their confidence in parliamentary democracy, and believed its weak and indecisive leadership was to blame. By 1933, industrial production had been cut in half and six million were unemployed.[23] These circumstances made the public especially susceptible to claims that a depletion of traditional values of discipline, hierarchical order, and selfless state service were responsible for the decline in Germany. The great flowerings of innovation in art could be interpreted as proof that the Weimar Republic represented an alien and degenerate break with the solid German traditional past. The Nazi movement in the thirties, with its aspect of "religious revival,"[24] incarnated the promise of a "third way" beyond the capitalist West and the communist East made by the nihilist writers of authenticity in the twenties.

The post-war moment presented a unique juncture in German history. The traditional authoritarian state had been lifted for the first time, and a new tradition of democracy was introduced. But it was introduced into an economy constructed by the old regime, and did not have time to take root. Vested interests, and perhaps people in general, were suspicious of the parliament. It was associated with military defeat, confusing social changes, and economic disaster. A combination of political nihilism and wonder at technological advancement informed the popular imagination of Germans living in the twenties. When, by 1929, the Weimar Republic appeared to hold only a future of poverty for the nation, people longed for an alternative but lacked faith in existing political forms. Authenticity discourse fed off this mood of despair with existing political forms and exploited the public wonder at technological innovation. The works by German nihilists in the 1920s – the "reactionary modernist" strand identified by Herf – fused technological imagery with traditional symbols. They promised a new form of nation-state – one strong, yet rooted in German tradition. They were intellectuals rather than leaders, but showed the power of intellectuals to affect the public choice of leadership. By articulating the intensity of a public mood, and manipulating nostalgia as a political axis, the nihilists showed the power of these forces to overthrow modern social systems in times of unrest. The imagination may be far from seizing power; but seizing the imagination is a crucial brick in laying the road to it.

The "discourse of authenticity" in Friedrich Nietzsche and Ernst Junger

The German discourse of authenticity had an intellectual grandfather in Friedrich Nietzsche. Though he spurned the masses and thereby overlooked the central pillar of the "movement," as well as its single hope for an actualized political future, he did tap into the sentiments which characterized its essence. As a critic of modernity, he understood the problem of vanishing roots, and felt strongly that in their absence humanity would dim to dross. This brought him into conflict with the whole tradition of liberalism, and particularly its conception of liberation as freedom from imposing social hierarchy. Nietzsche yearned for tradition to bestow greatness and nobility upon society – thus, he said "all that is good is inherited: whatever is not inherited is imperfect, a mere beginning."[25]

Nietzsche described the crisis of modernity on a metaphysical level as the loss of a higher human purpose, and called this nihilism. But the tradition Nietzsche longed for did not exist in any nation, people, or faith. He was forced to raise the banner of a different "tradition": the banner of an ontological undercurrent which had always existed in Western civilization, but which modern institutions had repressed. In *The Birth of Tragedy* he championed the Dionysian impulse in Western history, and lamented its suppression under Apollonian cultural forms, or the culture of mediocrity and reason. Tracing a decline in Western history, he showed the tradition of Platonism impressing itself upon reality right up to the present, and demanding a repressive and leveling order to society. Nietzsche's challenge to modernity was on a cultural level – he wanted to build cultural forms suited to reviving the Dionysian undercurrent, and placing its instinctual and passionate tendencies at the center of social destiny.

At the same time he attacked existing traditions of his day, most notably Christianity, which he accused of bringing about the sickness of nihilism. Christianity had sealed its own demise – by carrying the corrosive element of "absolute truthfulness," it ensured the demotion of its celestial authority to simply another perspective in a world of many. The result is a crisis in values, for unless Christianity can stand as an absolute, its metaphysical claim to truth is no stronger than any other worldly force of interpretation. Nietzsche saw the entire culture of "humanism," including democracy and socialism, as based in Christian metaphysics. Since these metaphysics were no longer legitimate, the championing of their values could only be a lie, an inauthentic posture. The cult of reason merely affords us a blindfold to shield our eyes from the crisis of values at the heart of our lives. Nietzsche reveled in the tensions produced by these contradictions, and saw them as bringing about a gradual collapse in the entire order of society.

Nietzsche called upon Western society to face up completely to this "death of God"; until we do so, he maintained, we will be living as unauthentic beings, acting in shallowness upon ideals we no longer believe in. To be authentic is to create new values and live by them – but until we face up to the crisis in the fullest sense, such creation is impossible. Nietzsche tried to demonstrate how this nihilism sprang logically and inexorably from the European-Christian tradition in particular. The flight into a mediocre culture of "sleep," he maintained, was a very specific form of nihilism, with hidden potentials behind the bleak surface:

The supreme values . . . were erected over man . . . as if they were commands of God, as "reality," as the "true" world, as a hope and future world. Now that the shabby origin of these values is becoming clear, the universe seems to have lost value, seems "meaningless" – but that is only a transitional stage.[26]

In the "death of God," Nietzsche saw possibilities for human liberation – if man stopped channeling his energies into an imaginary afterlife (or the fake ideals derived therefrom), he could begin to exploit his full human potential here on earth. In *Beyond Good and Evil* (1886), Nietzsche described a massive accumulation of human energy born of the self-repressive struggle in Western history:

. . . now that [Christian and Platonic dogmatism] is overcome, now that Europe is breathing freely again after this nightmare and at least can enjoy a healthier sleep, we, whose task is wakefulness itself, are the heirs of all that strength which has been fostered by the fight against this error . . . [this fight] has created in Europe a magnificent tension of the spirit the like of which has never yet existed on earth: with so tense a bow we can now shoot for the most distant goals.[27]

The goal is a "re-evaluation of all values" – the victory of "life affirming" values which center on danger and heroism. A "superman" is the only being capable of bringing about this transvaluation, by creating his own values while squarely facing the void of nihilism. Nietzsche sees modern life as rootless in the absence of a strong tradition, and lifeless in the lack of a higher purpose than mere everyday life. His message contains a contrasting call for a "new beginning" and an "authoritative tradition." There is a naked contempt for modernity blended with a modern longing for the creation of an alternative world. And yet Nietzsche is no populist. His condemnation of a "leveling age" takes the form of a reverence for the rare and unique individual. It is only the efforts of such individuals that can reverse the degenerate trend of universally imposed "herd mentality."

Nietzsche posits a different ethic than "leveling" justice and equality – one based on a mystical reverence for "unconditional life," beyond the inauthentic values and dead metaphysics to which we are enchained. This is the principle of "Eternal Recurrence" – the "triumphant idea of which [sic] all other modes of thought will ultimately perish," and the weapon to prevent "reduction to mediocrity." He prophesies that "the races that cannot bear it stand condemned, and those who find it the greatest benefit are chosen to rule."[28] The superman will implement it for all humanity: he posits a metaphysical will-to-power as the instrument the superman will use to wrench meaning out from nihilism, and bring the world's many under the "new beginning."

The superman would reconstitute metaphysical power through his "life affirming" and authentic deeds, drawing from the latent Dionysian powers embedded in Western society. Significantly, Nietzsche renounces any "ultimate reality," and the possibility of deriving any intellectual principle therefrom. Life, in essence, is not intelligible. Instead, he posits a fundamentally shared state of being, deep beyond reach of the intellect, but apparent in our world of lived practices (the will to power). This is a seminal point for "authenticity discourse" – the "recentering of 'reality' to a new locus in a depth separate from the surfaces of material or social human phenomena."[29] There is unquestionably a counterpart to the atheist in Nietzsche – a quasi-religious side, where the principle of Eternal Recurrence will act as "a vicious circle made God," dragging all humanity into a delirious festival of creative and destructive power.[30] But given Nietzsche's snide dismissal of "social questions," and his insistence on the "will," the discourse of authenticity remained on the level of individual revolt in his work. He lacked any in-depth critique of technology or modern politics – in fact completely rejecting the latter – and insisted upon speaking only to the select few, in disdain of the general public.

The most interesting points about Nietzsche in the context of authenticity discourse are the following: (1) He drew off a created tradition, with roots in a supposedly perennial struggle within his culture. (2) He claimed to go beneath the surface to these hidden roots, which, while lacking an institutional form, still contained a profound life. (3) He created an intellectual system (ideology) which he claimed had "ontological" legitimacy (in these roots) rather than mere intellectual legitimacy. (4) He rejected the "autonomy of reason" as mere intellectualism without roots in life – and a society founded on rational principle as therefore "rootless" – thus abstracting people from their true possibilities. He rejected "universalism" in favor of the unique and disorderly. (5) He claimed people were living inauthentically because of these two ideologies, and wanted to reestablish a unified, authentic basis or principle for life beyond the ideological anarchy and rootlessness of the modern era. (6) He centered the problem of authenticity on the creation of new values which supposedly already had a secret, repressed heritage.

Nietzsche's elitist attitudes did not inhibit other social visionaries who saw promise in "authenticity discourse" as a popular ideology. As Germany underwent modernizing procedures in the late nineteenth century, authors used "authenticity" to describe a contrast between the standardized life of modern mass society and the unique, "true" experience of German traditional culture. Wilhelm Dilthey (1833–1911) created his influential "philosophy of life" in opposition to the increased urbanization, industrialization, and secularization of everyday life. Dilthey also condemns liberalization for eroding the sense of hierarchy in German society.

But the political rendering of "authenticity discourse" as a revolutionary program occurred through the works of Ernst Junger. His work brought the articulation of such concerns from the elites to the masses. Junger was the son of a wealthy chemist in Hanover. He broke with his family at seventeen and joined the French Foreign Legion, traveling to Africa, where the mystery and beauty of the natural surroundings would influence his writings permanently. At nineteen, he went straight to the front line of World War I. He fought in the very worst battles of the war, but survived to tell the tale.[31] Junger always remembered the war as a time of fraternity and unity of purpose, and longed to transplant these conditions to German society as a whole. He also saw in the war a mystical fusion of "civilized man" and "nature," awakening ancient impulses, and ripping an entire generation free from the restraints of bourgeois civilization. The end of World War I brought chaos and rapid innovation to Germany, destroying old patterns of life without a firm substitute to replace them, and Junger seized upon this explosive intersection. After Germany's defeat, Junger wrote works glorifying the war experience, arguing that it had ushered in a new age:

The war is not the end but rather the emergence of violence. It is the forge in which the world will be hammered into new limits and new communities. New forms filled with blood and power will be packed with a hard fist. The war is a great school and the new man will be taken from our race.[32]

Naming the war a "school" shows Junger's idea of education – not the received knowledge of formal academic learning, but the hands-on experience of action on the battlefield. The pupils who graduate become:

[the] new man, the storm pioneer, the elite of Central Europe. A wholly new race, intelligent, strong, and full of will. What emerges here in battle . . . tomorrow will be the axis around which life revolves faster and faster.[33]

The most important lesson for Germany to come out of this "educational experience" is the recognition of German decline. Junger tells us that Germany is weaker than the rest of Europe because it has forsaken its roots to adopt the false ideologies of its Western neighbors. The war invites Germany to know itself once again as it truly is, shrugging off the inauthentic veil. By this reasoning, Germany had not really lost the war at all, but had seen its essential soul revived, in a calling to world transformation. Junger's work, on the one hand, provided consolation for a bruised and weakened nation, and on the other, promised a radical regeneration to sweep away all traces of national humiliation.

Junger transformed the "discourse of authenticity" from a mere philosophical-aesthetic position into a fully modern ideology of technology and politics. His essay on "Total Mobilization" (1930) refashioned elements of Nietzsche's philosophy, specifically the concepts of nihilism and will to power, for German nationalist purposes. He openly acknowledges his intellectual debt to Nietzsche, yet argues that Nietzsche fails precisely because he neglects to tackle the central issue of modernity: the "machine." In *Fire and Blood* (1926), he referred to the need for updating Nietzsche:

Yes, the machine is beautiful. It must be beautiful for him who loves life in all life's fullness and power. The machine must also be incorporated into what Nietzsche (who, in his renaissance landscape, still had no place for the machine) meant when he attacked Darwinism. Nietzsche insisted that life is not only a merciless struggle for survival but also possesses a will to higher and deeper goals. The machine cannot only be a means of production, serving to satisfy our paltry material necessities. Rather, it ought to bestow on us higher and deeper satisfactions.[34]

The war, in Junger's eyes, brought a great conflict into the open between the "cult of progress" (socialism and liberalism) and the underlying German soul. In the words of Junger's brother, Friedrich, one represents the "community of mind" and the other the "community of

blood."[35] The victory of the later is predetermined by the fact that conscious efforts at progress – i.e., imposing mental ideals upon reality – are
undermined by that reality itself. Reality is the "life force," with which
German Kultur has a privileged relation. Junger argued these points as
follows: while sharing Nietzsche's disdain for the "dullness and uniformity" of bourgeois progress, he senses a "source of much greater
significance underlying it."[36] He concluded from his participation in
World War I that "progressive movements produce results contradicting
their own innermost tendencies which suggests that here, as everywhere
in life, what prevails are not these tendencies but other, more hidden
impulsions." The "secret movement" within the war introduced the
"authentic, moral factor of our age," and destroyed the "nineteenth
century's great popular church" of bourgeois "progress."[37] He rejects the
ideal of "truth" and the possibility that reason might be employed to
create a just and transparent society beyond the violently unpredictable
instincts and passions of the human animal. Junger hailed the Great War
as a lesson for an effete and dying culture in the "spirit of life."[38] He interpreted the war as the righteous rebellion of "reality" against vain attempts
by Enlightenment bourgeois institutions to impose a false (Christian)
ethics on the world. Thus, he reduced Nietzsche's concept of "nihilism"
to a concrete historical basis: the loss of faith in bourgeois progress and
civilization following the First World War.

He saw the positive counterpart to this nihilism in the possibilities
unleashed by the war: a vindication of the deeper, unutterable truth of
instinct, blood, and tradition, and the material means to mobilize this
avenging spirit against decaying Civilization. The revelation of this true
human unity would restore conviction to a declining Europe:

Europe, whose area extends in planetary proportions, has become extremely thin,
extremely varnished: its spacial gains correspond to a loss in the force of conviction. New powers will emerge from it . . . Deep beneath the regions in which the
dialectic of war aims is still meaningful, the German encounters a stronger force:
he encounters himself. In this way, the war was at the same time about him: above
all, the means of his own self-realization . . . one that cannot be satisfied by any of
this world's ideas nor any images of the past.[39]

Just as the war produced "self-realization" for the German people, it
will produce the world leaders of tomorrow. Here, Junger has articulated
a pillar of authenticity discourse – the synthesis of "collective" self-
realization and revolutionary political commitment. Having identified
authenticity as the bonding experience of the war, he locates the cause of
social division in German society after the war: the alien imposition of
the Weimar Republic. For Junger, the residue of German defeat lingered
in this symbol of Western ideology. Parliamentary democracy was

an "unGerman" imposition, and coupled with "cosmopolitan mass culture," it constituted the encroachment of the effete West into Germany. Thus, the next war should begin at home with ridding the culture of foreign taint. In order to win the next war against the West, he argued that Germany needed a superior vision to overcome the "obvious, transparent dogma" of rationalism,[40] and a fully mobilized population to crush the enemy abroad and prevent the fermentation of revolution at home (due to unused human resources). With regard to modernization and the survival of the German soul, he considered the lesson of World War I for Germany. It turns out that the two are utterly inseparable, and anything short of total mobilization threatens the survival of the German soul:

We have . . . no desire to complain about the inevitable. We wish only to establish that Germany was incapable of convincingly taking on the spirit of "the age," whatever its nature. Germany was also incapable of proposing, to itself or the world, a valid principle superior to that spirit. Rather, we find it searching – sometimes in romantic-idealist, sometimes in rationalist-materialist spheres – for those signs and images that the fighting individual strives to affix to his standards. But the validity lying within these spheres belongs partly to the past and partly to a milieu alien to German genius; it is not sufficient to assure utmost devotion to the advance of men and machines – something that a fearful battle against a world demands . . . In this light we must struggle all the more to recognize how our elemental substance, the deep, primordial strength of the Volk, remains untouched by such a search . . . And yet, this smoldering fire, burning for an enigmatic and invisible Germany, was sufficient for an effort that left nations trembling to the marrow. What if it had possessed direction, awareness, and form?[41]

The war had unveiled the mysterious substance of German identity, but the simple revelation is not enough. It must be articulated and institutionalized into authentically German political forms. Junger tells us "the nation must penetrate . . . into the forces of our time: the machine, the masses, and the worker," and must "put aside the misguided romanticism which views the machine as in conflict with the Kultur."[42] The two can be combined with the transformation of every citizen into a "worker-soldier," for "unlimited marshaling of potential energies" toward chronic warfare.[43] This continual warfare would create meaning out of life and death struggle – in Nietzsche's words, "the fertile soil out of which humanity can grow," drawing every class into a single social unit, and fusing knowledge and practice into a singular collective purpose.[44] This was Junger's vision of the immanence of Nietzsche's will to power as a social system based on this "metaphysical truth."

As Herf has pointed out, Junger's work succeeded in ridding technology of its association with "alien" Western culture, and wedding it organically to German cultural nationalism. He used a language of Volkish

Romanticism, but integrated it with a reverence for technology. His theory had a wide impact on inter-war German society: in 1933, his most important book, *The Worker*, became a bestseller.[45] When the Nazis came to power, they did not fail to acknowledge his crucial assistance in paving their way. One year after their seizure of power, a Nazi commentator announced:

German youth owe a great debt above all to Ernst Junger for the fact that technology is no longer a problem for them. They have made his beautiful confessions to technics born from fire and blood their own. They live in harmony with it.

They require no more ideologies in order to "overcome" technology. Rather, they grasp it as the arm of the idea. This was something new for us, this incorporation of matter into the meaning of events. Junger has liberated us from a nightmare.[46]

Junger embraces technology not to overcome the inscrutability of experience, but to champion it. Not to vanquish the mysteries associated with religion, but to raise them anew as a triumphant social system and ideology. Just as the war was an "experience of mathematical precision and magical background," he aims to create a link between technology and mysticism, placing the former in the service of the latter.[47] Without explicitly mentioning religion, his message constantly refers back to a community whose bonds lie deeper than rational organization. Religion, for him, is in the life force itself. Like Nietzsche, he sees life as a mysterious substance that defies science and reason. The war is referred to as the "father of all things," having "hammered, chiseled, and hardened us into what we are."[48] If there is a god in his scenario, it is the temporal force of mass destruction ripping open layers of serenity imposed by bourgeois-materialist civilization, and unleashing the primordial "forces of nature." Only a technological state power could perform this liberating task. This is ultimately Junger's point: the scientific must be used in the service of the unknowable, the higher power of the "divine." The war must be turned into a political and religious institution. His work "strives to incorporate the labors of chemistry into the realm of alchemy." The "decisive aspect of . . . Total Mobilization" is "the force of faith" and the monotonous "technical side is not decisive."[49] He posits a metaphysical force of creation that gives birth to all truly great human accomplishments:

[Great creations] like pyramids and cathedrals, or wars that call into play the ultimate mainsprings of life – economic explanations, no matter how illuminating, are not sufficient . . . This is the reason that the school of historical materialism can only touch the surface of the process . . . To explain efforts of this sort, we ought rather focus our first suspicions on phenomena of the cultic variety.[50]

In a time when pyramids and cathedrals are mere artifacts of history, the Great War was the first event to involve the sheer mass of people in a great creative encounter which calls upon the true essence of life. The war is the marker of a new historical epoch, the departure from the bourgeois world which sought security and comfort in technology, but found instead the most elemental danger and terror. Only Germany, with its strong tradition of Romanticism and vivid memory of pre-rationalized modes of life, is in a position to seize this opportunity and fuse technology with elemental forces to produce "great events" once more. The legacy of the war should be a resistance to leveling rationalism from the West, and only the culture with roots in life's depths is qualified to lead such a struggle. Junger's prose mingles talk of supernatural beings and unconscious forces with snide dismissals of scientific understanding:

In the craters' depths, the last war possessed a meaning no arithmetic can master . . . the German demon's voice bursting forth mightily, the exhaustion of the old values being united with an unconscious longing for a new life.[51]

Junger's references to "cults" and mass movements suggest a desire for a mass cult – a form of religion to transcend nihilism. He is obviously interested in mass politics – but not the democratic sort, whether socialist or capitalist. The "dawn of the age of labor" is a mass cult of sacrifice and mystery, designed to break beyond bourgeois society:

Labor is an expression of national life and the worker is one of the parts of the nation. Every effort to rob the worker of his living bonds by placing him under the empty concepts like "humanity" or an international community of interest is high treason of the blood by the intellect. The meaning of labor does not lie in profit making or wage earning but in creating for the nation the fullness of values that it needs for its unfolding.[52]

Junger's "god," in effect, is the German nation. It is an abstract god whose meaning can be manipulated freely, using "culturally authentic" language. Junger is less concerned with fixing its meaning and more interested in the nation as a symbol of the "life force." Of course the "life force" takes priority over the lives of anyone living, whether in Germany or beyond its borders. He understands that a mass cult requires visual and sensual stimulation, and offers the religious ritual of sacrifice: "The deepest happiness of man lies in the fact that he will be sacrificed and the highest art of command consists in the capacity to present goals that are worthy of sacrifice."[53]

While Nietzsche vehemently attacked ideas of God and afterlife, Junger simply ignores them, inheriting Nietzsche's tacit "worldly" religion of Dionysian celebration. Although Junger was no Christian, his answer to the "spiritual crisis" of the nation had a deeply moving impact on another young scholar of the Front generation. The young Catholic, Martin Heidegger, agonized over the question of Germany's soul within the passage to modernity – it eventually cost him his faith. Thomas Sheehan, in his essay on Heidegger's life, wrote that shortly after losing his faith, Heidegger read Junger's *The Worker* and it "opened his eyes to a supra-metaphysical vision of the true meaning of the modern social, political, and economic order."[54] Heidegger had a lifelong preoccupation with the place of religious mystery in technological modernity, and extended the tradition of fusing political commitment with spiritual authenticity. For all Heidegger's complex explorations of the relationship between "Being" and "technology," his excursion into actual politics espoused nothing better than just such a "god" of unbridled brutality. Heidegger was for the most part a solitary man, preferring his cabin in the Black Forest to the company of others. His work raised the discourse of authenticity to an explicitly metaphysical level, and for this reason we shall use him here primarily to explore the metaphysical dimensions of authenticity discourse.

Martin Heidegger

Martin Heidegger's life and work were encircled by religious concern, and his religious life is a key to the unfolding of his philosophy as a discourse of authenticity. Heidegger (1889–1976) grew up in the Catholic farmlands of southern-central Germany, where his father was a sexton at St. Martin's Church. While studying for the Catholic priesthood in his twenties (1903–11), he spoke out against "the danger of 'Modernism' to the ageless wisdom of the Catholic tradition."[55] It has often been said that Heidegger had two religious turnings: his conversion from Catholicism to Protestantism in 1917 and his complete loss of religious faith in 1929.[56] These "turnings" did not occur in a rarefied intellectual atmosphere, but in a climate of terror and disaster. The first – in 1917 – occurred after the agony of the First World War shook his faith in religion. But rather than reject religion altogether, he decided that God could only be a personal savior, and could not be a caretaker for the world; thus, with a great measure of doubt and shame, he converted to Protestantism.[57] The second turning occurred after his experience of Germany in the twenties. During this time, he shook the ground at Freiburg University as a "radical phenomenologist." It appears that the absence of a worldly God in his thought encouraged him to conceptualize the life of God in the public world, which culminated in *Being and Time* (1927). Caputo has documented that a central aim of this book is to "recover authentic Christian experience" by "formaliz[ing] the structures of factical Christian life" through studies of New Testament communities.[58] But his project of preserving religious experience from the ravages of modernity was shifting onto political terrain as well. Heidegger began his first lecture following

the war in 1919 by announcing that national regeneration would necessi-
tate a "return to the authentic origins of the [German] spirit," and that
the "real reform" of the university had yet to begin. In the same lecture,
he also shouted "man, become essential!", quoting the seventeenth-
century German mystic Angelus Silesius.[59] His lectures were passionately
intense and his diatribe was obviously political, but he spoke on an
abstract level. He attacked Husserl's system for keeping human thought
too abstracted in theory, and missing the rich, pre-theoretical textures of
everyday life. He claimed that philosophy would "live or die" depending
upon whether or not it could shake off dominance by the theoretical. The
theoretical, he said, reduced experience to being "absolutely without
world, world-alien, a sphere where the breath is knocked out of you and
you cannot breathe."[60] There is an obvious subtext to such remarks which
expresses Heidegger's well-known disdain for the emergence of city life,
technology, and modernization in Germany at this time.[61] In his work, he
did consider the so-called "theoretical" as the intellectual system responsible for the development of modernity as a negative, soul-less thing. All
the while he tacitly described the necessity for a concrete immersion in
what it means to be authentically German. Although this tendency was
more manifest in his lectures, there are also strong traces of it in *Being and
Time*. *Being and Time* represents an important fusing of religious concern
and everyday culture as a seminal political intersection in Heidegger's
thought. In this famous book, Heidegger argues that the Western philosophical tradition has come to see humans and the world as mere objects
of scientific manipulation. The rational and efficient organization of
public life has gradually eaten away the spiritual content and value of
people's lives. Since this spiritual quality cannot be quantified for rational
scrutiny, it has been dismissed as unreal and secondary. In his effort to
counter this development, Heidegger begins his philosophical system at
the level of people's everyday lives, and considers what is primary in
average human existence. For the most part, people are not "perceiving"
beings (as in the Cartesian tradition of the rational subject), but "coping"
beings. Rather than staring at the world, as one would an object, they are
actively engaged within a totality. Humans encounter this world with an
implicit, pre-thematic "understanding," grounded in practices rather
than explicit pieces of knowledge. "Understanding" is a person's thorough yet unreflected grasp upon the domain, or region, of their life –
which constitutes a "temporal horizon." This organic grasp – which constitutes a network of normalized, familiar relationships within a region – is
what we call "home." If these relationships are brought out explicitly in
our everyday lives by some commonly shared understanding – like a religion – then we are in touch with Being, which manifests itself as culture.

Culture, in this sense, is a unique and shared progression which bears the impression of particular historical memories – ultimately creating a shared world which we love as a sentient being, and as the larger force underlying all individuals. For example: we certainly don't need an objective knowledge of our village or province to feel the compulsion to die for it if necessary. While an ethnographer might know the rainfall or soil content of a province, this knowledge is not the relation to it which makes one call it home in Heidegger's sense. The "forestructure of understanding" is inherently veiled in our everyday conduct (the mundane), but forms the only basis for any derivative practices such as scientific inquiry or intellectual speculation. The "forestructure" is prior to formal logic, occurring on a level where "action has its own sight."[62] This grounding is implicitly rooted in and colored by tradition. For Heidegger, the Western philosophical tradition has passed over and forgotten this "Being" – and as a result, gradually, so has Western society as a whole. Also, Western science and logic have become rootless because of this loss of connection. Instead of knowledge and facts, Heidegger posits "understanding" as the central feature of human experience in general. And whereas "knowledge" is grounded in a notion of ultimate or objective reality, "understanding" is grounded in a notion of "genuine, primordial understanding."[63] Accordingly, for Heidegger, the "truth" of "understanding" (and our lives in general) must be measured in terms of authenticity rather than accuracy. Authenticity is a recognition of the deep significance of "mood" as against formal belief or knowledge: "the possibilities of disclosure which belong to cognition reach far too short a way compared with the primordial disclosure belonging to moods."[64] Heidegger cites the orator to show the "truth" of moods – "he must understand the possibilities of moods in order to rouse them and guide them aright."[65] By centering his concepts of "understanding" and "authenticity," Heidegger tried to return the issues of "spiritual life" and "values" to the forefront of human concern.

Heidegger explains that when Being is forgotten, it remains as concrete as before, but ceases to endow collective life with meaning. Heidegger seeks a means to reignite this lost background, through creating institutions which will bring the buried spirit – i.e., German tradition – back to life explicitly in people's everyday lives. In this way, meaning would be restored to modern life. But Heidegger was quite hostile to many modern institutions – including democracy and secularism – and this became especially true when Heidegger began to articulate a binary between the declining West and the vitality of German Kultur in its privileged relationship to Being.

At this same time, Heidegger grew fascinated with the writings of

Nietzsche and Junger – there is evidence that the latter implanted the fusion of religious authenticity and radical politics in his mind.[66] In 1927, Heidegger admitted to having lost his faith completely – this second turning was most painful to him. Some combination of his spiritual anguish, his personal arrogance as a philosopher, his longing for social order, and his hatred for the West, emerged as his consciousness in the years prior to the Second World War.

Heidegger welcomed the Nazi revolution in 1933, and enthusiastically joined the crusade for "German regeneration." He saw Nazism as a means to crushing Marxism, one of his great hatreds. He also identified the Party with the far-right theories of Friedrich Naumann, whose visions of a militantly nationalistic and anti-communist "socialism" appealed to Heidegger.[67] But his work and his declarations at this time show an obvious confusion between his own philosophical ambitions and the true nature of the Nazi state. Heidegger was a mystic, not least of all in his views on social relations. He faced inevitable disappointment when the state failed to materialize in the form of his philosophical expectations.

Heidegger's writings at the time show the political nature of his philosophy. I will discuss: (1) the creative and hermeneutic nature of his view of tradition; (2) his view of political movements as grounded in ontological dispositions; (3) the conception of time as an elemental and willful force, beneath the historical chain of cause and effect; (4) his conception of "authentic knowledge" as a transcendence of rootless "universal knowledge"; (5) his sanctioning of a "metaphysical will" to politically redress the "social problem" of the "death of God."

Heidegger's mission is a type of spiritual revival, although he did not advocate a return to unconditional faith or to any religious past at all. While explicitly rejecting the possibility of such options, he insisted that spiritual revival required a shifting of meaning in human thought and practice to initiate a new beginning. Yet simultaneously, he promoted the revival of a "great and lost heritage" at the dawn of Western civilization. This apparent contradiction contains the essence of his challenge to modern conventions. He rejected the intellectual system which applies universal method to reality as an object in order to extract an essence, maintaining instead that we can only realize possibilities within a specific historical horizon and context. Thus, rather than retrieving a lost historical essence, a people must imaginatively re-explore the tacit possibilities of tradition to create the beginning anew. Hoy has described his work as shifting the locus of truth from the "epistemological model of perception" to the "hermeneutical model of reading."[68] In this regard, Heidegger can be read as a model for the insurrection of subjugated local knowledges against established dominant truths. Objective knowledge succumbs to "understanding," which is more akin to the expression "feeling at home" than the trans-cultural facts of scientific method. Heidegger's demonstration of these concepts as fundamental human structures in *Being and Time* has been seen as bringing into question the principles of rationalist universalism. On the level of practice and strategies for modernization, it also brings into question the conventional dichotomies between "superstition/reason" and "modernity/tradition" – and places these temporally conceived oppositions in a contemporary dialectic.

Heidegger's work around 1933 began to center definitively on the heroic will and he warned of an encroaching nihilism in the form of modern bourgeois-liberal institutions. He contrasted this with Germany as the spiritual nation in the middle of materialist-nihilist encirclement. It was both American consumerism and Russian Communism that threatened Germany's "soul." He described Germany's plight in his *Introduction to Metaphysics* (1935):

This Europe, in its ruinous blindness forever on the point of cutting its own throat, lies today in a great pincers, squeezed between Russia on the one side and America on the other. From a metaphysical point of view, Russia and America are the same; the same dreary technological frenzy, the same unrestricted organization of the average man . . . The spiritual decline of the earth is so far advanced that the nations are in danger of losing the last bit of spiritual energy that makes it possible to see the decline . . . We [Germans] are caught in a pincers. Situated in the center, our nation incurs the severest pressure . . . [Ours is] the most endangered [but also] the most metaphysical of nations. We are certain of this vocation, but our people will only be able to wrest a destiny from it if within itself it creates a resonance, a possibility of resonance for this vocation, and takes a creative view of its tradition. [To] move itself and thereby the history of the West beyond the center of their future "happening" and into the primordial realm of the powers of being . . . means nothing less than to recapture, to repeat, the beginning of our historical-spiritual existence, in order to transform it into a new beginning . . . we do not repeat a beginning by reducing it to something past and now known, which need merely be imitated . . . the beginning must be begun again, more radically, with all the strangeness, darkness, insecurity that attend a true beginning.[69]

In this passage, Heidegger pits his vision for Germany's future against the twin expressions of modernist-rationalist triumph: Western liberal capitalism and Soviet socialism. Both systems profess materialist ideologies and perceive progress as the transcendence of superstitious tradition in favor of rational secularism. Thus, for Heidegger, they are metaphysically the same despite their mutual opposition on a political level. Heidegger's attack is essentially a metaphysical attack on the paradigm of Enlightenment rationalism, which he sees as causing the "darkening of the world" through nihilism. On a more personal level, these passages express Heidegger's mind state as a Nazi activist. He is obviously concerned with religion in some form – though the prominence of "will to power" in his thought seems to exclude any but the most godless and bloodthirsty. He is concerned with the place of Germany, its autonomy and strength in the modern world, and the preservation of its authentic culture. How can these spiritual and national aspirations be reconciled? For Heidegger at this stage, God is Being endowed with a political will. German culture alone is in touch with this Being and will. German culture opposes the doomed and Godless West with the support of this Being. How, then, could a metaphysic of "will to power" not be justified in the execution of this "great" historical deed?

There is more. Heidegger anticipated a completely new world in the wake of overcoming bourgeois Zivilization. He reduced history to a primordial power play, utterly passing over the social forces which created the war, and attached Being to the will of the Nazi state. Volition was everything in his philosophy at this time, the only time when he was active in politics. From so isolated a vision, what but sheer volition could act as wings to drive his perception upon the world and reshape it? Heidegger never once deigned to enter politics as a process of negotiation: he never once recognized the real complex of social relations. Just as violently as Heidegger had philosophical wishes for the world, so this totalitarian state would implement them with an incontestable will. This, at least, was Heidegger's naive expectation.

His politicization changed the content of his writings. Whereas his formerly philosophical work had only implicitly referred to technology and politics, his new work began explicitly to discuss the preservation of German identity within modernity. Heidegger joined the party in 1933, and became Rector of the University of Freiburg that same year. His Rectorial address proclaims the necessity for a "spiritual mission" to salvage the "extreme distress of the German fate."[70] To provide the context for this "mission," Heidegger's lecture invites us to leave behind "historical time" and enter "elemental time." Ernst Junger's description of the difference between elemental and historical time is useful for understanding this pillar of authenticity discourse:

Success in history, as the conquest of Babylon, for example, shows, is fleeting and tied to names. The moment does not return in the same form; it becomes a link in the chain of historical time. But if we consider changes in the elemental world, neither names nor dates are important and yet changes take place time and again, not only below historical time, but also within it. They burst forth like magma from the crust.[71]

Elemental time seeks to shift the center of truth from surface events, in a chain of cause and effect, to a deeper and hidden level beyond rational scrutiny. Thus, Heidegger's Rectorial address could insist that ". . . the [Greek] beginning of [knowledge] remains its greatest moment," and although "Christian-theological interpretation" and the "mathematical technical thinking of the modern age" have caused degeneration, "the beginning still exists and stands before us." The "beginning" has "invaded our future" and issued "a distant decree [ordering us] to recapture its greatness."[72] He describes a European loss of roots in the Greek past, and insists that only Germany can revive this distant greatness. The context for this challenge is the onslaught of Western nihilism, and Heidegger's address offers an illustration of the contrast between decadent bourgeois nihilist society and the revived greatness offered by National Socialism.

Initially, the lecture dispenses with "historical time" as a method of analysis for comprehending the "spiritual mission" of the University:

Do we know of this spiritual mission? . . . Neither knowledge of the conditions that prevail today nor familiarity with its earlier history guarantees sufficient knowledge of the essence of the university unless we first delimit, clearly and uncompromisingly, this essence for the future; in such self-limitation, will it, and, in this willing, assert ourselves.[73]

Beneath the material surface of history, then, a fusion of created self-consciousness and political commitment are projected by the force of will. Heidegger has introduced the inseparability between self-realization and political commitment, a central feature of all authenticity discourse. He goes on to describe the "science," or "authentic," "true knowing," which shall serve as the "innermost necessity of [German] existence":

We regard the German university as the "high" school which from science and through science, educates and disciplines the leaders and guardians of the fate of the German Volk. The will to the essence of the German university is the will to science as the will to the historical spiritual mission of the German Volk as a Volk that knows itself in its state. Science and German fate must come to power at the same time in the will to essence. And they will do this then and only then when we – the teachers and students – expose science to its innermost necessity, on the one hand, and, on the other, when we stand firm in the face of German fate in its extreme distress.[74]

Science, then, is not conceived as a trans-cultural and universal method of inquiry. It is an agent for the spiritual revitalization of the German nation. Heidegger tells us it is worth having "only when we submit to the power of the existence." Such a science is motivated by a "passion to remain close to what is," and must be grounded in the "fruitfulness and blessing of all the world-shaping forces of man's historical existence: nature, history, language, the Volk, custom, the state, poetry, thought, belief, sickness, madness, death, law, economy, and technology." He contrasts this to dispassionate, universal, bourgeois science: "a calm, pleasurable activity, an activity free of danger, which promotes the mere advancement of knowledge."[75]

The realization of a world based on this science is entirely dependent on the will. But such a will exists already, with the "German students on the march," and needs only a purposeful vision. The university is to be the source of "spiritual legislation." The combination of "will" and German "science" will "create for our Volk a world of the innermost and most extreme danger, i.e., a truly spiritual world."[76] Spirituality is not the "busy practice of never-ending rational analysis," but "the determined resolve to the essence of Being, a resolve that is attuned to origins and knowing." Nor is "the spiritual world of the Volk" a "cultural superstructure" or "arsenal of useful knowledge and values," but a "preserving at the most profound level [of] the forces that are rooted in the soil and blood of a Volk."[77]

Perhaps most astonishingly of all, Heidegger speaks of creating a political reckoning for Nietzsche's philosophical poeticizing about the "death of God." Rather than letting the issue remain on the level of philosophical discourse, he wants to "take it seriously" on the level of real world politics:

[I]f our own most existence itself stands on the threshold of a great transformation; if it is true what . . . Nietzsche said: "God is dead"; . . . if we must take seriously the abandonment of man today in the midst of Being, what then does this imply for science?[78]

Here the answer is clear – the death of God can only be rectified if science submits itself to the authenticating conditions Heidegger has just described. National and spiritual regeneration have become completely intertwined, and the genocidal Nazi state forms the only bridge home to Being. Finally, the lecture contains a stinging indictment of bourgeois decadence, counterposed with the new reality emerging in Germany. Since the West is doomed to collapse under its own corruption, Germany can survive only by creating a path of its own:

Do we will the essence of the German university, or do we not will it?. . . But neither will anyone ask us whether we will it or do not will it when the spiritual strength of the West fails and the West starts to come apart at the seams, when this moribund pseudocivilization collapses into itself, pulling all forces into confusion and allowing them to suffocate in madness.[79]

In this light, bourgeois freedom appears as a "lack of concern, arbitrariness in one's intentions and inclinations, lack of restraint in anything one does." Labor service, Heidegger contends, will return "the German students' notion of freedom" to "its truth." Germans will no longer be permitted bourgeois "knowledge service," "the dull, quick training for an elegant profession." Rather, knowledge will "place one's existence in the most acute danger in the midst of overpowering Being."[80]

Yet twelve years later, the revolution which Heidegger so praised had fallen to the global forces that he most despised: Soviet Communism and "Western" liberal capitalism. While refusing to fully renounce Nazism, Heidegger renounced the possibility of human will-power effecting spiritual revival. Furthermore, he re-interpreted Nietzsche and the Nazis as expressions of the global "Will to Power" metaphysic, the detached subject seeking to completely manipulate the world as an object through will, without any intermediary relation to Being – allegedly the very thing he had joined the Nazi party to protest. Yet while he renounced the usefulness of activism and "will," his attitude towards the spiritual plight of humanity did not dramatically change. He simply cut himself off from political life, insisting that we are "too late for the gods, and too early for Being."[81] When, in his *Der Spiegel* interview, he was asked to contribute his philosophical talent to improving the nation, he responded that society must simply wait passively for a "god to save us."[82] Returning to his level of veiled abstraction, he focussed on the central danger to spirituality posed by modernity: the secular, technological world. Hence, we see the extent of his direct political activism. He was a philosopher who blindly fooled the instruments of a modern state for his philosophical castles in the sky.

I shall now confine myself to three remarks about the implications of Heidegger's thought for the discourse of authenticity and the politics which produce it. The first is the issue of "collective meaning" or "community." Heidegger's confrontation with the tradition has implications for politics around the issue of secularism. For secular modernism, the only true reality is everything you can see, touch, and measure. Everything else is your dream, your opinion, your moral sensibility – it is not certain. These uncertainties are confined to the individual, as private matters, or to particular institutions, such as the Church – they do not color the public sphere. Thus, "meaning" is contrasted with "truth" as the subjective to the objective. Conversely, Heidegger insists that meaning is embedded in the fullness of public life, and cannot be confined to individuals except when the very meaning of "life" itself has been lost. Heidegger's critique of modern religion is that it exists inside individuals and churches, but not in the world.[83] It is for this reason that Heidegger urges Germany to revive its buried tradition in the face of modernization from the "West." Heidegger's appeal lies in making "meaning" real again, as a source of authority to guide society towards a common goal. In situations of national developmental crisis, this issue of "meaning" can be a very powerful axis of politicization, especially where numerous cultural traditions exist and await the transformation into ideology.

The other point is about the nature of tradition in Heidegger's work. Whatever his personal feelings may have been regarding cities or technology, Heidegger's philosophical system articulates a very open and adaptive form of tradition. It is no innocuous or temporary effort to "return." His system loosens the foundations of conventional paradigms of tradition, and invites them to enter modern society as political agents without being "assimilated" or deleted. This achievement signals both positive and negative possibilities. On the positive side, it invites a more complex and less reductionist view of people's political subjectivities, and gives voice to political perspectives which have been historically deleted or submerged into larger identities. Again, Heidegger's philosophical system, rather than the man himself, must take the credit for these positive effects in that people have derived these uses from his work. On the negative side, Heidegger's system creates an openness in tradition while preserving the worst authoritarian tendencies of any tradition. Heidegger made no secret of being an enemy of democracy, and this factor plays out in his work. Anyone attempting to use Heidegger's system for progressive purposes must fully face up to this, or risk the pitfall of unbridled authoritarianism.

Finally, Heidegger's system has implications for ethnic politics. In criticizing the vacuous and diverse cluster of values posited by the rational society, Heidegger argues that there is a deeper, mysterious, background of real values already contained in our active, collective life. This, for him, is the spiritual foundation of a people, and liberation depends upon achieving a "conscious" alignment with it. Naming this background and transforming it into a uniform belief system is a political act. This type of "identity" seems most likely to surface where distinct ethnicities have recently suffered forced migration to cities, and are asked to assimilate with the "urban mass." Such "identities" are also likely where developing nations demand that their minority populations conform to some larger national identity for the sake of political integration.

Conclusion

Let us now outline some of the differences in content and then the shared ideological traits between the German and Iranian cases. The first obvious difference is in the political orientation of the German and Iranian intellectuals. Both Shari'ati and Al-e Ahmad had strong socialist, even Marxist, leanings – but their embrace of Islam forced them to create a radically alternative form of revolutionary socialism. They essentially viewed themselves as radicals of the Left, although their work helped to usher in a conservative theocracy. Shari'ati was especially explicit in envisioning a classless society for his goal. Junger and Heidegger, on the other hand, were explicitly right-wing, and championed only the most nationalistic forms of socialism which had nothing to do with an egalitarian society. Heidegger, especially, hated Marxism and its promise of a classless society, considering this a dreadful leveler of the human spirit. Junger's impassioned love for "merciless spectacle" and "mayhem" naturally aligned him with a politics of perpetual crisis – but at times the Soviet Union's modernization policies satisfied his appetite for this, and he frankly extended his warm admiration to the country. In this way Junger at times seemed dubiously apolitical, pledging his allegiance to anything that promised vital and chaotic upheaval. But this commitment in itself is a sabotage of any serious attempt to create a just and egalitarian society.

The parallels between the two sets of thinkers are abundant. Initially, there is a longing for an authoritative tradition to hold onto against the chaotic tide of modernization. This is set up as a critique of humanity's absence of conviction under modernity – or absence of a unifying social principle to endow collective life with a single, higher meaning. These types of sentiments, ultimately, are the very opposite of "multiculturalism," because they envision human worth in the uniformity of collective will and identity.

The desire for an authoritative tradition is conjoined with a longing for an absolutely new beginning. The "new dawn" is a common projection of modern ideologies of liberation. In this case, the potential for the new dawn is located in some repressed dimension of the prevalent tradition. Shari'ati argues that Shi'i Islam has a secret and essential revolutionary side, and Heidegger argues that our essential roots in Greek culture "demand" that we make a new beginning and reject the hollow "bourgeois civilization" that has evolved.

This tendency to raise "hidden traditions" shows a very creative relationship to tradition – the thinkers here are not afraid to utterly re-invent the traditions of their societies for radical political purposes. But the important thing is to disguise the intellectualization of the tradition, and to make the interpretation appear ontologically legitimized. It is not simply a new interpretation of an old tradition, but the true life blood of the tradition itself calling to us to restore its greatness under siege. Heidegger's Rectorial address, for example, issued a twisted imperative as he promised forms of damnation for those who refused to hear the "calling" of the "roots." There is no doubt that he deliberately manipulated this religious format, even calling himself "the spiritual leader."

Of course, ontological legitimacy must be contrasted with decline. Just as the tradition has become corrupted by the powers that be and the "Great Satan" outside, so the masses must be called upon, in their simple and untainted wisdom, to perform the gut-level imperative of destroying the ruling order and restoring the "spiritually authentic" truth.

The final and most significant dynamic in this whole scenario is the presence of a vast external civilization, an encroaching and powerful "Other," the living incarnation of evil, injustice, and decay. This enemy sets up the condition for pitting "universal standardization" against "authenticity." In both Iran and Germany, authenticity was supposed to constitute a third way through modernity.

Let us now observe some of the social conditions which give rise to movements of this kind. They will occur in societies being rapidly modernized from above, and where traditional modes of life are thus being violently displaced. The process of modernization will be imposed by a regime which is either perceived to be, or is in fact, behaving under the influence of a controlling foreign power. A history of intervention and domination by foreign powers is an important factor – though even the perception of a comparatively more advanced neighbor may incite such hostilities. The ideology of authenticity makes its strongest appeal in developing urban centers, where a rapidly growing new urban poor are witnessing a widening gulf between themselves and a new upper-class elite. This elite will be viewed as the infestation of the externally controlling foreign power. These movements frequently take on the character of being simultaneously populist and authoritarian.

Having then defined the conditions and tendencies associated with movements for authenticity, we can see how modernity in its conventional mode literally and systematically functions not only to incite such movements, but to proliferate them on an ever greater scale. The gridlock of antagonism implicit in modernity's own terms as a system of world domination, classification, and exclusion has the effect of "creating its own monsters"; i.e., reproductions of the exclusion and violence essential to its own system on a smaller but ever proliferating scale. In light of this, it is time we arrested the foolish game of pretending such formations are "aberrations," atavistic and freak insertions of a distant past, awaiting transcendence by the progress of history. We must dispense with all ludicrous distortions about an "age of faith" in the Third World and an "age of reason" in the West. Implicit in such totalizing and myth-making categorizations is a continuation of the violence endemic to the era of Western and colonial domination; the resurgence of this mythology and its accompanying practices will only guarantee that the pattern of resistance described herein is very far indeed from exhausting itself.

There is one more way in which we may profit from this example of the German discourse of authenticity. It shows the irrelevance of attempts to explain these movements, and their authoritarian leanings, in terms of some "non-Western spirit" – as, for example, we see in Huntington's desperate attempt to re-invent the East/West split (and its corresponding mind states) within Europe itself based on the "border line" separating the Islamic and Orthodox Slavs from the Catholic Slavs. The manifestations we have described are liable to transpire in any setting where the experience of modernization is inseparable from one of violent intervention, irrespective of totalizing demarcations dreamed up by intellectuals regarding the supposedly essential split between "East" and "West."

6   The tragedy of the Iranian Left[1]

Religious distress is at the same time the expression of real distress and
the protest against real distress. Religion is the sigh of the oppressed
creature, the heart of a heartless world, just as it is the spirit of a spiritless
situation. It is the opium of the people.   Karl Marx[2]

Introduction

The story of the Iranian Left in the build-up to the Revolution of 1979 is
instructive in several important ways. The telling of this story, of course,
amounts in the final analysis to the explanation of a tragic modernist
failure. In all fairness, however, one should consider that the Iranian Left
was confronted by a very difficult and complex situation for which it was
not ready. The Islamic discourse and the pre-eminent role of clerics were
explained away as "superstructural" manifestations, spontaneous religious expressions, and transiently superficial features of the revolutionary
process.[3] This overconfidence in theories of modernity and secularization
(which scientific Marxism, as well as a range of other modernist ideologies, embraced) mirrored, and perhaps exceeded, the Pahlavi state's own
dogmatic and unrelenting attachment to predigested and hegemonic
conceptions of modernity. The Left's dismissal of religious politics as
merely instrumental in their potential not only overlooked a towering and
important source of revolutionary force, but resulted in support of
Islamic politics, based on the same imperceptive reason, by many leftist
organizations and intellectuals.[4] We can say that the Left, not unlike many
other Iranian political forces, was a victim of the general modernist failure
to see Islam as the forceful and violent spring of power that it was. How
destructive and unhelpful it proved, in their case, to cling to those rigidly
preconceived modernist boundaries when things were unfolding in front
of their eyes along profoundly different lines; and the conceptual blindfold which dispensed with the need for self-doubt remained affixed seemingly until the final and bitter moment of reckoning. It is in this important
context that the story of the Iranian Left fits in neatly with the overall
dominant narrative of modernity we have been describing in this book.

On another level, a close look at the story of the Iranian Left will reveal that the Revolution was far from an exclusively Islamic phenomenon. Other forces, most notably the secular Left and liberal nationalists, provided ideas which fueled the Revolution and also fueled the Islamic radicals themselves. Significant and telling portions of society joined and participated in the Revolution from a secular/Left perspective. The seminal role of the Left, as we will show in this chapter, was no accident; the tradition of leftist activism runs deep in modern Iranian political history.

What is perhaps most interesting and most contrary to prevalent views of Islamic radicalism is the fact that the Islamists proved themselves to be far more pragmatic in political thinking than the Left itself. It was the Islamists who unabashedly appropriated large portions of leftist discourse for their own purposes, while the Left itself clung tenaciously to its abstract modernist boundaries to the utter detriment of practical politics. Ironically, it was so-called "fundamentalists" who were most willing to twist and interfuse divergent ideological streams with the sheer force of their political imaginations, while the Left remained blindly and resolutely bound to its received "scientific" categories of social analysis. Moreover, the implications of this massive intellectual appropriation remained lost on most thinkers of the Left, with well-known and disastrous consequences. The political disarming of the Iranian Left was prefigured well in advance by its intellectual disarmament at the hands of Islamic radicals, and this critical blow transpired all but completely without their notice or serious consideration.

Yet the very failings of the Left – particularly its naive, reductionist and dogmatic style of political thought – demonstrate that the conditions foreclosing the Left's failure in this instance hardly ensure the irrelevance or inevitable failure of the Left or secularist projects in themselves for Iran. The fact that the ideas of class inequality and secularism exercised such widespread appeal at crucial junctures in modern Iranian history only shows all the more that the failure of the Left in the Iranian Revolution sprang from its own self-induced and ultimately suicidal limitations, and not from any hostility to these ideas innate to the Iranian soil. Taking into consideration the highly significant role of Left, radical, and secular ideas in modern Iranian history, it would be entirely mistaken to presume such influences as de facto dead or irrelevant to the political and social development of the country.

A brief history of socialist movements

It is worth pointing out that the socialist movement in Iran is among the oldest not only in the Middle East but in Asia. Maxime Rodinson points out that at the beginning of the century there appeared in the Middle East a working-class trade union movement and various social democratic organizations in contact with the Second International. Among them were Iranian laborers working in the Russian Caucasus, notably in Baku.[5] Liberal thought had emerged in the previous century, and the small Iranian intelligentsia was active in the 1906–11 Constitutional Revolution in Iran,[6] in Rasht, Mashhad, Tabriz, and Tehran. The Constitutional Revolution allowed the socialist trade unions and political organizations to develop and become firmly rooted in Iran itself.[7] Iranian socialists took part in the Bolshevik Revolution in Russia and were also greatly inspired by it. Persia's Avetis Mikailian, better known as Sultanzadeh, was, along with India's M. N. Roy, among the prominent Marxists of Asia, and was a delegate to the Comintern.[8] The Iranian Communist Party took part in nationalist movements and autonomy struggles in the 1920s, and one of its leading figures, Haidar Amughli Khan, was a founder of the short-lived (1921) Gilan Soviet Republic.

The labor movement in Iran grew in tandem with the socialist and communist parties, as has been the case in many other countries. The earliest unions – of printers and telegraphers – were formed in 1906 in Tehran and Tabriz and by 1944 one of the largest labor confederations in Asia existed in Iran and was associated with the communist Tudeh Party.[9] The making of the Iranian Left spanned several decades and left an indelible mark on the political culture. Certain words and concepts, understood to be left-wing or socialist in origin, have become part of popular and intellectual vocabularies. The evolution of the Left has been by no means smooth or uninterrupted; over the years, the socialist movement has suffered serious setbacks and lost many of its cadre and leading intellectuals to prisons and firing squads. Nonetheless, throughout the century and right up to the recent Revolution it managed to be a consistent social and political force which also represented a cultural alternative to both the traditionalism of Islamic forces and the "pseudo-modernism"[10] of the monarchists.

To summarize the trajectory of the Left's growth and activities up until the recent Revolution, we have identified four distinct phases (see Table 1). The first was the period 1906–37, representing its genesis and growth as a militant, revolutionary communist movement with strong ties to the emerging working class and an emphasis on trade unions. This period ended with the rise of the autocrat Reza Shah (ruled 1926–41), who put an end to left-wing activity through the promulgation of laws and through armed force. The second period was 1941–53, the interregnum between the two dictatorships, when activists from the 1920s reemerged from prison, exile and underground existence to form the Tudeh (masses)

Table 1. *Iranian secular radical organizations*

Period	Political Parties	Activities
1906–37	Social Democratic Party (later Edalat and (Communist parties) Arani Group	Trade-union organizing, women's associations, Gilan Soviet Republic Published *Donya*
1941–53	Tudeh Party	Trade-union organizing, parliamentary and political activities
	Ferqeh Democrat	Azerbaijan Autonomous Republic (1945–46)
	Kurdish Democratic Party	Mahabad Republic
	Niroye Sevom	Intellectual and political activities
1954–70	Tudeh Party	In exile; student organizing in Europe
	National Front II, Niroye Sevom	Brief resurgence 1960–63; thereafter active in student movement in Europe and the U.S.
1970–78	New Communist Movement	Urban guerrilla actions and underground activities
	People's Fedayee Peykar Revolutionary Organization Palestine Group Tufan	
	Tudeh Party	Anti-regime activities
	Confederation of Iranian Students (U.S., Europe)	Raising international awareness; anti-regime activities
	People's Mojahedin	Urban guerrilla actions

Party. With close ties to the Soviet Union, the party became a major political actor with formal links to the labor confederation, one of the largest in Asia. The other major force during this period was the National Front, a grouping of liberal and nationalist parties which favored constitutional rule and a strong parliament. This period ended with the CIA-sponsored coup d'état against prime minister Mohammad Mosaddeq (August 1953), and the resumption of autocracy. The third period, 1954–70, began in a post-Comintern context with no communist center; the Cold War and U.S. hegemony reigned internationally, and the Shah was closely identified with American global and regional economic and military interests. Regionally, the period was characterized by the rise of anti-Zionist and anti-imperialist movements. Domestically, the Tudeh Party and the labor unions were suppressed and banned; a project for capitalist development was initiated and jointly undertaken by the second Pahlavi ruler, Mohammad Reza Shah, in concert with Western, particularly

American, capital. During this period, the locus of underground Left activity shifted from the factory to the university. In the early 1960s there was a brief resurgence of dissident activity, mainly by the National Front. In what Abrahamian has called a dress rehearsal for the 1978–79 Revolution, protests in 1963 against the Shah's autocracy and growing ties to the U.S. involved students, teachers, bazaaris, the Tudeh Party, and a leading cleric who was subsequently exiled – Ayatollah Ruhollah Khomeini.[11]

In the fourth phase, 1970–78, a new type of Left emerged: political-military organizations espousing armed struggle against the Pahlavi regime as the regional pillar of U.S. imperialism. In Iran, as elsewhere, this period saw the full formulation of an anti-imperialist paradigm which posited a military strategy of revolution and a vague socio-economic program. During these years, guerrilla activity was undertaken principally by the Organization of the Iranian People's Fedayee Guerrillas (OIPFG, or Fedayee), and the Organization of the Mojahedin of the People of Iran (OMPI, or Mojahedin), in addition to smaller guerrilla groups. These groups were (and are in this chapter) referred to as the "militant Left" or "new communist movement."

In his discussion of the contention between "fundamentalism" and secular criticism in the Arab world, Sharabi notes the "double disadvantage" of the latter: "It enjoys limited power in the political arena (lacking political organization), and as state censorship erodes, restricts, and deflects its effectiveness, it finds itself also opposed by mass (religious) opinion."[12] He points out that while the new radical critics are routinely attacked, muzzled, and suppressed under most Arab regimes, fundamentalist spokespersons are not only allowed to proclaim their doctrines freely and publicly but are often provided with substantial aid by the state institutional machinery and media. So it was in Iran.

It is important to note that throughout the 1960s and 1970s, while the Left and liberal/social democratic forces and their institutions were hounded and banned by the Pahlavi state, the religious establishment expanded considerably and its institutions proliferated.[13] Networks of mosques, seminaries, and lecture halls, the publication of religious journals and books, access to the print and electronic media, and the steady stream of mullahs (clerics) emerging from the theological schools of Qom and elsewhere provided the leaders of political Islam with an important social base, organization, and resources.[14] The Shah's political war against the Left and the liberals resulted in a diminution of secular political discourse, left-wing organizational resources, and democratic institutions. The dominant language of protest and opposition against the Pahlavi state was religious, even though elements of other discourses (third worldist, Marxist, populist) were also present. When the Army and monarchy collapsed in February 1979, the clerics were in a far more advantageous position than any other political force to assume power and to command popular allegiance.

The Revolution and the Left

In Iran, uniquely, the revolution was "made" – but not, everyone will note, by any of the modern revolutionary parties on the Iranian scene: not by the Islamic guerrillas or by the Marxist guerrillas, or by the Communist ("Tudeh") Party, or by the secular-liberal National Front.[15]

In providing an account of the experiences of the Left during and after the 1979 Revolution, four phases may be identified. The first was the revolutionary conjuncture itself, 1978–79, which catapulted the Left as a mass force, a situation for which it was largely unprepared. The second important period was 1980–81, when the battle between the Left, liberals, and Islamists intensified. The third phase began in June 1981, when Left organizations went underground and lost the battle with the Islamists. The fourth and present phase is that of the resumption of the politics of exile and a shift in political thinking and practice.

When the revolution erupted, the odds were seriously stacked against the Left. Twenty-five years of systematic suppression of the socialist and liberal forces, and the absence of any democratic institutions, left a political and institutional vacuum which the religious establishment quickly occupied. The consolidation of Islamist rule, however, was by no means predetermined; rather, it followed protracted political conflict and ideological contention between Islamists, socialists, and liberals. The absence of an understanding of the nature of political Islam, on the part of the Left, disunity within its ranks, and unwillingness to forge a liberal–Left alliance undermined the secular project and facilitated Islamist domination.

It may come as a surprise to learn that the Iranian Revolution occurred in the absence of any political parties openly operating in the country. The parties, organizations and groups which were written about during the revolution – the National Front, the Freedom Movement, the Islamic Republican Party (IRP), the Tudeh Party – existed in name only. (The IRP was formed immediately after the Revolution, but had distinct advantages which will be discussed in a subsequent section.) Years of underground existence and exile had left the Tudeh Party, National Front, Fedayee Guerrillas, Mojahedin and others without the social bases, resources, large memberships, and other political means necessary for real and viable political organization. This is especially true of the new revolutionary organizations formed during the 1970s. Our interviews with past and present activists and leaders of Peykar, Fedayee, the Tudeh Party and smaller Maoist groups reveal that on the eve of the revolution in 1977, most of their cadres were in prison. Some were residing and working outside of Iran, and the rest of the membership was small in number and very disorganized. A former leader of Peykar told us that his organization had about 50 members in late 1977; a Fedayee leader estimated that there were about 25 remaining members. Not withstanding the Tudeh Party's long history of political activity and the fact that it had refrained from armed struggle (and therefore had lost fewer cadres), it was only able to organize two or three cells. Compared to its large numbers in the early 1950s, the Tudeh Party on the eve of the revolution was quite small. Indeed, the student movement abroad, organized in the Confederation of Iranian Students, was actually larger than any of the internal parties. As the revolutionary situation intensified in 1978, the existing Left organizations began to disagree internally as to the proper approach, method, and action to take. Within the Fedayee organization, major disputes around theoretical and political issues led some members to leave the group and join the Tudeh Party.

The revolutionary conjuncture

The revolutionary conjuncture transformed the Left's situation and gave it an open space within which to maneuver. With a base among university students and former political prisoners, the Left gained in stature and prestige as a result of its engagement in armed struggle against the Shah. Indeed, the moral and psychological impact of the urban guerrilla movement was an important factor in attracting large numbers of radicalized youth and intellectuals to the Fedayee. In the process of the revolution, therefore, the Left emerged as a mass force and came to represent a serious challenge to the Islamists in 1979. Its social base was principally among university and high school students, but included teachers, engineers, and some skilled workers.[16] In addition, the Left was active among the ethnic and religious minorities, especially the Kurds and Turkomans. The student supporters were organized into different student groups (Pishgam, Daneshjooyan-e Mobarez, Demokrat, etc.); teachers and engineers became members or active supporters; workers' councils were supported or organized; and left-wing organizations promoted the struggle around ethnic rights and regional autonomy. Table 2 lists the main secular left-wing organizations and their characteristics.

It is important to stress the conjunctural nature of left-wing support. It was tied very much to revolutionary enthusiasm, the political space

Table 2. *Characteristics of principal secular left-wing organizations, 1979–83*

Organization	Orientation	Formation/Duration
Iranian People's Fedayee Guerrillas (OIPFG)	Independent, non-aligned communist	Formed 1970; split 1980 into minority and majority wings
Peykar	Maoist	Formed 1974 out of Mojahedin; disbanded 1983
Tudeh Party of Iran	Pro-Soviet communist	Formed 1941; leadership arrested early 1983; split in 1985 declared People's Democratic Party of Iran
Kumaleh	Formerly Maoist, non-aligned	Formed 1978 as a leftist alternative to KDPI; remains active in Kurdestan
Kurdish Democratic Party of Iran (KDPI)	Social democratic/ nationalist/federalist	Formed 1945; split in 1988 created "Revolutionary KDPI"
Fedayee-Guerrillas (Ashraf Dehghani Group)	Armed-struggle advocates	Formed 1978 out of OIPFG; underwent several splits
Rah-e Karger	Independent communist	Formed 1978; still active
Ranjbaran	Maoist	Formed 1979; dissolved 1985
Ettehade Mobarezan	Maoist	Formed 1979; dissolved 1981
Union of Communists	Maoist	Formed 1976; dissolved 1982
Hezbe Kargaran Sosialist	Fourth International Trotskyist	Formed 1979; dissolved 1982

created by the Revolution with the dissolution of the old regime, the absence of a new central authority, and the respect accorded to the guerrilla organizations which grew when SAVAK torturers on trial in early 1979 recounted their horrific treatment of communist prisoners. The Left's expanding base of support was not the result of years of political organizing and mobilization – this was a luxury they had never been allowed.

It should also be recalled that the Left was being challenged by a very difficult political and ideological situation. Political Islam was something that was not well understood; the Left had nothing to go by theoretically or experientially to help it better come to grips with this new phenomenon. To be sure, Iranian leftists were not the only ones who were confused by the situation and could not respond to the challenge of political Islam. Both within Iran and internationally, many liberal, progressive and radical groups and individuals did not recognize the hazards of the politi-

Table 3. *Selected leftist candidates in the Tehran elections for the Assembly of Experts*

Candidate	Votes	Affiliation
R. Daneshgari	115,334	Fedayee
M. Madani	100,894	Fedayee
H. Raisi	90,641	Fedayee
M. Hajghazi	56,085	Fedayee
M. Aladpoosh	49,979	Peykar
E. Tabari	47,225	Tudeh
N. Kianouri	32,627	Tudeh
M. Amooye	25,792	Tudeh
M. Farmanfarmaiyan	25,435	Tudeh
B. Zahrai	16,446	Hezbe Kargaran Sosialist

Source: Ettela'at, 12 August 1979

cal Islam which under the leadership of Ayatollah Ruhollah Khomeini took over state power in 1979. The rise of Islam as a mass movement could not be explained by class analysis or other modernist sociological categories.

Expansion and contention

The year 1979 was one of expansion for the Iranian Left. The Revolution created the possibility for their increased involvement on the political terrain, including participation in electoral politics. Leftist candidates ran for seats in the Assembly of Experts and the Parliament (see Table 3). A serious drawback to left-wing activity, however, was the absence of a long-term perspective and program. Instead of building a movement, Iran's socialists were constantly responding to regime actions. For example, any measure taken by the regime which appeared progressive, such as nationalization of the banks and its confrontation with the United States, would spark a discussion within the socialist organizations as to the nature of the regime and its future course of development. In this way the totality of political Islam was ignored and a comprehensive analysis of the regime escaped them.

The theoretical discourse that most Iranian leftist organizations and intellectuals had adopted did not permit them to see the realities of political Islam and the course of events in Iran. Socialism was equated with nationalization of the economy and anti-imperialism. The Fedayee Organization published its program one year after the Revolution, in

February 1980. The main concern of the program was the elimination of dependent capitalism and imperialism, and the nationalization of industries and foreign trade.[17] Thus, the nationalization program undertaken by the Islamic regime, and its anti-U.S. rhetoric and policies, confused the Iranian Left – as it did many international leftists. When "Islam" was seriously considered, it was done so within an economistic and reductionist discourse which viewed religion, culture and ideology as superstructural, and thereby derivative.[18] For example, in analyzing the results of the Assembly of Experts elections, the Fedayee suggested that the people's support for Khomeini was symbolic and emotional and did not represent any class interest.[19]

Analytically oblivious to the compelling nature of political Islam, and incapable of recognizing political Islam as a class project, the Left was also inattentive to the theocratic, anti-secular and anti-democratic nature of the regime. A line of argument in the newspaper *Kar*[20] was that the Islamic fanatics were unimportant and without a future and that the Liberals were to be the focus of the struggle. Because the struggle against imperialism and dependent capitalism was presumed to be paramount, the socialist organizations gave a short shrift to democratic concerns, including "bourgeois feminism." While socialists paid lip service to women's rights, freedom of the press, and political freedoms, the major Left organizations, following a brief period of cooperation, ended ties with the National Democratic Front, which was making democratic rights its priority. Left-wing discourse was strongly populist in its appeal to "the toiling masses" and to peasants. None of the socialist groups had specific references to the problems and needs of women or young people; all were inattentive to questions of education, recreation, personal freedoms and rights. As a result the Left deprived itself of a solid base among the modern social strata, a foundation which any socialist program would need to realize its goals. In its inability to formulate an alternative democratic-socialist program, the Left missed the chance to present itself as a serious political and ideological contender.

Another missed opportunity was the construction of a Left united front. Even after the anti-democratic and anti-communist nature of the Islamist regime was obvious to all, the Left remained fragmented and sectarian and proved incapable of uniting to counter the Islamists' moves. In retrospect it is astounding that the many left-wing groups and organizations ignored the obvious fact that post-revolutionary Iranian society was being transformed into an Islamic-totalitarian state and made no effort to form a broad secular-radical united front to oppose this trend. It is conceivable that a Left–liberal alliance would have altered the balance of power. But such a prospect was never even considered. In some cases, opportunism and organizational fetishism precluded cooperation; this was especially true of the Mojahedin and the Tudeh Party, both of which had grand plans for themselves. In other cases, dogmatic insistence on ideological and political purity not only prevented cross-party alliances but eventually split certain key organizations (such as the Fedayee in 1980 and 1981) nearly into oblivion. Meanwhile the IRP, the party of the Islamists, was extending its sphere of influence and easing out liberal control within the government and bureaucracy. Without a perspective for the future and by adopting a naive and simplistic anti-imperialist position, the Left found that the seizure of the American Embassy by pro-Khomeini students in November 1979 represented a serious political and theoretical challenge. Following this event, disagreements within the Fedayee organization as to the nature of the regime intensified, and the organization formally split in early 1980. The Fedayee-Majority adopted the Tudeh Party position that the regime was "anti-imperialist" and deserving of left-wing support.

In sum, this critical period was marked by the expansion of the Left organizations and their bitter internal debates over the nature of the new regime; the efficacy of Islamic populism in mobilizing popular support and challenging the received wisdom of the communist groups; errors and missed opportunities in the areas of women's rights and democracy; electoral confusion; and the absence of a united front. Guided by the anti-imperialist paradigm, the Left organizations frequently slid into a populist rhetoric that echoed many of the themes of the Islamists. They seemed unable to offer a distinct, separate, and alternative socialist agenda. Moreover, during this period regime harassment of the Left increased; violent battles were fought in Kurdistan (August 1979) and Turkaman Sahra (January 1980). Abolhassan Bani-Sadr was elected president but joined the "Islamic cultural revolution," which was spearheaded by his rival Ayatollah Beheshti, head of the IRP, to weed out communist influence in the universities (April 1980). In September 1980 the Iraqis invaded Iran, forcing the Left to face another challenge and to formulate a "line" on the war.

The seizure of the American Embassy, the split within the Fedayee, the Iraqi invasion of Iran, and the growing rift between Bani-Sadr and the IRP each presented a new and apparently overwhelming challenge to the Left. Each time a problem was resolved or at least dealt with, a new one emerged to preoccupy the Left organizations. Like Lewis Carroll's Red Queen, it took all the running they could do to keep up, and still they were constantly overtaken by events. During this period the Islamists gained considerable political leverage; the program of Islamization in the juridical and cultural spheres continued apace without a serious contestation from Liberals and Leftists.

This was a period of considerable internal conflict and political confusion for the Left. The Mojahedin organization occupied the central position in the opposition while the secular organizations became secondary and marginalized. The Fedayee-Majority and the Tudeh Party were keen to be the "legal Marxists"; their only concern was that the IRP and Ayatollah Khomeini had rejected their suggestion of the formation of an anti-imperialist popular front.[21]

On the other hand, the militant Left (Fedayee-Minority, Peykar, the Kurdish organization Kumaleh, Ashraf Dehghani, Organization of Communist Unity) adopted a hardline and receptionist policy during this period. Attempts were made to join the Mojahedin in an anti-regime front, but the secular Left could not countenance the Mojahedin's unilateralism and commandism. The Mojahedin threw their support behind the beleaguered Bani-Sadr and staged large street demonstrations in his support in the Spring of 1981. As the political contest between the Islamists and their erstwhile liberal associates intensified, the IRP-dominated Majlis voted to impeach and prosecute Bani-Sadr. When the Mojahedin took to the streets to protest, they were violently attacked. In a rapid-fire series of events, Bani-Sadr and the Mojahedin leader Massoud Rajavi formed the National Council of Resistance and fled to Paris. The bombing of IRP headquarters (attributed to the Mojahedin but still mysterious in origin), in which nearly a hundred of its top leaders were killed, was met with arrests and executions by the authorities. A vicious cycle of regime brutality and Mojahedin assassinations plunged the country into a situation of near civil war and total repression as the Islamists attempted to restore order and reassert their power.

The Tudeh Party and the Fedayee-Majority sided with the regime, criticizing "ultra-leftists." At first the secular Left organizations remained at the sidelines, unhappy with the turn of events and their own powerlessness. Eventually, though reluctantly, they elected to join the battle and subsequently suffered tremendous losses. When the mini-civil war finally ended in late 1982, the regime had won it. In 1983 the Islamists then turned their attention to the Tudeh Party and the Fedayee-Majority, and a new wave of arrests, executions, and repression ensued. Ironically for a party that had for so long toed Khomeini's line, the Tudeh Party suffered even greater losses than the other organizations, mainly because it had naively publicized names and addresses of its cadre who were consequently more easily rounded up. In the wake of the repression, those Tudeh activists who were not arrested fled to Afghanistan and to Europe, where they resumed an existence in exile.

The social bases and composition of the Left

In a book on Arab society, Sharabi states that Islamism constitutes a "mass grassroots movement while secularism still consists of an internally diverse, largely avant-garde movement of critical intellectuals, writers, professionals, scholars, and students."[22] In Iran, the secular Left is also composed of intellectuals, professionals, and students. In this section we will discuss the class composition and the social bases of the Left in post-revolutionary Iran. We intend to show that the left-wing organizations, ideologies, and discourses correspond to specific social and cultural groups within the population. Our first observation is that the socio-economic base and status of Iranian leftists in Iran and abroad was largely student and modern middle class, and included men and women, and members of the religious minorities and all ethnic groups. But to render this impressionistic analysis more objective, and to give it an empirical content, we have analyzed the social background of some 900 members of socialist groups who were killed in one way or another (that is, under torture, in prison, through executions, or in street battles) in the period 1981–83, and in the case of the Tudeh Party in the post-1983 period.

The data reveal that in the case of the new revolutionary organizations, members were largely urbanized, educated, and youthful. In the case of the Tudeh Party, its members tended to be heavily represented by older people in the professions. Iranians attracted to left-wing organizations are primarily from the non-religious, highly educated, modern and urban middle classes (see Table 4). Notwithstanding the Left's populist leanings and desire to attract khalq ("popular masses"), our data reveal that Left organizations were largely composed of urban, highly educated, and professional Iranians. Bazaaris, traditional urban petty bourgeois, rural elements, and the urban poor were not to be found in the Left ranks in any significant numbers. The latter were in fact more likely to be attracted to the various Islamist groupings. There was some, but not significant, working-class participation. Our political conclusion from the empirical findings, supported by the evidence in the tables, is that the Left organizations could and indeed should have taken a more explicitly secular and modern cultural and political stance without alienating their social bases.

A note on sources is in order before proceeding. The following data are compiled from a list of 10,231 names of individuals who were in one way or another killed by the Islamic regime. The listing is contained in the June 1984 issue of *Mojahed*, the magazine of the People's Mojahedin organization. Our tables do not include the Mojahedin casualties, which were by far the highest (9,368). We focus instead on the secular Left groups. Because the data reflects the period 1981–83, the Tudeh Party

Table 4. *Summary characteristics of Iranian communists*

	Sex			Age			Occupation											Total
	M	F	NA	A	AA	NA	C	HS	NA	S	T	E	W	P	MD	M	O	
Fedayee-Minority	205	13	6	97	24	127	37	62	125	43	10	6	6	1	1	2	8	224
Peykar	164	27	3	67	26	127	60	32	102	53	5	10	8				1	194
Kumaleh	142	7	8	41	23	116	18	24	115	18	7	7	5	1	1	3	3	157
Fedayee-Guerrillas	97	7	4	41	23.5	67	11	40	57	25	4	2	6				1	108
Union of Communists	58	3	2	17	24	46	14	9	40	8		5	1				2	63
Rah-e Kargar	36	3	1	18	26	22	13	3	24	15	1	1	1	1			1	40
Ranjbaran	22	1		8	27	15	6	5	12	6	1						1	23
Tufan	18	1	1	13	25	7	4	5	11	1		1	2		2			20
Razamandegan	11			6	28	5	6		5	5								11
Union of Militant Communists	1	2	2	3	27	2	2	1	2	1								5
Pouyab Group	4					4			4									4
Communist Unity	2		1	1	28	2	1		2	1								3
Others	8	3		4	31	7	6		5	1	1	1						11
Total	738	67	28	316		547	178	181	504	177	29	33	29	3	4	5	17	863

Notes:

Key to headings: M, male; F, female; NA, not available; A, numbers for whom age was available; AA, average age; C, college; HS, high school; S, student; T, teacher; E, engineer; W, worker; P, peasant; MD, medical doctor; M, military; O, other.

Source: These data were compiled from a list of 10,231 individuals who were in one way or another killed by the Iranian State. The greatest number of "martyrs" belongs to the Mojahedin Organization, and these are excluded from this table. The table is based on characteristics of 863 members of secular left-wing organizations, mostly self-described communist groups, and excluding the Tudeh Party.

The list was published in a special issue of *Mojahed*, the journal of the Mojahedin Organization, in June 1984. The data refer to the period 1981–82, with some deaths occurring in 1983.

Table 5. *Fallen Tudeh Party members, 1983–84*

Members	Total
Male	30
Female	0
Average age	40
NA	21
High School[a]	4
College[b]	17
Student	2
Teacher	4
Worker	6
Military	6
Pasdar	2
Civil servant	2
Engineer	1
Total	30

Notes:
[a] Includes people with a few years of education, high school students, and high school graduates.
[b] Includes college students and graduates.

and Fedayee-Majority are not represented, as they were legal parties at that time and supported the regime. However, a separate table (Table 5) illustrates the Tudeh Party victims of the regime's repression. There are no data for the two Trotskyist groups. In a developing context, engineering is an elite occupation, with a strategic role to play in modernization and the rational re-ordering of the world. Engineers therefore tend to be politically active (unlike engineers in advanced industrialized countries who tend to be conservative or quiescent). In Iran, for many years the most radical academic settings were the Technical College of Tehran University and other engineering universities.[23]

Out of 863 dead communists, the occupation of 566 of them could not be identified. It is highly likely that many of these individuals were professional revolutionaries and therefore did not hold regular jobs. Indeed, we are familiar with many of the names, recognize many of them as leading cadre, and know that they were previously university students. Hence the number of students in the tables is actually a conservative figure.

Table 4 provides a summary of the characteristics of Iranian communists. Twelve major left-wing organizations are listed (again, excluding the Tudeh Party and Fedayee-Majority, which at this time were not targets of regime repression), and their fallen members are described by sex, age, education, and occupation. The organization with the largest number of dead is the Fedayee-Minority; Peykar, Kumaleh, and the Fedayee-Guerrillas (Ashraf Dehghani Group) also lost many members. The vast majority of their martyrs are male; the average age is 25; nearly all have at least a high school education; almost half are college students or graduates; engineering is the most frequent occupation for those communists on whom occupational information is available.

Table 4 provides more information on the occupations of the fallen leftists. It reveals that more than half were students (177 out of 307). Professionals are also represented (teachers, doctors, engineers, etc., that is, the modern, salaried middle class), while traditional occupations and class locations (such as peasant, bazaari, and so on) are insignificant. Workers are represented, but not in a significant way. For example, out of a total of 307 dead leftists of identified occupations, 39 were workers, the largest number of which were affiliated to Peykar.

Out of 835, the fallen men comprise 768 (92 percent), and the women 67 (8 percent). This is suggestive of the skewed sexual distribution patterns. This does not necessarily mean an under-representation of women among the rank-and-file. It does indicate, however, that leadership positions were occupied by men. In this regard, we can put forward the proposition that the Left's insensitivity to women's rights was in part related to the male-dominated leadership and the fact that the women cadres were less powerful in their respective organizations than were the men.

Nearly all of the fallen communists were highly educated. Slightly less than half (49.58 percent) of the total were college students or graduates and the remaining 50.42 percent were high school students or graduates. Once again, this confirms the Left organizations' base among modern, educated and professional social groups.

The data in Table 4 confirm our impressions and earlier speculation that the average age of those within the "new communist movement" was the mid-twenties. It should be noted that as a result of its high birthrate, Iran has a large youthful population.[24] As we mentioned earlier, young people tended to be attracted more to the new and militant Left organizations than the older and more traditional parties. However, the same criticism that we raised above pertains here as well: that is, that the Left organizations' programs did not reflect their own social base. They did not address themselves to the needs, problems, and aspirations of the modern, educated, professional middle class, including its youth and women.

In 1983 the regime turned against the Tudeh Party, and a sudden wave of arrests and executions nearly decimated it. Our data (Table 5) indicate that 30 Tudeh members lost their lives in 1983 and 1984. This information comes from the Tudeh Party's own sources, notably *Donya*, the political and theoretical organ of the Central Committee of the Tudeh Party of Iran, no. 2 (new series), 1985. Table 5 provides information on the fallen Tudeh members. It must first be noted that the table is based on 30 individuals described in the issue of *Donya*. While this is a small numerical base, we feel that it is fairly representative of the Tudeh Party's general characteristics. In the table, all of the members are male; the average age is 40; most of the members are university educated; most are employed in the professions. In contrast to the "new communist" organizations, the Tudeh Party cadres were more heavily male, older (average age 40 rather than 25), and more highly educated (predominantly university graduates rather than high school graduates). The militant Left was largely composed of students, while the Tudeh Party was heavily represented by professionals. Another difference between the Tudeh Party and the new communist organizations is that the party had a base within the military. Party policy was to enter the civil service, bureaucracy, the military, or the revolutionary guard (*pasdaran*). Indeed, a high-ranking military officer who was also a Tudeh Party member was Admiral Bahram Afzali, the commander of the Iranian Navy. He was arrested and executed in 1983.

Critiques of the Left

In the wake of the defeat of the Mojahedin, the communists and the liberals, and the consolidation of the Islamist State, recriminations and accusations abounded. In particular, the Left has been charged with all of these things: naiveté and inexperience, collaboration and opportunism, sexism, betrayal of socialist ideals, excessive workerism, Third Worldism, populism, being "out of touch" with Iranian culture and language, being inappropriately atheistic, being insufficiently irreligious. In this section we survey the sources of the main criticisms, and offer our assessment of them. These arguments were especially heated during the 1980s.

We begin with the conservative wholesale attack of Left praxis. The major argument of the monarchists and other Iranian conservatives is that the Left was responsible for the emergence and dominance of the political Islam; it facilitated Khomeini's assumption of power and collaborated with the Islamists after the Revolution.[25] The conservative critics have also regarded the contemporary Left as a clear and present danger (to borrow a phrase from the American context). In their speeches and writings (which appear in the newspaper *Kayhan-in-exile*, published in

London, as well as the journal *Sahand*) they have sought to expose the continuing left-wing threat, and warn of left-wing infiltration of the military and bureaucracy in Iran. They presented a very unflattering picture of the Left, depicting the Left as unpopular, without social roots, and thoroughly discredited in the eyes of the people. Herein lies the contradiction in their argument: the Left is presented as both unpopular and present in almost all political events in Iran. This characterization of the Left derives from the Right's fundamentally conspiratorial mentality, which at one point led them to insist that a certain high official of the Islamic Republic, Prosecutor-General Khoiniha, was a pro-Soviet communist. The intellectuals of the Right were obsessed with the Left and sought to attribute the Shah's fall and the success of the Islamists to the left-wing organizations. In the process they both exaggerated the role of the Left in the anti-Shah movement and offered a mere conspiracy theory of communist influence in the Islamic Republic.

For the liberals and nationalists, the main problem with the Left was that it was alien to Iranian culture and politics. In often patronizing terms the Left is presented as too young and inexperienced to be effective and too radical for the Iranian setting. They also accused the Islamic regime of adopting leftist discourses, a revolutionary course, and a set of policies which are non-Islamic and non-Iranian. Thus, in the liberal and nationalist critique, both the Left and the Islamists are alien, attempting, with various degrees of success, to impose languages, ideas and institutions that are foreign, strange, and inappropriate.

In the liberal and nationalist account, the Left is blamed for the post-revolutionary turmoil and conflict because it insisted on radical change and revolutionary transformation and thereby both encouraged the Islamists in that direction and undermined the liberals' gradualist program. The Left was also bitterly denounced (in this case correctly) for favoring the Islamists and attacking the liberals in 1979, and for being insufficiently sensitive to the need for democracy. They argue that as a result of all its mistakes and the defeat it suffered at the hands of the regime in the period 1981–83, there is no future for the Left in Iran.[26] Thus the liberal/nationalist critique of the Left's record and its prospects focussed on the following points: (1) the Left is alien to the Iranian culture; (2) the Left has suffered a serious defeat and is too weak, fragmented, and demoralized to be of any future use; (3) a leftist program is too radical for the realities of Iranian society, religion and nationalism being structural obstacles to any socialist movement in Iran; (4) the Left is anti-democratic and authoritarian, and it collaborated with the regime when it should not have – that is, after the liberals were eliminated from the political terrain in 1981. In this regard they are especially hostile to the Tudeh Party, which remained supportive of the regime until its own demise in 1983.

The Islamists' critique of the Left echoes some of the themes found in the right-wing critique and among the liberals and nationalists. The Left is charged with being too Westernized, non-traditional, and economistic; before, during and after the Revolution it was completely divorced from and therefore irrelevant to the lives and aspirations of ordinary Muslim people. The Islamists perceive the Left project as an alien intrusion into the politics and culture of traditional Iranian life; a corollary view is that left-wing activity is part of a Western conspiracy against Islamic values and practices. Islamists also accuse leftists of immorality in their personal lifestyles and in their program for gender equality. The Islamist critique includes philosophical arguments against Marxism and materialism, and an alternative emphasis on the spiritual dimension of life.

A response to the critiques

The conservative critique of the Left is politically motivated and very ideological. There is no logic to the claim that the Iranian Left is responsible for the Revolution or for the hegemony of political Islam. Nor is there any reality to the myth of an international and intellectual conspiracy to overthrow the Shah. The fact is that (a) at the time of the Revolution there was no powerful left-wing organization, and (b) the Iranian Revolution was a truly mass movement in which all classes and social strata participated. To suggest that the Left supported the Islamist regime and was responsible for its coming to power is also a distortion of the record. In the referendum of April 1, 1979, the Islamic Republic had the vote of more than 90 percent of the electorate; moreover, the Left (with the exception of the Tudeh Party) boycotted the referendum because it objected to the wording "Are you for or against the Islamic Republic?" The Iranian Left is responsible for many mistakes, but the claim that the Left is responsible for the rise of political Islam is an absurdity.

We also take issue with the characterization of the present Islamic regime as leftist. The ideology of political Islam (*velayat-e faghih*) and the practices of the Islamic Republic in the past ten years should dispel the myth of a convergence with the left-wing politico-cultural project. Only on some aspects of economic organization, such as nationalization, is there a convergence. The liberal critique of the Left is based on a double standard. For example, all of the main points of their case against the Left – that leftists were alienated from the Iranian masses, that they collaborated with the Islamic regime, were disunited, paid insufficient attention

to democratic rights, suffered a serious defeat at the hands of the
Islamists, no longer have the trust and confidence of Iranians – can be
turned around and used against the liberals themselves. The first and
most obvious point to be made is that it was the liberals, and not the Left,
that were part of the new state structure. Members of the principal
liberal/nationalist groupings, the National Front and the Freedom
Movement, occupied Cabinet posts and were part of the formal governmental structure as well as the shadowy Revolutionary Council in 1979.
It was a liberal, Abolhassan Bani-Sadr, who became the first president of
the Islamic Republic. Liberals were not the first dissidents; they joined the
opposition movement much later. Secondly, liberals are themselves
accused of *Gharbzadegi*, or of being too Westernized. Thirdly, unlike the
leftist organizations – which resisted the regime and were defeated only
after a bloody conflict – almost all the major liberal groupings and individuals dispersed as soon as the situation became difficult. Today, the
only liberal or nationalist organization active in Iran is the Freedom
Movement (Nehzat-e Azadi), led by former Prime Minister Mehdi
Bazargan.

There is another critique of the Left which is more sophisticated and
merits more serious attention. A number of Iranian intellectuals in exile
and certain European and American scholars have argued that the modernist vision as represented in particular by the Left is an alien one, and
that clerics or Muslims of various hues are "closer to the people" and represent "authentic" Iranian culture and identity. The essential point is that
the Left is too Westernized, does not "speak the language of the people"
and is divorced from and ignorant of the culture and sensibilities of the
traditional Iranian population. This critique is based on a dubious claim
to "authenticity" and is ultimately the manifestation of a view informed
more by nostalgia and romanticism than the realities of the Iranian cultural context. Like ideology, culture should be seen not as primordial and
fixed but as contingent and changing. In a complex, developing, and
heterogeneous society there is not one culture but many, all of which are
"legitimate" and "authentic." Furthermore, it seems that behind the
propositions about the "authentic culture" of Iran, there is a subtext: the
Left is being attacked for being leftist, that is, for subscribing to ideas,
objectives, and institutions that are associated with the social democratic,
socialist or communist traditions.[27]

As for those whose critique of the Iranian Left is based on the notion of
the greater "authenticity" of political Islam, and who regard Ali Shari'ati
and Al-e Ahmad as quintessential Iranians, we would point out the many
conflicts that have characterized post-revolutionary Iran and question the
utility of notions of "authenticity" in heterogeneous and complex

societies. Obviously there is no consensus as to what "Iranian identity" is; who defines "identity" and "culture"; how different cultural practices and discursive traditions can coexist within one society. What has the struggle in post-revolutionary Iran been about, if not the imposition of a central idea of what the Islamic Republic should look like, and the many reactions to it? The "return to Islam" – with its inherent ambiguity and multiple meanings, as well as absolutist underpinnings – is hardly the solution to the political and cultural crisis in Iran.

What is needed in Iran is political and cultural openness and not the monolithic and totalizing political-cultural model that the Islamists have sought to impose. The latter is based on the erroneous assumption of a uniform "Muslim culture" and of a population prepared for and receptive to direct clerical rule and constant ideological exhortation, mobilization, and manipulation.

The "Islamic mind"

Having observed the extraordinary lengths to which Orientalists will go in order to sculpt an imagined model of the "Islamic mind," with extended forays into premodern history, ancient textual sources, and elaborately based ontological arguments designed to evoke a causal relation between some primitive impulse and an entire people in the context of the modern world, one is tempted to demand why they refuse to merely *speak* with this other, rather than consistently *imagining* its voice. Given that modernity has been the defining factor in shaping the issues and conditions of the contemporary Islamic world, surely it is more productive to hear people's actual voices and read their literature in the context of modernity, rather than consulting exclusively premodern texts in order to construct a teleological model of Islamic motivation in the modern world. The difference between these two approaches constitutes a fundamental question of methodology in analyzing the peoples and cultures of Islamic societies. The Orientalist approach betokens an assumption that the voices of contemporary Muslims – of whatever political shade – can only be less valuable and informative than whatever the Orientalist has dreamed up and presented beforehand as the essential Islamic mind. The voices and literature of contemporary Muslims could do no better than to conform to what the Orientalist already knows from "expertise." To criticize this method is surely second to letting it stand in juxtaposition with people's actual voices, whereby the inevitably greater complexity of human reality will override the chimera nurtured in the Orientalist tradition.[1] In recent years a more liberal current in Islamic studies, critical of Orientalism, has tried to focus on contemporary Middle Eastern and Islamic societies. Unfortunately, this current too functions in accordance with Orientalist tradition by imagining and defining politics in these societies almost exclusively within the boundaries of Islam. In these texts, secularism is either presented as nonexistent or simply ignored.

In the Fall of 1995, I visited my home country of Iran after sixteen years in the United States. During this visit, I interviewed several Iranian intellectuals with diverse political backgrounds and cultural sensibilities, speaking with both Islamic and secular intellectuals on their opinions concerning Iranian *Tajadod* (modernity). These interviews and conversations confirmed my already growing belief that much has changed in the Iranian intellectual, and perhaps public, scene in the past decade.

Hassan Taromi, director of the history of Islamic sciences at the *Encyclopedia Islamica* Foundation, offered the following autobiographical account of what he believes to be the underlying reason for the transformation of intellectual attitudes about modernity in Iran:

I have gone through various stages in my attitude towards modernity and the West. I sincerely believed in the righteousness of Islam. At first, I felt that one could approach modernity selectively. For example, we can take technology, industry, and science, and leave the rest. I had a change of heart in the 1970s while at Tehran University. One reason was the oppressive political situation under the Shah. On the face of it, Iran was a fast-developing nation. But radical political movements were quite active, prisons were filled with political prisoners, censorship was prevalent, and so on. That made me quite disillusioned with my future career and with the future of modernization in Iran. I felt, now that we have all these experts we are supposedly modern, but what can we do? We were nobody.[2]

If this remark gives a glimpse into an Islamic activist's disillusionment with "modernity," it certainly does not show a spirit with an innate hostility to change, nor one preoccupied with merely the religious dimension of political injustice. It reveals, rather, a person of changing attitudes and frustrated hopes regarding modernity, a person who found disillusionment above all in the undemocratic nature of the Pahlavi regime. I asked him what particular event or concern had turned him away from the modern and "universalist" project of modernization and compelled him to seek a more "local" solution to Iran's social and political problems. His answer is telling:

Sometime in 1975, Ivan Illich came to Iran and gave a series of lectures at Tehran University. His critique of Western sciences and technology, the limitation of "development" and failures of other aspects of Western modernity, coming from a genius and an expelled bishop, had quite an eye-opening power on me. I concluded that one cannot approach modernity selectively, rather it has to be rejected in its entirety. As a result, I did not even learn how to drive until 1980. In the late 1970s, I left Tehran University and went to Qum to study Islamic theology. I spent eight years in the seminary.[3]

In a startling way, his reply undermines the Orientalist fetish for the "Islamic impulse," which portrays Muslims as oblivious to non-Islamic discourses, and as having little intellectual curiosity for non-religious questions. His account brings a more cosmopolitan discourse into the debate about the roots of the Islamic critique of modernization and the West. This young college student, already disillusioned with the actual experience of modernization in Iran (political oppression, lack of popular participation, etc.), heard his misgivings articulated and doubts affirmed by the analysis of a respected Western intellectual and subsequently gave up his faith in modernization as the answer to his country's problems.

Ironically, the coming of the Islamic Republic led to another personal and intellectual crisis and to yet another transformation in his perspective towards modernity and Islam. I asked him what he currently thinks about global modernity and its relation to Iran:

> I feel now that we cannot separate ourselves from what is going on in the world. The wheel that turns the world, and the philosophical traditions and assumptions which move that wheel, may have quite unacceptable results in practice, but we have to face that philosophy and appreciate it even though we may have reservations and doubts. The base of contemporary social life is modern rationality and I feel that religion should have only a corrective mission at best. That is why, as a religious community, [the Ulama establishment] should not try to confront modernity. They should try to come to terms with it.[4]

Here is an Islamic clergyman with a history of involvement in Islamic politics, detailing an analysis of modernity undermining the characterizations of Islamist views by such intellectuals as Samuel Huntington, Bernard Lewis, and Ernest Gellner. These, and a number of other Western intellectuals, have been warning the Western world that the new Islamic political movements are maliciously anti-modern and historically hostile to the Western cultural tradition. In contrast, what I hear from a Muslim intellectual such as Hassan Taromi, as well as many others, is that he embraces modernity as a "fate of our time," and proposes that Islam should withdraw from many aspects of public life to make room for secular and practical concerns.[5] Despite any ambivalence he may feel, his remarks show a willingness to imagine and explore the possibility of new cultural and political configurations, revealing an attitude of pragmatic adaptation rather than one of rigid adherence to immutable doctrine.

Hassan Taromi shows a daring flexibility when he proposes that modernity should occupy the central and defining position in Iranian public life and that Islam should perform only a marginal moral function. He comes to this position after eight years in an Islamic seminary and a personal involvement in the Islamic Revolution. One wonders if those intellectuals and scholars in the West who are seriously talking about the "clash of civilizations," or "fundamentalist fanaticism" have ever listened to a person like Hassan Taromi.

A few days before talking to Hassan Taromi, I interviewed another Iranian scholar in the same institution. Javad Tabataba'i is a well-known political theorist in Iran, a secularist and outspoken modernist. Although his views are conspicuously different from his colleague Hassan Taromi, I detected a somewhat common understanding of the issue and a similar approach to the questions raised in our discussion. I asked him how, as an Iranian secular intellectual, he defines Iran's cultural and political identity, and how he locates Iran within larger global communities, such as the "Third World," the "Orient," the "Islamic World," or any other larger cultural or political context:

We are not part of the "Third World," nor of the "Orient." Since rationality has historically been an ingrained part of our culture, we are part of the West. Our traditional philosophical and political thought employed a logic that was Greek, and even our religious thought was an interpretation of Greek logic, mostly its Aristotelian branch. Our dilemma today is how to understand the gap that has developed between us and the West since the Renaissance. On the one hand, we need to re-link to this part of our tradition that also inspired the West. On the other hand, we should come to terms with modern Western values. We can divide the history of our political thought into two parts: during the first, we interpreted the *sha'ar* [religious law] logically, and during the second, which continues to this day, we have interpreted reason according to *sha'ar*.[6]

Tabataba'i, a staunchly modernist thinker (in the most conventional sense of the term), extends the model of modernity/other within his own context, identifying strands within Iranian society and history which locate Iran "outside" of modernity and the West, in contrast to "disconnected" rational elements that historically bind Iran to the West. I asked him if he were proposing a return to an earlier period in Iranian history, and if so, how the Iranian rationalist tradition could be revitalized.

We have to express new ideas with our medieval vocabulary and language. Historically, we are in an era similar to the German "Kulture Kritik." It is not until we pass this stage that we can expect the emergence of a new mode of thinking and new thinkers who can revolutionize our language and also our thoughts. For we can re-read ibn-Sina [Avrceina] with a Western horizon in mind. There are others in Iran who are engaged in re-reading this tradition as well. However, they have religious concerns, or as they themselves say they have a religious "anguish." For me the problem is cultural, and religion is only one constituent part of it and no more.[7]

We see from these remarks a secular Iranian Muslim, who is more than ready to compare his own culture to the former experiences of a Western country, with a view to revolutionizing Iranian language, traditions, and thought along lines reconciling Islam with Western modes of thought. It would seem that if any modernist should feel threatened with annihilation by Islamic politics, Tabataba'i would be the one. I asked him how he evaluates the effects of Islamic politics in relation to his idea of a cultural revival of Iranian *Tajadod*:

For now, the religious tradition and the Revolution have entrapped many and this, in a way, is fine because Ayatollah Khomeini has forced the religious tradition into a situation where it does not belong. This offers an opportunity whereby our cultural traditions can be re-evaluated in its [sic] entirety. In my last book, I focussed on the tradition of monarchy, and you may ask why it is important to deal with monarchy in the aftermath of the Islamic Revolution. It is my belief that in Iranian political thought monarchy has many bodies. We need to deal with it so that its reincarnation in the theory of the "rule of jurist" [velayat-e faghih] does not last long.[8]

I also asked him how he could reconcile his ethnic and national identity as an Azari, in the context of what is going on in Iran and in the world, with his conspicuously modernist and universalist theory of Iranian identity:

As an Azari [an ethnic minority in Iran], I enjoy Azari music as much as French music. I believe national minorities are to be defined in terms of the Iranian cultural tradition. Even if the boundaries of national minorities were somewhat demarcated before, the Islamic Revolution has removed some of the color. Since Shahnameh [the Persian epic], we are a unified nation. Of course it is true that national unity is built upon national interests, and we still can't define our national interests.

I have even spoken of the Greater Iranian Cultural Sphere. Samarkand and Tashkent belong to this Cultural Sphere. We can even speak of Armenia as part of the Iranian cultural tradition. Today, Farsi is the primary foreign language being taught in Armenian schools. I believe that Iran acted very naively during the past five years of the dismantling of the Soviet Union. In reality, we have lost these lands, which belong to our cultural sphere.[9]

These discourses articulate a considerable range of concerns notably discordant with the characterizations made by such "experts" as Lewis. Taromi's political views reflect an obvious concern for human rights, and he willingly imagines a political space beyond the commanding influence of Islam. His secularist colleague, Tabataba'i, goes even further in this regard. Above all, neither of their statements evokes an antithetical "clash of civilizations" scenario. Their intellectual energies are marshaled towards reconciling their culture with the West rather than in destroying Western civilization. Also, implicit in their discourse is a view of a common fate for humanity, and nothing to suggest a radical separation between Muslims and "ancient historical opponents." Indeed, there is no trace of obsession with such opponents whatsoever. The only negative reference made to the "West" or "modernity" stems from Taromi's own experiences of the Western backed Pahlavi regime, and exhibits neither a linkage to "ancient hostility" nor a projection of inevitable hostilities to come. Modernity is a subject broached with familiarity and concern.

To those with strong secular and Eurocentric sensibilities, inclined to

inflate any Islamic presence in politics to the scale of clashing civilizations, the possibility of a reflexive and reconfigured modernity may be
hard to absorb. However, there is little doubt in my mind that the era of
fixed, Euro-centered, and non-reflexive modernity is on the verge of
reaching its end. This is far from suggesting that modernity, as a sociological project, has exhausted its material grounding or its intellectual allure
in the context of the Middle East or the "Third World." On the contrary,
the current struggles in the non-Western world are for the heart and soul
of modernity.

Yet, for modernity to survive, it must recognize its own inner capacity
for flexibility and creativity, and transcend the totalizing narrative in
whose grip it has been enchained in theory if not always in practice. The
actually existing narrative of modernity, a European invention rooted in
Western culture, is intellectually too rigid and historically too hostile to
non-Western cultures and histories. It is incapable of coming to terms
with the emerging challenges of our world and their complex realities.
Theories of modernity desperately need to reexamine a historical record
revealing a far more open-ended structure of modernity than its theoretical representations have ever before had the courage to concede. New
modernities are required with built-in ambiguities about their truth
claims, so that the very concept of modernity in itself may grow with the
contribution of new voices and experiences.

However, the dominant discourse of modernity unyieldingly resists any
possibility of reflexive modernities with ambiguous boundaries. The idea
of lifting modernity's universalist veil seems too radical and politically
dangerous. Modernist orthodoxy looks at this as an attack on "reason"
and "rationalism." After all, if modernity is a universal discourse and is
rooted in scientific legitimacy, any subjective or cultural representations
of it will automatically lead to the collapse of the project altogether. These
perceived dangers are based as much on precepts about the other as they
are on modernity's own self-definitions (though the effort to disentangle
these two might prove gravely formidable); which is to say, instead of perceiving an instance of violence in its context, an "essence" is posited
whereby the object (in this case, Islam) is condemned "by nature" to be of
a terminally violent disposition. This pretense of a "scientifically based"
disclosure of a timeless "essence" acts as a substitute for dialogue and
analysis, and succeeds only in proliferating enemies and flooding the
channels of international communication with distortion.

The contemporary "order of things" must be changed in favor of a
reflexive conception of modernity. Such a theory engages issues in terms
of its own point of departure, acknowledging its own circumstances in
relation to discourse, rather than assuming the veneer of a "universal"

voice to disguise its own biases and interests. Mass movements based on religious, ethnic, cultural and other forms of identity are already beginning to shape the emerging faces of modernities in our time. It is pointless to try to deny the implications of their existence, to stuff them back into the box of conventional paradigms by way of either intellectual reduction or military force. Rather, we should listen to them and draw political and theoretical conclusions from their experiences and voices. It is *only* on this basis that there is a valid foundation for either accepting or rejecting, in part or in whole, what they have to offer.

Modernization and the survival of cultures

The Middle East is not exempt from the global process of modernization, or from its aggressive tendency to expand, penetrate, dominate, and transform all parts of the world.[10] An important consequence of the global expansion of modernization is the predicament of "local" cultures which are undergoing this process. The contestation over "cultural modernity" pits "Western values" against "local" cultures, values, and symbols, representing sources of individual, communal, and national pride, as well as identity for the people of these societies.

From the beginning of the Middle Eastern encounter with modernity and the West, several different forms of accommodation have evolved. Throughout most of the twentieth century, Middle Eastern versions of modern ideology have generally dominated the social and political discourses of these societies: Kamalism, Nasserism, Pahlavism, Bathism, and, to a lesser extent, socialism became powerful ideologies in the Middle East. These ideologies, largely involved with the state structure and/or the colonial powers, adopted a national ideology that viewed Islam and Islamic culture as fundamentally opposed to modernity.

A second group, of "traditional" intellectuals such as Jamal al-Din Al Afghani, inserted a discourse of accommodating modernity into Islamic culture. Al Afghani, who worked closely with the Iranian constitutionalist movement, combined Islamic cultural precepts with Western science, technology and nationalist politics in an attempt to articulate an anti-colonial, pan-Islamic nationalism. The goal of such thinkers was to make an Islamic reform movement compatible with modern science and ideas, but retentive of the values and culture of Islamic society.

The crisis of secular ideology in the Middle East led to the growth of Islamist ideologies challenging Western ideologies and forms of modernity on "nativist" grounds. These forms of "nativism" have a relevance beyond their own particular domain, for their basic element can be viewed with consistency in many social settings where "Western modernity" has been experienced as an imposition. Just as answers turn back into questions, these movements place an immense question mark at the end of the conventional modernist narrative which proclaimed itself the "absolute answer" to the riddle of history.

The current rise of Islamic politics is part of a long and difficult attempt to adapt to the modern culture of social change within the historical and cultural context of Iranian society.[11] The complexities, tensions, and even the contradictory nature of political Islam reflect the struggles of particular groups with the culture of modernity. Islam, as an ideology and as a cultural system, is attempting to provide an indigenous cultural context.

We have seen (chapter 1) how the supposedly universal representation of modernity is an inflation and abstraction of Europe's particular experience of modernization, raised to the level of a categorical truth for humanity, and externally imposed accordingly. In the absence of a "local" cultural representation of modernity in the non-Western world, the experience of modernization is almost always a violent imposition. This was the case during the colonial era as well as the early nation-building period, and is the case today, when modernizing states are trying to keep their grasp on power. Moreover, as long as Western modernity arrogantly refuses to come to terms with cultures and experiences outside of its earlier origins, modernity will be correctly perceived as an extension of foreign domination and alien cultural hegemony.

When experienced as domination, modernization frequently triggers an explicit and innovative synthesis of culture and politics, resulting in a form of protest we have called the "discourse of authenticity." This tendency was illustrated in detail in our comparative study of Iran and Germany. Under conditions of cultural marginalization and political oppression, culture becomes a powerful axis for politicization. Certain modes of being – traditional ways and lifestyles – are initially destroyed by modernization. Under the influence of intellectuals, society turns to a revitalization of traditional culture to cope with the challenge of modernity. The previously unthematized modes of being, now lost, are filtered through the minds of intellectuals, and "traditional" culture is transformed from a mode of being into a political ideology, presenting itself as the vanguard of the "soul." The soul here represents memories of rural life. It is as though the modes of being have an afterlife, or experience a resurrection in ideology. The lost modes of life, or rather their surviving symbols, are turned into an ideological vision that promises continuity in the face of violent change, and draws power from collective nostalgia. The most interesting thing about this ideological rebirth is that an earthly residue of "being" lingers, giving the ideology an ontological aura that elevates it above mere intellectualism in the minds of its followers. This ideology is designed for a mass movement in an urban setting, and raises a banner of spiritual regeneration.

The aim of ideologies based on discourses of authenticity is to bring about modernity, not to return to the past. It is simply that the nostalgic mode of politicization is extremely effective in the battles among competing modern ideologies, and this power has been recognized. The movements inspired by these ideologies aim for a specific form of modernity, one considered consistent with national tradition. Since tradition has already been physically displaced and proven futile by modernity, then in order to spearhead any movement, tradition (real or imagined) must integrate itself with the objective foundations of modernity. There is a curious magic to this moment in that "tradition" picks up the objects of modernity as though they were never in any way alien, but completely consistent with an "ancient" and "indigenous" destiny. Of course, the point of rooting these "objective" forms in the subjectivities of the mass is to turn them into a revolutionary weapon against the encroaching enemy.

It is important to note that "tradition" does not simply dissolve in the natural course of time, but is perceived as being conquered by a stronger, alien "tradition." The enemy is within and without, and society is called upon to purge itself collectively of all traces of enemy infestation. In the cases presented here, this universal culture of modernity is explicitly associated with a "soul-less" materialism that preys upon the "natural order" of things. The "natural order" is implicit in the "given" forms of pre-modern social organization: family, clan, tribe, ethnicity and religion. The shift from these horizontal forms of social organization to vertical forms such as class and occupation represents the uprooting of a self-evident identity, forcing people to seek a new one. The ideology of authenticity invites people to embrace these new forms while referring them to old principles, thereby creating a bridge of continuity where there once was a hole in the people's souls.

In the post-independence era the secular-modernizing elite monopolized state power structures in many Middle Eastern countries. Many initially enjoyed some level of popular support (Turkey, Egypt, Iran). As I have argued in detail earlier in this study, the crisis of secular and nationalist states, in the Middle East generally but Iran in particular, resulted from their failure to achieve basic socio-economic and human needs (political participation, human rights, etc.) and led to a decline in the legitimacy of universalist ideological foundations.

It is only with the crisis of secular political institutions and ideas that we have seen the rise of social movements based on newly constructed Islamic and even ethnic identities. These movements promote social and political institutions that are modern and intended to push modernization, yet are symbolically rooted in "local" and "traditional" cultures and experiences. Based on notions of identity, these movements represent the disjointed and uneven global process of material modernization on the one hand, and the "localization" (or cultural accommodation) of modernity on the other. These seemingly contradictory configurations should be understood as the new and significant faces of the modernities of our time. We should attempt to understand them and their causes in their specificity, without resorting to simplistic distortions about the "resurgence of ancient impulses" or "religious fanaticism."

Predicament of secularism

Political Islamic movements arose in the Middle East at the same time that secular states were in crisis. Modern states suffered from the lack of popular legitimation; citizens blamed them for economic mismanagement and corruption, and in general the states did not enjoy a viable social or class base of support. Some scholars have conceptualized the crisis as "state exhaustion."[12] Others have suggested that the current rise of the Islamic movement is largely due to the "fragile foundation of secularism" in Islamic societies.[13] In either case, political Islam only became a viable popular social movement after it became conspicuously clear to all that different models of the modern secular state had exhausted themselves without producing political participation or viable economic development. We should not forget that modern Middle Eastern states rarely, if ever, enjoyed popular legitimacy based on popular will and legal processes. Most of these states are results of coups d'état or some other form of violent, non-popular action.

For these reasons, modern and secular-democratic institutions and ideas in the Middle East have usually enjoyed only a fragile foundation, and could hardly stand any serious challenge. Secular-democratic politics in the Middle East are underdeveloped because they were routinely undermined by an autocratic state. Autocratic ideologies on the banners of nationalism (Nasserism in Egypt, Bathism in Syria and Iraq), Westernization (Pahlavism in Iran, and to some extent, Kemalism in Turkey) and socialism (Algeria) organized a world view where the state dominated power and enjoyed a privileged position over any other societal structures or elements. In many cases the traditional structures of "civil society" were destroyed or subjugated to the arbitrary will of the political state. Autonomous institutions and organizations were destroyed and all the power concentrated in the hands of the state.

Ironically, although not surprisingly, the autocratic and interventionist nature of states in a country such as Iran made the state weak, not strong.

Ervand Abrahamian, in his study of the Iranian Revolution and the reasons for the dramatic collapse of the Shah's regime, points out that "[u]nder the Pahlavi monarchy, state autonomy brought not institutional strength but social isolation, [which] in turn brought weakness and vulnerability to revolution."[14]

But the crisis of the political state in Iran was not due to the fact that the state did not have a class base or was too interventionist. Iran, and many other Middle Eastern states, suffered from the lack of popular and viable modern political institutions. Mangol Bayat, an Iranian historian, makes an interesting observation with respect to the predicament of secularism in Iran: "The 1978 Revolution has pointed out the most fundamental weakness of Iranian political life in modern times – namely, the absence of a secular, nationalist ideology strong enough to sustain a war on two fronts: both against the absolutist regime of the Pahlavis, and against the predominant clerical presence in politics."[15]

Modern states in the Middle East tend to be selectively modern, randomly secular, and only rhetorically democratic. Modernity and modernization apply primarily to the structure of the state: centralization of state power, modernization of the national military, policing, particular means of surveillance and control, a state capitalist economy, promotion of Western consumer and commercial culture, and in some countries Western modes of formality (e.g., dress codes, formal bureaucracy). These modernized state appendages expend their energy and resources in systematically crushing the prospects for modernization in other, non-state controlled areas of society – political parties, trade unions, citizens' organizations and other aspects of civil society. Even more self-destructively, most Middle Eastern states adopted a policy of mistrust towards institutions which attempted to integrate the ideas and practices of modernity, such as the national education system, the media, communications, and the judicial system. They squandered enormous resources to obstruct the furthering and "normal" functioning of the very modern institutions which they had sponsored and created themselves.

Thus, the relationship between the modern state, its secular ideology and the society at large became ironic and at times comic. In the case of Iran, for example, the Pahlavi state transformed the education system, developed a literacy campaign, and established institutions of higher education, secular law and a legal system. In conjunction with those developments, it created a huge state police system to make sure that the population, which it had helped to educate, could read, write, and express only politically "safe" views and have limited access to information. If the modernization program alienated traditional social groups from the state, repressive and neopatriarchal policies alienated another important social base of the state: the middle class. Further, many of these states suppressed other modern or secular movements and ideologies which may have offered alternatives to the neopatriarchal ideology. As a result of these contradictory policies, many socio-political and cultural problems and tensions in Middle Eastern societies remained intact (ethnic, religious, gender, class, etc.) while new problems were simultaneously created by the state in the process of modernization (the urban poor, modern political repression, the gap between haves and have-nots, etc.). The deterioration of modern state systems created a counterculture among intellectuals, the middle class, and the urban poor against Westernization, apparent in anti-Westernism, and in the tendency toward nativism and cultural authenticity. This counterculture, with a very strong nostalgic tone, reflected itself in a language and a culture that romanticized the purity of the past and harshly criticized "alien" and modern culture.

Theoretical and political implications

Calling for a different and more tolerant project of modernity, at a time when modern secular ideas and institutions seem to be under Islamist attack, may be perceived as politically risky, intellectually naive, and practically unthinkable. I will be the first person to admit that any serious challenge to the prevalent Eurocentrist narrative of modernity may also be perceived as a challenge to certain modern sensibilities that many hold so critical for our political and individual well-being: modern ideals, such as respect for human rights, the role of law, the democratic process, and individual liberties. Other historical experiences, such as Nazism, ethnic nationalism and nativism teach us the hazards of anti-liberal politics and the violent impulses of culturally rooted critiques of modern rationalism. There are already conservative and even leftist intellectual trends attacking postmodernist and post-colonial discourses for instigating all sorts of dangerous trouble, from inciting tribalism, destroying "reason," to glorifying primitivism.[16]

I am very much aware of the anxieties felt by secularists and their quest to hold on to stable and fixed categories and boundaries. I see how some Islamist intellectuals appropriate anti-Orientalist and postmodernist critiques and welcome them as a reaffirmation of their troubling and narrow-minded agenda. For example, in Iran, the most extreme form of anti-liberal Islamism and intellectual intolerance is articulated by a circle of Islamic intellectuals who proudly and freely borrow theoretical and critical ideas from Heidegger and postmodernism.[17] I am also aware of the fact that some dark moments in the history of the modern West are associated with movements and intellectuals seeking to redefine modernity. We have already pointed to the relationship between the German "reactionary modernism" and Nazism and the roles of Junger and Heidegger in that movement.[18]

I have some understanding for the argument that while postmodern/post-colonial perspectives offer a timely critique of modernity's totalizing ideology, they nevertheless underestimate the intense desire of new social movements for a more inclusive and unifying narrative within modernity. This argument usually points out that the postmodern critical imagination can be helpful and liberating in societies where modernity is institutionalized and fully installed. However, such a radical critique of liberalism, in the difficult context of "Third World" societies, may lead to the catastrophic collapse of institutions and orders with gravely undesirable consequences.

Emerging global social movements are challenging this configuration of modernity. There may still be hope for modernity to open itself up to new possibilities. We would like to think that elemental shifts in the paradigm – such as freeing its center from an exclusively Western anchor – could open up a midway for every conceivable form of dialogue within the limits of non-violent communication; we hasten to add that should the "voice" of the paradigm remain concentrated upon the inflation of a single hegemonic and totalizing mind – extending communication by way of imagining its "other" rather than conversing with actual people – then the likelihood of violence is all too implicit. For if violence occurs where dialogue breaks down, then the discourse of modernity in its most basic precepts incites violence by severing dialogue before it has begun. It may still be premature to theorize about new social movements and knowledges within postmodern/post-colonial discourses. It remains to be seen whether a reflexive modernity is possible to achieve. However, positioning new possibilities as marginal has costs. Here we refer to the potential costs of new groups defining themselves on the margins, and also to the forced marginalization of new groups by authority and the resulting danger. For example, the dismissal of Islamic insurrection as "irrational" banishes it to a marginal category in the scheme of political colloquy: yet this mere conceptual deflation, while providing temporary reassurance to Western public and politicians, in no way reduces the actual significance or complexity of these movements in the long run. It is above all ignorance that makes a situation dangerous. On the one hand, for new groups to define our time in terms of postmodernity/post-colonialism runs the risk of avoiding having to confront the mainstream – that is, the actually existing power arrangements as they confront people in everyday life. Being in the margins may be a fascinating or intriguing *intellectual* possibility; however,

pe
co
sul

and
fyii
nit
mo
to
tha
on
lead
gies
Iran
thes
soci
of W
dict
ofter
(Sad
has
and
state
Euro
great
timiz
chang
mode

tellectual movements)
rely given the chance to

new social knowledge
tal collapse of the uni-
magination. If moder-
s, we will have new
en. Only a willingness
challenges can assure
rvive. Angry assaults
magination will only
dern secular ideolo-
ocieties (in this case
to reevaluate, and at
as. Middle Eastern
ry or so at the hands
ular authoritarians,
nspired elites, who
hic consequences
orary Middle East
lerance, brutality,
Western-inspired
movements. The
velopment has a
ce, and with legi-
name of social

represent the darker face of
mode ... our respect for the liberal and "enlightened" ideals of
modern rationalism do not justify ignoring or overlooking the troubling
history and experiences of modernity.

Notes

INTRODUCTION: MODERNITY AND "CULTURE"

1. Lawrence D. Kritzman, ed., *Michel Foucault: Politics, Philosophy, Culture: Interviews and Other Writings, 1977–1984* (New York: Routledge, 1988), p. 224.
2. Ibid., p. 211.
3. As Marshall Berman suggests in *All That is Solid Melts into Air: The Experience of Modernity* (New York: Penguin, 1988).
4. By "local" I do not claim a clearly defined or authentically constructed local experience. The local is often imagined in contrast to a totalizing modern cosmopolitan. The local in our times incorporates many of the global experiences, desires, hopes, and practices. However, it is important to define certain experiences and imaginaries as local because of the subversive and democratic function of place-based experiences. For interesting discussions of the global/local, see: Rob Wilson and Wimal Dissanayake, eds., *Global/Local* (Durham: Duke University Press, 1996). Arif Dirlik ("The Global in the Local") and Mike Featherstone ("Localism, Globalism, and Cultural Identity") are particularly relevant to this issue. Arjun Appadurai, *Modernity at Large: Cultural Dimensions of Globalization* (Minneapolis: University of Minnesota Press, 1996), offers a very insightful analysis of local/global relationship.
5. For a discussion of different views on modernity and their relevance to reflexive modernization, see Scott Lash and Jonathon Friedman, eds., *Modernity and Identity* (Oxford: Blackwell, 1992)
6. Weber is perhaps the most consistent in articulating the idea that only a "Protestant ethic" is compatible with the rationalism of modernity.
7. This is what distinguishes Marx from the liberal Enlightenment. His insistence on materialist epistemology helped him articulate a radical critique of capitalism and its liberal modernity. However, Marx's criticism of liberalism is class reductionist and does not take into account issues such as colonialism and ethnicity.
8. That is, if materialism implies an understanding the "social" based on the everyday life experiences, I will argue that it is inadequate. This rather mechanistic materialism is a closed system which forecloses any non-Western experiences.
9. Berman, *All That is Solid*, p. 15.
10. Marshall Berman, "Why Modernism Still Matters," in Lash and Friedman, eds. *Modernity and Identity*, p. 37.
11. Berman, *All That is Solid*, p. 125.

12. Ibid., p. 126.
13. Berman, "Why Modernism Still Matters," p. 36.
14. Berman, *All That is Solid*, p. 345.
15. Berman, "Why Modernism Still Matters," p. 34.
16. This is similar to Perry Anderson's argument. See his "Modernity and Revolution," *New Left Review* 144 (1984), pp. 96–113.
17. Berman, *All That is Solid*, p. 348.
18. See Jurgen Habermas, "Modernity – An Incomplete Project," *The Anti-Aesthetic: Essays on Postmodern Culture*, ed. Hal Foster (Seattle: Bay Press, 1983), pp. 3–16.
19. Jurgen Habermas, *The Theory of Communicative Action*, vols. 1 and 2, trans. Thomas McCarthy (Boston: Beacon, 1984).
20. Thomas McCarthy, "Translator's Introduction," *The Theory of Communicative Action*, vol. I, p. xxxix.
21. John Tomilson, *Cultural Imperialism* (Baltimore: John Hopkins University Press, 1991), p. 168.
22. Anthony Giddens, *The Consequences of Modernity* (Stanford: Stanford University Press, 1990), pp. 174, 175.
23. Edward Said, *Culture and Imperialism* (New York: Vintage, 1994).
24. Timothy Mitchell, *Colonizing Egypt* (Berkeley, CA: University of California Press, 1991), p. 165.
25. Peter Dews, ed., *Autonomy and Solidarity: Interviews with Jurgen Habermas* (London: Verso, 1986), p. 187.
26. Jurgen Habermas, *The Philosophical Discourse of Modernity* (Cambridge: MIT Press, 1987), p. 344.
27. See Peter Hulme, *Colonial Encounters: Europe and the Native Caribbean 1492–1797* (New York: Routledge, 1992) and Tzvctan Todorov, *The Conquest of America: the Question of the Other*, trans. Richard Howard (New York: Harper, 1984) for two surveys.
28. See Peter Hulme, "The Spontaneous Hand of Nature: Savagery, Colonialism and the Enlightenment," *The Enlightenment and its Shadows*, eds. Peter Hulme and Ludmilla Jordanova (New York: Routledge, 1994) and James Tully, *An Approach to Political Philosophy: Locke in Contexts* (Cambridge: Cambridge University Press, 1993).
29. This is particularly the case in Turkey, and many Arab states such as Iraq and Lebanon. It is also interesting that in modern Iran most social movements and political conflicts have ethnic roots (those of the Azaris, Kurds and Arabs, for example).
30. See Mitchell, *Colonizing Egypt*; Arturo Escobar, *Encountering Development: The Making and Unmaking of the Third World* (Princeton: Princeton University Press, 1995); Edward Said, *Orientalism* (New York: Pantheon Books, 1978), for example.
31. Escobar, *Encountering Development*, p. 18.
32. Roy Mottahedeh's book *The Mantle of the Prophet: Religion and Politics in Iran* (New York: Simon and Schuster, 1985) offers an interesting insight into the duality of modern cultural life in contemporary Iran.
33. Samuel P. Huntington, "The Clash of Civilizations?," *Foreign Affairs*, vol. 72 no. 3 (Summer 1993), pp. 22–49.

1 WESTERN NARRATIVES OF MODERNITY

1. Edward Said, *Orientalism* (New York: Pantheon Books, 1978).
2. This is a reference to a debate on "The Scholar, the Media, and the Middle East," organized by Middle East Studies Association, November 1986. In this debate Bernard Lewis, who was challenged by Edward Said, appeared very defensive.
3. "Orientalism Revisited: An Interview with Edward Said," *Middle East Report* (January/February 1988), p. 3.
4. For an analysis of stereotypical images of Muslims and Middle Eastern people in the American media and popular culture, see Reeva S. Sirnon, *The Middle East in Crime Fiction: Mysteries, Spy Novels and Thrillers from 1916 to the 1980s* (New York: Lillian Barber Press, 1989).
5. "Orientalism Revisited," p. 6.
6. Thierry Hentsch, *Imagining the Middle East* (Montreal: Black Rose Books, 1992), p. ix.
7. Montesquieu, *Persian Letters* (Harmondsworth: Penguin Books, 1973), p. 41.
8. Jonathon Friedman, "Cultural Logics of the Global System: A Sketch," *Theory, Culture and Society* 5: 2–3 (June 1988), p. 448.
9. Montesquieu, *Persian Letters*, p.170.
10. Ibid., p. 190.
11. Ibid., p. 189.
12. Ibid., p. 66.
13. Ibid., p. 81.
14. Ibid., p. 73.
15. Ibid., p. 87.
16. Ibid., p. 46.
17. Ibid., p. 271.
18. The emotion of jealousy, Montesquieu tells us, is something infrequently nurtured in the free atmosphere of French society: "There are men whom everybody detests: jealous husbands . . . Consequently, in no country are there so few in number as in France . . . Married men here resign themselves with a good grace, and consider their wives' infidelities to be inevitably destined by the stars. A husband who wanted to have his wife all to himself would be looked upon as a disturber of the public pleasure, or as a madman who wanted to enjoy the sunshine to the exclusion of other men."
19. Jurgen Habermas, *The Philosophical Discourse of Modernity.* (Cambridge: MIT Press, 1991), p. 4.
20. Peter Singer, *Hegel* (Oxford: Oxford University Press, 1983), p. vii.
21. Georg Wilhelm Friedrich Hegel, *The Philosophy of History* (New York: Dover Publications Inc., 1956), p. 13.
22. During his youthful time as a tutor in Frankfurt, in the company of Hölderlin and Schelling, Hegel expressed exceptionally radical views on a number of issues. Among them were his reflections on the role of myth in philosophy: "Before we make the ideas aesthetical, i.e., mythological, they have no interest for the *people*; and on the other hand, before mythology is rational, the philosopher must be ashamed of it." (Quoted from Habermas,

Philosophical Discourse, p. 32). Writings in later years showed this view to ebb.
23. Habermas, *Philosophical Discourse*, p. 16.
24. Ibid., p. 12.
25. Ibid., p. 11.
26. Robert C Solomon, *In the Spirit of Hegel* (New York: Oxford University Press, 1983), p. 36.
27. Ibid.
28. Ibid., p. 39.
29. Ibid., pp. 41, 104.
30. Ibid., p. 62.
31. Ibid., p. 195. Hegel has a talent for expressing the same concept in a bewildering myriad of ways. On this occasion, Hegel is referring to the East/West split in terms of the superiority of Western monotheism; hence, nature is only the "creature" of God. When Spirit comes to full realization of itself in the West, human beings realize they are essentially one with the Spirit and hence perceive (and treat) nature as a subordinate entity. However, this particular angle on the matter also raises interesting questions concerning Europe's shared religious and cultural heritage with the Middle East. Later in the chapter we will devote attention to the "special relationship" between Europe and the Middle East as it is presented in Hegel.
32. Ibid., p. 99.
33. Ibid., p. 221.
34. Ibid., p. 223.
35. Ibid.
36. Ibid., pp. 174–75.
37. Ibid., pp. 141, 138.
38. Ibid., pp. 104, 142.
39. Ibid., p. 117.
40. Ibid., pp. 175, 114.
41. Ibid., p. 199.
42. Ibid., p. 220.
43. Ibid., p. 112.
44. Ibid., p. 174.
45. Ibid., p. 222.
46. Ibid., p. 99.
47. Ibid., p. 96.
48. Ibid., pp. 98, 98, 82.
49. Ibid., pp. 96, 81, 82.
50. Ibid., p. 96.
51. Ibid., p. 99.
52. Bryan Magee, *The Great Philosophers* (London: BBC Books, 1987), p. 207.
53. Karl Marx, "The British Rule in India," in Marx and Engels, *On Colonialism* (New York: International Publisher, 1972), pp. 35–41. pp. 37, 38.
54. Ibid., p. 40.
55. Ibid., pp. 40, 41.
56. Karl Marx, "The Future Results of British Rule in India," in ibid., p. 81.

57. Ibid., p. 83.
58. Ibid., p. 85.
59. Ibid.
60. Ibid., p. 87.
61. Steven Seidman (*Contested Knowledge: Social Theory in the Postmodern Era*, 2nd edn. (Malden, MA: Blackwell, 1998), pp. 32–54) argues, convincingly, that Marx's problematic is rooted in the tension between his moral and scientific visions.
62. Samuel P. Huntington, "The Clash of Civilizations," *Foreign Affairs*, vol. 72 no. 3 (Summer 1993), pp. 22–49.
63. Bernard Lewis, "The Roots of Muslim Rage," *The Atlantic Monthly* 266 (September 1990), pp. 47–54.
64. Ibid., pp. 47–54, 56, 59–60.
65. Ibid., p. 49.
66. Ibid.
67. Ibid., p. 56.
68. Ibid., p. 59.
69. Ibid., p. 53.
70. Ibid.
71. Ibid.
72. Ibid., p. 55.
73. Ibid., p. 59.
74. Ibid., pp. 56, 57.
75. Ibid., p. 56.
76. Ibid.
77. Huntington, "Clash of Civilizations," p. 29.
78. Ibid., p. 29.
79. Ibid., pp. 35, 45.
80. Ibid., p. 32.
81. Ibid.
82. Ibid., pp. 39, 49.
83. Ibid., p. 40.
84. Ibid., p. 31.
85. Ibid., p. 23.

2 RECONCILING WITH THE WEST'S OTHER

1. *Kaveh* (new series) vol. 1, no. 1 (January 22, 1920), pp. 1–2, quoted in Edward G. Browne, *A Literary History of Persia*, vol. IV (London: Cambridge University Press, 1978), pp. 485–86.
2. This is true of most standard histories of the Constitutional Revolution: Ahmad Kasravi, *History of the Constitutional Revolution*; Malek Zadeh, *History of the Constitutional Movement*; Morteza Ravandi, *Social History of Iran;* Nazen al-Islam Kirmani, *History of Iranian Awakening;* as well as Fereydun Aday'at's extensive writings on the intellectual history of the Constitutional Revolution.
3. This is particularly true of Adamiy'at's writings. In almost all of his writings on the Iranian constitutionalism he conceptualizes ideologies and intellec-

tual figures as either modern or traditional. Melkum Khan, Kirmani and Talibof are considered modernist with little qualification.

4. See note 2 above.
5. Morteza Ravandi, *Social History of Iran* [in Persian] (Tehran: Amir Kabir Publisher, 1975), vol. II, p. 541.
6. Ibid., p. 526.
7. Ibid., p. 535–36.
8. Ibid., p. 541.
9. Ibid., p. 526.
10. Ibid., p. 535.
11. Fereydoun Adami'yat, *Thoughts of Mirza Agha Khan Kermani* [in Persian] (Tehran: Payam Publisher, 1978), p. 2.
12. Fereydoun Adami'yat, *The Idea of Progress and Legal Government: Time of Sepahsalar* [in Persian] (Tehran: Kharazmi Publisher, 1972), p. 13.
13. Mehdi Malik Zadeh, *History of the Constitutional Revolution in Iran* (Tehran: Elmi Publisher, 1984), vol. I, p. 87.
14. Ibid., p. 87.
15. Ibid., p. 88.
16. Ibid., p. 87.
17. Yahya Dowlat Abadi, *Hayat-e Yahya* (Tehran: Ferdowsi Publisher, 1982), vol. II, p. 103.
18. Malik Zadeh, *History of the Constitutional Revolution in Iran* (Tehran: Elmi Publisher, 1984), vol. I, pp. 89–90.
19. Mahdi Quli Khan Hidayat, *Khatirat va Khatarat*, Memories and Dangers (Tehran, 1950), p. 9.
20. Fereydoun Adami'yat, *The Idea of Social Democracy in the Iranian Constitutional Movement* [in Persian] (Tehran: Payam Publisher, 1975), p. 6.
21. Yahya Arian Poor, *From Sabba To Nima* [in Persian] (Tehran: Amir Kabir Publisher, 1974), p. 344.
22. Mangol Bayat, "Mirza Aga Khan Kirmani: A Nineteenth Century Persian Nationalist," in E. Kedouri and Sylvana Haim, eds., *Towards a Modern Iran* (London: Frank Cass, 1980), p. 67.
23. Fereydoun Adami'yat, *The Idea of Freedom and the Making of the Constitutional Movement* (Tehran: Sukhon Publisher, 1961), pp. 113–49.
24. Ibid., pp. 113–14.
25. Ibid.
26. Ibid., p. 114.

3 THE CRISIS OF SECULARISM AND THE RISE OF POLITICAL ISLAM

1. Lawrence D. Kritzman, ed., *Michel Foucault: Politics, Philosophy, Culture: Interviews and Other Writings* (New York: Routledge, 1988), p. 218.
2. For discussion of modernity vs tradition, see Reinhard Bendix, "Tradition and Modernity Reconsidered," *Comparative Studies in Society and History* 9 (1967).
3. N. Keddie, "Islamic Revival in the Middle East: A comparison of Iran and

Egypt" in S. K. Farsoun, *Arab Society* (London: Croom Helm, 1983), pp. 65–82.

4. For an interesting discussion of the populist character of the Islamic movement during the Revolution in Iran, see: Ervand Abrahamian, *Khomeinism* (Berkeley, CA: University of California, 1993), pp. 13–38.

5. Philip S. Khoury, "Islamic Revivalism and the Crisis of the Secular State in the Arab World," in I. Ibrahim, ed., *Arab Resources* (London: Croom Helm, 1983), p. 214.

6. Raouf Abas Hamed, "Factors Behind the Political Islamic Movement in Egypt," a paper presented at the 24th MESA Conference, Texas, 1990.

7. Following Niyazi Berkes in *The Development of Secularism in Turkey* (new edn., New York: Routledge, 1998), pp. 3–8, I make the following conceptual distinctions: "secularization" is a social process (transformation of institutions, offices, properties, etc.), independent of an individual's control. "Secularism," on the other hand, is an intellectual project, which advocates temporal views and attitudes. "Secular" refers to individuals or states of society that are normally capable of maintaining a degree of differentiation and flexibility in their value systems.

8. M. Bayat, *Mysticism and Dissent: Socioreligious Thought in Qajar Iran* (Syracuse: Syracuse University Press, 1982) p. xi.

9. For analysis of the politics of this period, see H. Ladjevardi, *Labor Unions and Autocracy in Iran* (Syracuse: Syracuse University Press, 1985); F. Azimi, *The Crisis of Democracy in Iran* (London: I.B. Tauris, 1989); and Ervand Abrahamian, *Iran Between Two Revolutions* (Princeton: Princeton University Press, 1982).

10. Both Hedayat and Nima Yoshij started their literary careers in the 1930s, but the open environment of the 1940s made it possible to publicize and popularize these experiences inside the country and in a real public arena. The new poetry of Nima Yoshij, modernist fiction, and other forms of literary production are examples of the new wave of experimentation in literature and the arts.

11. In fact, some of the prominent political figures of the period were either journalists or newspaper publishers. Hossein Fatemi, Mosaddeq foreign minister, and the publisher of *Bahktare Emrowz*, was the most important of them.

12. Hassan Aboutorabian, *Iranian Press: 1940–1946* [in Persian] (Tehran: Ettela'at Publisher, 1987). This is an expanded bibliography of the Iranian press based on L. P. Elwell-Sutton, "The Iranian Press 1941–1947," *Journal of the British Institute of Persian Studies* 6 (1968).

13. For an analysis of traditional and modern forms of social organization in the Third World, see H. Sharabi, *Neopatriarchy: A Theory of Change in Arab Society* (New York: Oxford University Press, 1988).

14. Abrahamian, *Iran Between Two Revolutions*, p. 353.

15. For a more comprehensive analysis of the labor union movement in this period, see Abrahamian, *Iran Between Two Revolutions*; and Ladjevardi, *Labor Unions*.

16. This party was formed under the leadership of Ghavam Al-saltaneh (the prime minister of Iran), in 1946.

17. For a more informative analysis of the politics of this period and the history of ethnic politics in Iran, see Abrahamian, *Iran Between Two Revolutions*.
18. R. Cottam, *Nationalism in Iran* (Pittsburgh: University of Pittsburgh Press, 1964).
19. It is important to note that even a prominent religious political figure such as Ayatollah Kashani was an ally of Mosaddeq and worked within the National Front. It was only at the end of the Mosaddeq premiership that Kashani abandoned him and his movement.
20. For discussions on the rise and the demise of the nationalist and communist movements at this period, see Jami, *Gozashteh Cheraghe Rahe Ayandeh Ast, The Past is the Light of the Future* (Tehran: Ghoghnous, 1978).
21. Cottam, *Nationalism in Iran*, pp. 212–17.
22. For an informative analysis of the Tudeh Party's role during this period, see Jami, *Gozashteh Cheraghe Rahe Ayandeh Ast*, pp. 679–717.
23. Anva Khamenh'i, *Forsate Bozork-e Az Dast Rafteh*, The Big Chance that Was Lost (Tehran: Hafte Publisher, 1983), pp. 108–10.
24. For a brief exposition of Mosaddeq life and ideas, see R. Mottahedeh, *The Mantle of the Prophet: Religion and Politics in Iran* (New York: Simon and Schuster, 1985), pp. 114–33.
25. For a more detailed discussion of Iranian politics under Mosaddeq, see Jami, *Gozashteh Cheraghe Ayandeh*.
26. Ladjevardi, *Labor Unions*.
27. For an account of the suppression of the trade union organizations in post-coup (1953) Iran, see ibid.
28. The Shah's security police almost destroyed the two main guerrilla organizations (the People's Fedayee Guerrillas and the People's Mojahedin of Iran). Abrahamian's study of the Iranian radical political organizations gives a very informative analysis of this subject: E. Abrahamian, *Radical Islam: The Iranian Mojahedin* (London: I.B.Tauris, 1989).
29. Although the student movement was active in the political affairs of the country during the 1940s, there is an important difference between this and the student movement which developed in the 1960s and 1970s. While the former was the extension of the political activities of the major party of the country, the latter was the principal political party and had almost no connection to any other larger political organization. Another important change in the politics of Iran in the post-coup era was the eroding political role of the *Asnaf* (guilds), which had historically played an important part in modern Iranian politics from the constitutional movement to that time.
30. For an analysis of the concept of the Karbala paradigm, see M. Fischer, *Iran: From Religious Dispute to Revolution* (Cambridge, MA: Harvard University Press, 1980).
31. During the 1960s and 1970s, the urban guerrilla movement dominated radical Iranian politics. The two major guerrilla organizations were the People's Fedayee Guerrillas and the People's Mojahedin of Iran.
32. On the other hand, we know that there has almost always been a bazaar–mosque alliance. For a discussion of the role of the bazaar in the protest movement in modern Iran, see Ahmad Ashraf, "Bazaar–Mosque

Alliance: The Social Bases of Revels and Revolutions," *International Journal of Politics, Culture and Society*, vol. 1 no. 4 (Summer 1988), pp. 538–67.

33. Iranian student activists formed the largest and most organized student movement in the U.S. and Western Europe. The Confederation of Iranian Students was originally organized in January 1961 and was politically active during the 1960s and 1970s.

34. They were mainly a different variety of Marxist-Leninist and Maoist groupings.

35. They were mainly but not exclusively organized into the *Jebheye Meliee Khavare Miane* (the National Front in Middle East).

36. G. Afkhami, *The Iranian Revolution: Thanatos on a National Scale* (Washington, D.C.: Middle East Institute, 1985).

37. G. Afkhami, a high-level official of the Shah's regime, later admitted to the fact that the regime's secret police, SAVAK, in fact did not take the Islamic challenge seriously: ibid.

38. The reign of Naserdin Shah of Qajar is described as the period when the idea of modernity and the politics of constitutionalism were introduced in Iran. The whole period has been called the Period of Awakening (Asre Bidari). See F. Adami'yat, *Andish-ye Taraghi Va Hokumat-e Ghanoon*, The Idea of Progress and Legal Government: Time of Sepahsalar (Tehran: Kharazmi Publisher, 1972).

39. For an analysis of the socio-economic changes during the 1960s and 1970s, see F. Halliday, *Iran: Dictatorship and Development* (London: Penguin, 1979).

40. For an interesting analysis of the land reform in Iran, see E. Hoogland, *Land and Revolution in Iran* (Austin: University of Texas Press, 1982).

41. An interesting analysis of the politics of modernization in Iran is given in J. Green, *Revolution in Iran: The Politics of Countermobilization* (New York: Praeger, 1982).

42. This point, which was ignored during the period of modernization in Iran, is now acknowledged by almost everyone. G. Afkhami, a high official of the Shah's government, in his recent book admits to this fact. See Afkhami, *The Iranian Revolution.*

43. On the nature of the state power in Iran under the Shah, see Abrahamian, *Radical Islam*, pp. 9–41.

44. As has already been pointed out, "There is no such thing as modernity in general. There are only national societies, each of which becomes modern in its own fashion." Jeffrey Herf, *Reactionary Modernism: Technology, Culture and Politics in Weimar and the Third Reich* (New York: Cambridge University Press, 1984), p. 1.

45. A. Parsons, *The Pride and the Fall* (London: Jonathan Cape, 1984).

46. There are many examples of the elitist approach of the government in implementing its programs. "In order to make way for new streets and avenues, the mayor of Tehran sent bulldozers to demolish private houses in working class districts, and in 1978 riots occurred as a result of this policy. To create agroindustries, the government forced villagers to sell their farmland and often razed entire villages." S. Bakhash, *The Reign of the Ayatollahs* (New York: Basic Books, 1984), p. 11.

47. E. Abrahamian, "Structural Causes of the Iranian Revolution," *MERIP Reports* (May 1980), p. 23.
48. Ladjevardi, *Labor Unions*, p. 236.
49. F. Kazemi, *Poverty and Revolution in Iran* (New York: New York University Press, 1980), p. 60.
50. A brief but interesting analysis of the social stratification of the Iranian society in the 1960s and 1970s is presented in M. Milani, *The Making of Iran's Islamic Revolution* (Boulder, CO: Westview Press, 1988); and Abrahamian, *Radical Islam*.
51. Kazemi, *Poverty and Revolution*, p. 60.
52. Ibid.
53. Ibid., p. 63.
54. Abrahamian, *Radical Islam*, p. 17.
55. J. Bill, *The Politics of Iran: Groups, Class and Modernization*, (Columbus, OH: Charles E. Merrill Publishing Co., 1972), p. 74.
56. Hassan Abedini, in the second volume of his *One Hundred Years of Fiction Writings in Iran 1963–1978* (Tehran: Tondar Publisher, 1989), gives a very interesting analysis of the literary currents of Iran in this period, the shift to the national and traditional context and experiences by the Iranian novelists and intellectuals.
57. Ibid., p. 14.
58. Abrahamian, *Radical Islam*, p. 15.
59. For a brief appraisal of Al-e Ahmad's life and thought, see Mottahedeh, *Mantle of the Prophet*, pp. 287–336.
60. A very interesting study of Shari'ati's views is Abrahamian, *Radical Islam*, pp. 105–25.
61. Ernest Gellner, "Forward," in Said Amir Arjomand, ed., *From Nationalism to Revolutionary Islam* (Albany: State University of New York Press, 1984), p. viii.
62. For a critique of Al-e Ahmad's idea of Gharbzadegi from a liberal perspective, see F. Adami'yat, *Ashoftegi Da Fekre Tarihki*, Bewilderment in Historical Thought (Tehran: Jahan-e Andisheh, 1981).
63. Bendix, "Tradition and Modernity Reconsidered," p. 326.
64. For an analysis of the anti-modernist discourse of Iranian intellectuals in this period, see A. Ashtiani, "A Historical Sociology of Three Discourses of the Iranian Intellectuals" [in Farsi], *Kankash*, vol. 1 nos. 2 and 3 (1987), pp. 87–137.
65. Many intellectuals who occupied relatively important positions in the government are included in this category. They include figures like H. Nassr, E. Narahgi, and D. Shayegan. Narahgi's critique of the West instigated controversies and was debated at the time: E. Narahgi, *Ghorbat-e Gharb*, The Alienation of the West (Tehran: Amir Kabir Publisher, 1975).
66. For discussion of the role of the Left in the Iranian Revolution, see: Ali Mirsepassi and Val Moghadam, "The Left and Political Islam in Iran," *Radical History Review* 51 (Fall 1991), pp. 27–62.
67. There is a tendency to treat Islam as an autonomous force that transcends any other social or political variables in a given social formation. This essentialistic interpretation of Islam basically precludes any societal or historical

specificities to the Islamic movement or its politics. Here we are providing a social context and a time period in order to promote the proper understanding of the Islamic movement. For an interesting analysis of Islam as an ideology and a critique of the autonomous conception of Islam see the introduction section of F. Halliday and H. Alavi, eds., *State and Ideology in the Middle East and Pakistan* (New York: Monthly Review Press, 1989), pp. 1–8.

68. E. Browne, *A Literary History of Persia* (London: Cambridge University Press, 1978), vol. IV, p. 18. Edward Browne looks at the Shi'i and Suni dispute as a reflection of "the essentially antagonistic doctrines of Democracy and Divine Right of Kings. The Arabs are, and always have been, in large measure democratic in their ideas, while the Persians have ever been disposed to see in their Kings divine or semi divine beings." Hegel, in his *Philosophy of History*, makes the same argument about the nature of political authority in pre-Islamic Iran, and the East generally. While one cannot reject the mythological accuracy of these assertions, there is an orientalist attitude in both of the authors' analyses of the Persian concept of divine rule.

69. A. K. S. Lambton, *Theory and Practice in Medieval Persian Government* (London: Variorum Reprints, 1980), p. 404.

70. W. Montgomery Watt, "The Significance of the Early Stages of Imami Shi'ism," in N. Keddie, ed., *Religion and Politics in Iran: Shi'ism From Quietism to Revolution* (New Haven: Yale University Press, 1983), p. 31.

71. S. Amir Arjomand, *The Turban For the Crown: Iran's Islamic Revolution* (New York: Oxford University Press, 1988), p. 13.

72. A well-researched study on the role of Shi'i clerics in the Iranian Revolution of 1906–11 is: Vanessa Martin, *Islam and Modernism* (Syracuse: Syracuse University Press, 1989).

73. For a discussion on the Akhbari/Usuli debate, see S. Amir Arjomand, *The Shadow of God and the Hidden Imam* (Chicago: Chicago University Press, 1984).

74. The clerics' debate on constitutionalism is covered in A. Hairi, *Shi'ism and Constitutionalism in Iran* [in Farsi] (Tehran: Amir Kabir Publishing, 1985); H. Enayat, *Modern Islamic Political Thought* (Austin: University of Texas Press, 1982).

75. For a biography of the earlier life of Khomeini in English, see H. Algar, "Immam Khomeini, 1902–1962: The Pre-Revolutionary Years," in E. Burke and I. Lapidus, *Islam, Politics, and Social Movement* (Berkeley, CA: University of California Press, 1988), pp. 263–88.

76. Bakhash, *Reign of the Ayatollahs*, p. 40.

77. R. Khomeini, *Islamic Government* [in Farsi] (Tehran: no publisher, 1977) Although the idea of Velayat-e Faghih is often associated with Khomeini, it is suggested that E. Narahgi is the earlier proponent of this theory: H. Dabashi, "Early Propagation of Wilayat-i Faqih and Mulla Ahmad Naraqi," in H. Nasr, H. Dabashi, and M. Nasr, eds., *Expectation of the Millennium: Shi'ism in History* (New York: State University of New York, 1989), pp. 288–300.

78. For a more detailed analysis of Khomeini's view on State and society, see Abrahamian, *Khomeinism*.

79. Bakhash, *Reign of the Ayatollahs*, p. 41.
80. *Bahsi Dar Bare-e Rowhaniyat va Marja'yyat*, An Inquiry into Marja'yyat and Religious Institutions (Tehran: Enteshar Publisher, 1962).
81. *Anjoman-e Islami-ye Iran* (Islamic Association of Iran) was organized by Mehdi Bazargan and the regime tolerated its efforts to limit the appeal of Marxism on the college campuses. On the issue of the regime's espousal of Shi'ism, see Abrahamian, *Radical Islam*, p. 19.
82. *Bahsi . . .*, pp. i–ii.
83. S. Akhavi, *Religion and Politics in Contemporary Iran* (Albany: State University of New York Press, 1980), p. 119.
84. M. Motahhari, "Ijtihad Dar Islam," in *Bahsi . . .*, pp. 21, 20.
85. M. Tabataba'i, "Valayat Va Za'amat," in *Bahsi . . .*, pp. 39–81.
86. Therefore, in contrast to the view that he was opposed to the concept of the Velayat-e Faghih and the Islamic State, he is one of the earlier proponents of clerical rule.
87. Ibid., p. 41.
88. M. Motahhari, "Moshkele Asasi Dar Sazemane Rowhaniyat," in *Bahsi . . .*, pp. 105–30.
89. Ibid., p. 105.
90. Ibid., p. 120.
91. Ibid., p. 107.
92. Ibid., p. 118.
93. Akbar Rafsanjani, the current president of Iran, was among those who initiated the "Maktab-e Tashayo" in 1957 in Qum. For more information on Rafsanjani's activities, see *Vijenameye Ayatollah Morteza Motahhari*, The Sixth Anniversary of the Martyrdom of Ayatollah M. Motahhari (Tehran: Islamic Republican Party, 1985), pp. 323–91.
94. *Maktabe Tashayo* (Qum: Elmiye Publisher, 1959, 1960, 1965).
95. "Moshkelate Ma Va Elale Paydayeshe Anha," in *Maktabe Tashayo* (1959), pp. 3–6.
96. Ibid., pp. 3, 4.
97. Ibid., p. 6.
98. M. Tabataba'i, *Maktabe Tashayo* (1960).
99. Tabataba'i's activities go back to the 1940s at the height of the Tudeh Party's popularity.
100. *Maktabe Tashayo*, vol. III, p. 3.
101. Ibid., p. 6.
102. *Goftare Mah Dar Namayandane Rahe Raste Din* (Tehran: Sadugh Publisher, 1960–61), p. 3.
103. Ibid.
104. *Goftare Mah Dar Namayandane Rahe Raste Din* (Tehran: Sadugh Publisher, 1962), p. 1.
105. Akhavi, *Religion and Politics*, p. 144.
106. Arjomand, *The Turban For the Crown*, pp. 91–2.
107. Ibid., p. 92.
108. Ibid., p. 93.
109. S. Amir Arjomand, ed., *From Nationalism to Revolutionary Islam* (Albany: State University of New York Press, 1984), p. 216.

110. Kazemi, *Poverty and Revolution*, p. 153.

111. Bakhash, *Reign of the Ayatollahs*, p. 44.

112. It appears that theories of revolution are either involved with long-term structural determinants or are concerned with the politics of moments and spontaneity. For a structuralist approach to the theory of revolution, see T. Skocpol, *State and Social Revolution* (London: Cambridge University Press, 1979). For an "interpretive" theory of revolution, see F. Furet, *Interpreting the French Revolution* (London: Cambridge University Press, 1981). A more critical approach to the dichotomous conception of revolution is L. Hunt, *Politics, Culture, and Class in the French Revolution,* (Berkeley, CA: University of California Press, 1984), pp. 218–20.

113. For an excellent study of the role of symbols and rhetorical language in revolutionary politics, see Hunt, *Politics, Culture and Class*.

114. In regard to the contemporary character of the Iranian Revolution, Halliday makes an interesting observation: "If Iran's upheaval was unique in the prominence occupied by this traditional feature, it was equally so for the opposite reason: the modern character of the event. The Iranian Revolution took place in a society far more socio-economically developed, in major respects, than was Russia in 1917 or China in 1949." F. Halliday, "The Iranian Revolution: Uneven Development and Religious Populism," in F. Halliday and H. Alavi, *State and Ideology in the Middle East and Pakistan* (New York: Monthly Review Press, 1989), p. 35.

4 ISLAM AS A MODERNIZING IDEOLOGY: AL-E AHMAD AND SHARI'ATI

1. Jeffrey Herf, *Reactionary Modernism: Technology, Culture and Politics in Weimar and the Third Reich* (New York: Cambridge University Press, 1984), p. 1.

2. Jalal Al-e Ahmad, *Gharbzadegi*, Westoxication (Tehran: Revagh Publisher, 1962), p. 227. The term *Gharbzadegi* has been translated in English as "Occidentosis," "Westoxication," and "Euromania." This book has been translated into English: Jalal Al-e Ahmad, *Occidentosis: A Plague From the West,* trans. R. Campbell (Berkeley, CA: Mizan Press, 1984).

3. Al-e Ahmad, *Karnamahi Sih Salah* (Tehran: Revagh Publisher, 1979), p. 159.

4. That is how he talked about his family background: "I come from a religious, Shi'i Muslim family. My father, older brother, and one of my brothers-in-law died in religious dignity." "An Autobiography of Sorts," in Michael Hillmann, ed., *Iranian Society* (Lexington, KY: Mazda Publishers, 1982).

5. Michael Hillmann, *Iranian Culture: A Persianist View* (New York: University Press of America, 1990), p. 119.

6. Hamid Dabashi, *Theology of Discontent: The Ideological Foundation of the Islamic Revolution in Iran* (New York: New York University Press, 1993), p. 63.

7. Jalal Al-e Ahmad, "Masalan Sharh-e Ahvalat," in Hamid Tbrizi, *Jalal Al-e Ahmad: Mardi da kesh Keshe Tarikh-e Moaser* (Tabriz: Nashr-e Kave, 1978), p. 63.

8. For a brief exposition of Kasravi's life and ideas, see Ervand Abrahamian, "Kasravi: The Integrative Nationalist of Iran," in Elie Kedouri and Sylvana Haim, *Towards a Modern Iran* (London: Frank Cass, 1980), pp. 271–95.

9. Al-e Ahmad, "An Autobiography of Sorts," in Hillmann, ed., *Iranian Society*, p. 15.

10. Ibid.

11. Hillmann, *Iranian Culture*, p. 14.

12. Jalal Al-e Ahmad, *Our Suffering*, in Hillmann, ed., *Iranian Society*, p. 16.

13. Al-e Ahmad, *Dar Khedmat va Khyanat-ye Rowshanfekran* (Tehran: Kharazmi Publisher, 1979), vol. II, p. 146.

14. Ibid., p. 175.

15. Al-e Ahmad, "An Autobiography of Sorts," in Hillmann, ed., *Iranian Society*, p. 16.

16. In an introduction to Gide's *Return from the Soviet Union*, Al-e Ahmad praises him as a man who fights against any forms of orthodoxy, "religious or otherwise" (Tehran: Akhtar Shoma Publishing, 1954), p. 4.

17. Al-e Ahmad, *Iranian Society*, p. xi.

18. Jalal Al-e Ahmad, "Eftar-e Bimogheh," in *Did va bazdid* (Tehran: Amir Kabir Publisher, 1960), pp. 55–69.

19. Jalal Al-e Ahmad, *Khasi Dar Mighat*, A Traveler's Diary (Tehran: Amir Kabir Publisher, 1966). This book has been translated into English: Jala Al-e Ahmad, *Lost in the Crowd*, trans. John Green (Washington, D.C.: Three Continents Press, 1985).

20. Jalal Al-e Ahmad, *The Seh'tar* (Tehran: Sepehr Publisher, 1978).

21. Ibid., p. 11.

22. Ibid.

23. Al-e Ahmad, "An Autobiography of Sorts," in *Iranian Society*, p. 16.

24. Ibid.

25. Hillmann, *Iranian Culture*, p. 128.

26. Dabashi, *Theology of Discontent*, p. 59.

27. Al-e Ahmad, *Iranian Society*, p. 17.

28. Jalal Al-e Ahmad, *Occidentosis [Gharbzadegi]: A Plague From the West*, trans. R. Campbell (Berkeley, CA: Mizan Press, 1984), p. 27.

29. For a critique of Al-e Ahmad's idea of Gharbzadegi from a liberal perspective, see F. Adami'yat, *Ashoftegi Da Fekre Tarihki*, Bewilderment in Historical Thought (Tehran: Jahan-e Andisheh, 1981).

30. "Reactionary modernism" was a movement in Germany which embraced modern technology but rejected Enlightenment reason. Herf, *Reactionary Modernism*, p. 15.

31. Ibid., p. 27.

32. Al-e Ahmad, *Occidentosis*, p. 25. It is worth noting that Al-e Ahmad translated Junger's work into Persian. See Ernst Junger, *Obour As Khat*, trans. Al-e Ahmad and Mahamud Human (Tehran: Kharazmi Publisher, 1965).

33. Roy Mottahedeh, *The Mantle of the Prophet: Religion and Politics in Iran* (New York: Simon and Schuster, 1985), p. 299.

34. Ibid., p. 301.

35. Ibid., p. 303.

36. Al-e Ahmad, *Occidentosis*, pp. 27, 28.
37. Ibid., p. 29.
38. Ibid., p. 28.
39. Ibid., pp. 31, 136.
40. He also notes how Africa, Latin America, and non-Islamic parts of Asia stand no chance against Western hegemony because of overwhelming religious diversity, and *only* Islam can unify and defend the Third World. *Occidentosis*, p. 33.
41. Ibid., p. 34.
42. Ibid., p. 71.
43. Ibid., pp. 57–58.
44. Ibid., p. 59.
45. Ibid., p. 59.
46. Ibid., p. 71.
47. Ibid., p. 78.
48. Ibid., p. 31.
49. Ibid.
50. Ibid., p. 79.
51. Mottahedeh, *Mantle of the Prophet*, p. 308.
52. Al-e Ahmad, *Dar Khedmat va Khyanat-ye Rowshanfekran*, vol. 2, p. 149.
53. Ibid., p. 83.
54. Al-e Ahmad, *Khasi Dar Mighat.*
55. Hillmann, *Iranian Culture*, p. 141.
56. Al-e Ahmad, *Khasi Dar Mighat*, pp. 84–85.
57. Ibid., p. 127.
58. Ibid., p. 129.
59. Ibid., p. 131.
60. Jalal Al-e Ahmad, *Safar be Vellayate Ezrail* (Tehran: Revagh Publisher, 1984), p. 50.
61. Ibid., p. 52.
62. Al-e Ahmad, *Karnamahi Sih Salah*, p. 164.
63. Al-e Ahmad, *Lost in the Crowd*, p. 64.
64. Mostafa Zammani Nia, ed., *Fahang-e Jalal Al-e Ahmad*, The Encyclopedia of Jalal Al-e Ahmad (Tehran: Pasargad Publisher, 1984), p. 173.
65. See the preface to Al-e Ahmad's *Safar be Vellayate Ezrail*. This long preface, written by his brother Shams, to Al-e Ahmad's Diary to Israel is very informative.
66. *Iran va Jahan*, October 1982, in Hillmann, *Iranian Culture*, p. 140.
67. For a detailed analysis of the relationship between the Mojahedin and Shari'ati, see Ervand Abrahamian, *Radical Islam: The Iranian Mojahedin* (London: I.B. Tauris, 1989).
68. For more detailed information on his life see Ali Shari'ati, *Kavir* (Mashhad: Ashtiani Publisher, 1970).
69. Abrahamian, *Radical Islam*, p. 108.
70. Ibid.
71. Shari'ati, *Kavir*, pp. 78–107.
72. His critical attitude toward the Shi'i clerical hierarchy made him the target of hostile attacks by the Shi'i establishment.

73. Ali Shari'ati, *Marxism and Other Western Fallacies: An Islamic Critique* (Berkeley, CA: Mizan Press, 1980), p. 32.

74. Ali Shari'ati, *On the Sociology of Islam* (Berkeley, CA: Mizan Press, 1979), p. 119.

75. Shari'ati, *Marxism and Other Western Fallacies*, p. 95.

76. Dabashi, *Theology of Discontent*, p. 141.

77. Shari'ati, *Marxism and Other Western Fallacies*, p. 67.

78. Shari'ati, *Sociology of Islam*, pp. 9, 108.

79. Ibid., p. 109.

80. Yann Richard, "Ali Shari'ati" in Niki Keddie, ed., *Roots of Revolution* (New Haven: Yale University Press, 1981), p. 224.

81. Dabashi, *Theology of Discontent*, p. 104.

82. Shari'ati, *Sociology of Islam*, p. 71.

83. Ibid., pp. 104, 106.

84. Dabashi, *Theology of Discontent*, p. 140.

85. Abrahamian, *Radical Islam*, p. 115.

86. Ibid.

87. Ibid.

88. Ibid., p. 116.

89. Shari'ati, *Sociology of Islam*, p. 79.

90. Abrahamian, *Radical Islam*, p. 115.

91. Ibid., p. 116.

92. Shari'ati, *Sociology of Islam*, p. 79.

93. Robert Lee, "Authenticity in the Political Thought of Shari'ati," a paper presented at the Middle East Studies Association, North Carolina, Nov. 1993, p. 4.

94. Shar'iati, *Sociology of Islam*, p. 79.

95. Dabashi, *Theology of Discontent*, pp. 122, 141.

96. Ibid., p. 142.

97. Shari'ati, *Sociology of Islam*, pp. 79, 123.

98. Ibid., pp. 59, 50.

99. Lee, "Authenticity," pp. 4, 5.

100. Shari'ati, *Sociology of Islam*, p. 79.

101. Ibid., pp. 82, 85.

102. Ibid., p. 95.

103. Dabashi, *Theology of Discontent*, p. 105.

104. Ibid., p. 110.

105. Ibid., p. 114.

106. Abrahamian, *Radical Islam*, p. 119.

107. Shari'ati, *Sociology of Islam*, p. 49.

108. Dabashi, *Theology of Discontent*, p. 116.

109. Ibid., p. 117.

110. Abrahamian, *Radical Islam*, pp. 114, 113.

111. Dabashi, *Theology of Discontent*, p. 143.

112. Richard, "Ali Shari'ati," p. 215.

5 GERMAN INTELLECTUALS AND THE CULTURE OF MODERNITY

1. Friedrich Nietzsche, *Twilight of the Idols* in *The Portable Nietzsche*, ed. Walter Kaufmann (New York: Penguin, 1982), p. 543.
2. Jeffrey Herf, *Reactionary Modernism: Technology, Culture and Politics in Weimar and the Third Reich* (New York: Cambridge University Press, 1984), p. 21.
3. Ibid., p. 23.
4. Felix Gilbert and David Clay Large, *The End of the European Era: 1890 to the Present* (New York: W.W. Norton and Co., 1991), p. 76.
5. Ibid., p. 78.
6. Ibid.
7. Ibid., p. 80.
8. Ibid., p. 81.
9. Ibid., p. 20.
10. Barbel Schrader and Jurgen Schebera, *The Golden Twenties: Art and Literature in the Weimar Republic* (New Haven: Yale University Press, 1990).
11. Herf, *Reactionary Modernism*, p. 1.
12. Ibid., p. 22. This was Hitler's promise to the nation.
13. Schrader and Schebera, *The Golden Twenties*, p. 75.
14. George Mosse. *Fallen Soldiers: Reshaping the Memory of the World Wars* (New York: Oxford University Press, 1990), p. 111.
15. In his *Imagining the Middle East* (Montreal: Black Rose Books, 1992), Thierry Hentsch writes in a very interesting way about this "loss of faith" in imagined metaphysical-historical categories, and Spengler's anguished conviction that "even if such categories do not exist, it is necessary to invent them."
16. Schrader and Schebera, *The Golden Twenties*, p. 89.
17. Ibid., p. 86.
18. Ibid., p. 89.
19. Ibid.
20. Mosse, *Fallen Soldiers*, p. 58.
21. Schrader and Schebera, *The Golden Twenties*, p. 129.
22. Ibid.
23. Gilbert and Large, *European Era*, p. 244.
24. Ibid., p. 234.
25. Nietzsche, *Twilight of the Idols*, p. 551.
26. Ibid.
27. Friedrich Nietzsche, *Beyond Good and Evil*, trans. Walter Kaufmann (New York: Vintage Books, 1989), p. 2.
28. Friedrich Nietzsche, *The Will to Power*, trans. by Walter Kaufmann and R. J. Hollingdale (New York: Random House, 1967), p. 544.
29. Marcus Bullock. "Ernst Junger: Literature, Warfare, and the Intoxication of Philosophy," *Mosaic: A Journal for the Interdisciplinary Study of Literature* (Fall 1986), p. 109.
30. Ibid., p. 68.
31. Raymond Furness and Malcolm Humble, *A Companion to Twentieth-Century German Literature* (New York: Routledge, 1991), p. 154.

32. From Ernst Junger, *The Battle as Inner Experience* (1922). Quoted in Herf, *Reactionary Modernism*, p. 67.
33. Ibid., p. 75.
34. From Ernst Junger, *Fire and Blood* (1929). Quoted in Herf, *Reactionary Modernism*, p. 79.
35. Ibid., p. 28.
36. Ernst Junger, *Total Mobilization* (1930), in Richard Wolin, ed., *The Heidegger Controversy* (Boston: MIT Press, 1992), p. 123.
37. Ibid., p. 124.
38. Herf, *Reactionary Modernism*, p. 90.
39. Junger, *Total Mobilization*, p. 139.
40. Ibid., p. 133.
41. Ibid.
42. From Ernst Junger, *Metropolis and Countryside* (1926). Quoted in Herf, *Reactionary Modernism*, p. 86.
43. Junger, *Total Mobilization*, p. 126.
44. Friedrich Nietzsche, "Homer's Contest" (1872), in *The Portable Nietzsche*, p. 32.
45. Herf, *Reactionary Modernism*, p. 101.
46. Ibid., p. 80.
47. Ernst Junger, *Nationalism and Modern Life* (1927). Quoted in Herf, *Reactionary Modernism*, p. 82.
48. Junger, *The Battle as Inner Experience*. Quoted in Herf, *Reactionary Modernism*, p. 90.
49. Junger, *Total Mobilization*, pp. 124, 129.
50. Ibid., p. 129.
51. Ibid., p. 138.
52. Ernst Junger, *Our Battle Position* (1927). Quoted in Herf, *Reactionary Modernism*, p. 90.
53. Ernst Junger, *The Worker* (1932). Quoted in Herf, *Reactionary Modernism*, p. 103.
54. Thomas Sheehan, "Reading a Life: Heidegger and Hard Times," in *The Cambridge Companion to Heidegger*, ed. Charles Guignon (New York: Cambridge University Press, 1993), p. 88.
55. John Caputo, "Heidegger and Theology," in *The Cambridge Companion to Heidegger*, p. 270.
56. Ibid., p. 272.
57. Sheehan, "Reading a Life," p. 70.
58. Caputo, "Heidegger and Theology," p. 272.
59. Sheehan, "Reading a Life," p. 77.
60. Ibid., pp. 78, 79.
61. Ibid., p. 87.
62. Martin Heidegger, *Being and Time* (San Francisco: Harper and Row, 1962), p. 99.
63. Ibid., p. 182.
64. Ibid., pp. 173, 195.
65. Ibid., p. 178.
66. Caputo, "Heidegger and Theology," p. 277.

67. Sheehan, "Reading a Life," p. 86.
68. David Hoy, "Heidegger and the Hermeneutic Turn," in *The Cambridge Companion to Heidegger*, p. 36.
69. Martin Heidegger, *Introduction to Metaphysics* (1935; New Haven, CT: Yale University Press, 1986), p. 37.
70. Martin Heidegger, "The Self Assertion of the German University," in *The Heidegger Controversy*, p. 30.
71. Bullock, "Ernst Junger," p. 110.
72. Heidegger, "Self Assertion," p. 32.
73. Ibid., p. 29.
74. Ibid., p. 30.
75. Ibid., pp. 31, 33, 32.
76. Ibid., pp. 37, 33.
77. Ibid., p. 33.
78. Ibid.
79. Ibid., p. 38.
80. Ibid., p. 34.
81. Martin Heidegger, *Poetry, Language, and Thought* (1935; New York: Harper Collins, 1985), p. 4.
82. "Only a God Can Save Us": *Der Spiegel*'s interview with Martin Heidegger (1976), in *The Heidegger Controversy*, p. 91.
83. In his *Poetry, Language, and Thought*, Heidegger tells us "the era is defined by god's failure to arrive, by the 'default of god'. But [this default] does not deny that the Christian relationship lives on in individuals and in churches. The default of god means that no god any longer gathers men and things unto himself, visibly and unequivocally, and by such gathering, disposes of the world's history and men's sojourn in it" (p. 91).

6 THE TRAGEDY OF THE IRANIAN LEFT

1. This chapter is based on an earlier article that I co-authored with Val Moghadam and which was published in *Radical History* ("The Left and Political Islam in Iran," *Radical History Review* 51 (Fall 1991)). I have revised the earlier article for this book. I would like to thank Val Moghadam for giving me permission to include this piece here.
2. Karl Marx, *Contribution to the Critique of Hegel's Philosophy of Right* (New York: International Publishers, 1979), p. 42.
3. By the Left here we mean the dominant trends and groups among many different leftist organizations. There were some leftist groups which had a more critical analysis of the situation during the Revolution.
4. Several leftist groups and many radical intellectuals were critical of the political Islam during this period.
5. Maxime Rodinson, "Marxism and Socialism," in Michael Adams, ed., *Marxism and Socialism in the Middle East* (New York: Fact on Files, 1988), p. 641.
6. Fereydoun Adami'yat, *Fekre Democratis-e Ejtemaee dar Nehzate Mashtoyyate Iran*, The Idea of Social Democracy in the Constitutional Movement in Iran (Tehran: Payam Publisher, 1975), p. 38.

7. Rodinson, "Marxism and Socialism," p. 641.

8. Ervand Abrahamian, *Iran Between Two Revolutions* (Princeton: Princeton University Press, 1982); Cosroe Chaquerie, "Sultanzade: The Forgotten Revolutionary Theoretician of Iran: A Biographical Sketch," *Iranian Studies*, vol. 17 no. 203 (Spring–Summer 1984), pp. 215–36; Sepehr Zabih, *The Communist Movement in Iran* (Berkeley, CA: University of California Press, 1966).

9. Fred Halliday, *Iran: Dictatorship and Development* (Harmondsworth: Penguin, 1979); Abrahamian, *Iran Between Two Revolutions*; Habib Ladjevardi, *Labor Unions and Autocracy in Iran* (Syracuse: Syracuse University Press, 1986).

10. Homa Katouzian, *The Political Economy of Modern Iran* (New York: New York University Press, 1981).

11. Abrahamian, *Iran Between Two Revolutions*.

12. Hisham Sharabi, *Neopatriarchy: A Theory of Change in Arab Society* (New York: Oxford University Press, 1988), p. 12.

13. Said Amir Arjomand, *The Turban For the Crown: Iran's Islamic Revolution* (New York: Oxford University Press, 1988), p. 91.

14. Shahrough Akhavi, *Religion and Politics in Contemporary Iran* (Albany: State University of New York Press, 1980); Michael Fischer, *Iran: From Religious Dispute to Revolution* (Cambridge, MA: Harvard University Press, 1980).

15. Theda Skocpol, "Rentier State and Shi'a Islam in the Iranian Revolution," *Theory and Society*, vol. 11 (1982), pp. 265–83.

16. Abrahamian, *Iran Between Two Revolutions*.

17. *Kar* no. 44.

18. But the hostage takeover forced a break in the Fedayee's political position. Now they became almost exclusively concerned with the atrocities of U.S. imperialism, and the collaboration with it of the liberals and monarchists. The best example of Left confusion is reflected in the Fedayee positions in the first year of the Revolution. At the beginning, they adopted a highly critical position against the regime and defended the cause of democracy. They participated in the National Democratic Front's meeting in commemoration of the late Prime Minister Mosaddeq (*Kar* no. 1). Many of the editorials and headlines of *Kar* cover the repressive policies of the Islamic regime and support basic human and democratic rights (*Kar* nos. 8, 12, 13). They support the independent Kayhan editors and condemn the regime's attempt to remove them (*Kar* no. 14), and also condemn the Hezbollah's attack on the National Democratic Front (*Kar* no. 17). In this period *Kar* ran several editorials and analyses in defense of the freedom of the press (*Kar* no. 12 on Ayandegan, no. 11 the suppression of the press, no. 14 the Iranian lawyers' editorials condemning the Iranian liberals as tools of the U.S.). In *Kar* nos. 28–61, they published special issues containing secret documents that revealed the liberal connections to the U.S. (*Kar* no. 40). At the same time there was hardly any mention of the issue of democracy or of the regime's attempt to monopolize political power. They even criticized the Mojahedin for advocating freedom from all political parties, including the liberal parties (*Kar* no. 44).

19. *Kar* no. 29.

20. *Kar* no. 53.
21. "Only the united actions of all revolutionary organizations and institutes under the proven and wise leadership of Imam Khomeini will be able to complete this great task that has already started" (*Donya*, Tudeh Party, p. 45).
22. Sharabi, *Neopatriarchy*, p. 11.
23. We should note that in recent years, engineering is no longer an elite occupation and therefore engineers are no longer predictably radical/secularist in Iran.
24. *National Census* (Tehran, Statistical Center of Iran: 1986).
25. G. Afkhami, *The Iranian Revolution: Thanatos on a National Scale* (Washington, D.C.: Middle East Institute, 1985); Arjomand, *The Turban For the Crown*, 1988; Sepehr Zabih, *The Left in Contemporary Iran* (London: Croom Helm, 1986).
26. Katouzian, *Political Economy*; Mehdi Bazargan, *Enghelab-e Iran dar do Harakat*, The Iranian Revolution in Two Phases (Tehran: Naraghi Publisher, 1984).
27. It is worth pointing out that the Bolsheviks were also seen as having imported an "alien" European ideology. For Adam Ulam, author of *The Unfinished Revolution* (Boulder, CO: Westview Press, 1979), the Bolsheviks are seen as a tight-knit party of intellectuals, almost literally divorced from their society. They bring to Russia from the outside, from exile, an alien European ideology, i.e., Marxism, and they come to power with the support of the newly urbanized proletarians, uprooted from the countryside and disoriented by industrial life. One could actually apply Ulam's thesis to the Islamists rather than to the leftists!

7 MODERNITIES OF OUR TIME

1. The question of how a chimera could become a substitute for living people presents a whole field of inquiry in itself.
2. Interview conducted by the author with Hassan Taromi, Tehran, October 1995.
3. Ibid.
4. Ibid.
5. Ibid.
6. Interview conducted by the author with Javad Tabataba'i, Tehran, October 1995. Javad Tabataba'i's works include: *A Philosophical Preface to the History of Political Thought in Iran* (Tehran: Kavir, 1993); *The Decline of Political Thought in Iran* (Tehran: Kavir, 1993); and *Ebn Khaldun and the Social Sciences* (Tehran: Tarhe No, 1995).
7. Interview with Tabataba'i.
8. Ibid.
9. Ibid.
10. Anthony Giddens, *The Consequences of Modernity* (Stanford: Stanford University Press, 1990).
11. Hamid Enayat, the late Iranian political scientist, in an article, "The Resurgence of Islam," *History Today* (February 1980), argues that the Islamic resurgence is a movement that is both contemporary and a part of a

larger political attempt by people of the Middle East for independence and cultural identity.

12. Philip S. Khoury, "Islamic Revivalism and the Crisis of the Secular State in the Arab World," in I. Ibrahim, ed., *Arab Resources* (London: Croom Helm, 1983), p. 214.

13. Raouf Abas Hamed, "Factors Behind the Political Islamic Movement in Egypt," paper presented at the 24th MESA Conference, Texas, 1990.

14. Ervand Abrahamian, *Radical Islam: The Iranian Mojahedin* (London: I.B. Tauris, 1989), p. 11.

15. M. Bayat, *Mysticism and Dissent: Socioreligious Thought in Qajar Iran* (Syracuse: Syracuse University Press, 1982), p. xi.

16. The leading figure of this circle is Davari: their writings are published in magazines such as *Mashregh* and *Nameh-ye Farhang*.

17. Mehrzad Boroujerdi, *Iranian Intellectuals and the West: The Tormented Triumph of Nativism* (Syracuse: Syracuse University Press, 1996), pp. 156–65.

18. See the discussion of the German intellectuals in chapter 5.

Bibliography

Abadi, Yahya Dowlat. Hayat-e Yahya (Tehran: Ferdowsi Publisher, 1982).

Abedini, Hassan. *One Hundred Years of Fiction Writings in Iran 1963–1978* [in Farsi] (Tehran: Tondar Publisher, 1989).

Aboutorabian, Hassan. *Iranian Press: 1940–1946* [in Persian] (Tehran: Ettela'at Publisher, 1987).

Abrahamian, Ervand. *Iran Between Two Revolutions* (Princeton: Princeton University Press, 1982).

"Kasravi: The Integrative Nationalist of Iran," in Kedouri, Elie, and Haim, Sylvana. *Towards a Modern Iran* (London: Frank Cass, 1980).

Khomeinism (Berkeley: University of California Press, 1993).

Radical Islam: The Iranian Mojahedin (London: I.B. Tauris, 1989).

"Structural Causes of the Iranian Revolution," *MERIP Reports* (May 1980).

Adami'yat, Fereydoun. *Andish-ye Taraghi Va Hokumat-e Ghanoon*, The Idea of Progress and Legal Government: Time of Sepahsalar (Tehran: Kharazmi Publisher, 1972).

Ashoftegi Da Fekre Tarihki, Bewilderment in Historical Thought (Tehran: Jahan-e Andisheh, 1981).

Fekre Azadi va Moghaddameh-ye Mashrutiyat-e Iran, The Idea of Freedom and the Making of the Constitutional Movement (Tehran: Sufhon Publisher, 1961).

Fekre Democratis-e Ejtemaee dar Nehzate Mashtoyyate Iran, The Idea of Social Democracy in the Iranian Constitutional Movement (Tehran: Payam Publisher, 1975).

Thoughts of Mirza Agha Khan Kermani [in Persian] (Tehran: Payam Publisher, 1978).

Adams, Michael. *Marxism and Socialism in The Middle East* (New York: Fact on Files, 1988).

Adams, Michael, ed. *Marxism and Socialism in the Middle East* (New York: Fact on Files, 1988).

Afkhami, G. *The Iranian Revolution: Thanatos on a National Scale* (Washington D.C.: Middle East Institute, 1985).

Ahmad, J. Al-e. *Dar Khedmat va Khyanat-ye Rowshanfekran* (Tehran: Kharazmi Publisher, 1979), vol. II.

Did va Bazdid (Tehran: Amir Kabir Publisher, 1960).

Gharbzadegi, Westoxication (Tehran: Revagh Publisher, 1962).

Iranian Society, ed. Michael Hillmann (Lexington, KY: Mazda Publishers, 1982).

Karnamahi Sih Salah (Tehran: Revagh Publisher, 1979).

Khasi Dar Mighat, A Traveler's Diary (Tehran: Amir Kabir Publisher, 1978).
Lost in the Crowd, trans. John Green (Washington, D.C.: Three Continents Press, 1985).
"Masalan Sharh-e Ahvalat" in Tbrizi, Hamid. *Jalal Al-e Ahmad: Mardi da kesh Keshe Tarikh-e Moaser* (Tabriz: Nashr-e Kave, 1978).
Occidentosis: A Plague From the West, trans. R. Campbell (Berkeley, CA: Mizan Press, 1984).
Safar be Vellayate Ezrail (Tehran: Revagh Publisher, 1984).
The Seh'tar (Tehran: Sepehr Publisher, 1978).
Akhavi, Shahrough. *Religion and Politics in Contemporary Iran* (Albany: State University of New York Press, 1980).
Al-Azmeh, Aziz. *Islams and Modernities* (London: Verso, 1993).
Algar, H. "Immam Khomeini, 1902–1962: The Pre-Revolutionary Years," in Burke, E., and Lapidus, I., eds. *Islam, Politics, and Social Movement* (Berkeley, CA: University of California Press, 1988).
Alvarez, Dagnino, and Escobar, Arturo, eds. *Culture of Politics Politics of Cultures: Re-visioning Latin American Social Movements* (Boulder, CO: Westview Press, 1998).
Anderson, Perry. "Modernity and Revolution," *New Left Review* 144 (1984).
Appadurai, Arjun. *Modernity at Large: Cultural Dimensions of Globalization* (Minneapolis: University of Minnesota Press, 1996).
Arian Poor, Yahya. *From Sabba to Nima* [in Persian] (Tehran: Amir Kabir Publisher, 1974).
Arjomand, Said A. *The Shadow of God and the Hidden Imam* (Chicago: Chicago University Press, 1984).
The Turban For the Crown: Iran's Islamic Revolution (New York: Oxford University Press, 1988).
Arjomand, Said A., ed. *From Nationalism to Revolutionary Islam* (Albany: State University of New York Press, 1984).
Arkoun, Mohammed. *Rethinking Islam* (Boulder, CO: Westview Press, 1994).
Rethinking Islam Today (Washington, D.C.: Georgetown University, Center for Contemporary Arab Studies, 1986).
Asad, Talal. *Genealogies of Religion: Discipline and Reasons of Power in Christianity and Islam* (Baltimore: Johns Hopkins Press, 1993).
The Idea of An Anthropology of Islam, Occasional Papers Series (Washington, D.C.: Georgetown University, Center for Contemporary Arab Studies, 1986).
Ashraf, Ahmad. "Bazaar–Mosque Alliance: The Social Bases of Revels and Revolutions," *International Journal of Politics, Culture and Society*, vol. 1 no. 4 (Summer 1988), pp. 538–67.
Ashtiani, Ali. "A Historical Sociology of Three Discourses of the Iranian Intellectuals" [in Farsi] *Kankash* nos. 2 and 3 (Fall 1987), pp. 87–137.
Azimi, F. *The Crisis of Democracy in Iran* (London: I.B. Tauris, 1989).
Bahkash, Shaul. *The Reign of the Ayatollahs* (New York: Basic Books, 1984).
Bahsi Dar Bare-e Rowhaniyat va Marja'yyat. An Inquiry into Marja'yyat and Religious Institutions (Tehran: Enteshar Publisher, 1962).
Bayat, Mangol. *Mysticism and Dissent: Socioreligious Thought in Qajar Iran* (Syracuse: Syracuse University Press, 1982).

Bazargan, Mehdi. *Enghelab-e Iran dar do Harakat.* The Iranian Revolution in Two Phases (Tehran: Naraghi Publisher, 1984).

Beck, Ulrich, Giddens, Anthony, and Lash, Scott. *Reflexive Modernization* (Stanford, CA: Stanford University Press, 1994).

Bendix, Reinhard. "Tradition and Modernity Reconsidered," *Comparative Study in Society and History* 9 (1967).

Berkes, Niyazi. *The Development of Secularism in Turkey*, new edn. (New York: Routledge, 1998).

Berman, Marshall. *All That is Solid Melts into Air: The Experience of Modernity* (New York: Penguin, 1988).

Bill, J. *The Politics of Iran: Groups, Class and Modernization* (Columbus, OH: Charles E. Merrill Publishing Co., 1972).

Browne, Edward G. *A Literary History of Persia* (London: Cambridge University Press, 1978).

Bullock, Marcus. "Ernst Junger: Literature, Warfare, and the Intoxication of Philosophy," *Mosaic: A Journal for the Interdisciplinary Study of Literature* (Fall 1986).

Burke, Edmund, and Lapidus, I. *Islam, Politics, and Social Movement* (Berkeley, CA: University of California Press, 1988).

Caputo, John. "Heidegger and Theology," in Guignon, Charles, ed., *The Cambridge Companion to Heidegger* (New York: Cambridge University Press, 1993).

Chaquerie, Cosroe. "Sultanzade: The Forgotten Revolutionary Theoretician of Iran: A Biographical Sketch," *Iranian Studies*, vol. 17 no. 203 (Spring–Summer 1984).

Cottam, Richard. *Nationalism in Iran* (Pittsburgh: University of Pittsburgh Press, 1964).

Dabashi, Hamid. "Early Propagation of Wilayat-i Faqih and Mulla Ahmad Naraqi," in Nasr, H., Dabashi, H., and Nasr, M., eds. *Expectation of the Millennium: Shi'ism in History* (Albany: State University of New York Press, 1989).

  Theology of Discontent: The Ideological Foundation of the Islamic Revolution in Iran. (New York: New York University Press, 1993).

Dews, Peter, ed. *Autonomy and Solidarity: Interviews with Jurgen Habermas* (London: Verso, 1986).

Dowlat-Abadi, Yahya. *Hayat-e Yahya* (Tehran: Ferdowsi Publisher, 1982).

Elwell-Sutton, L. P. "The Iranian Press 1941–1947," *Journal of the British Institute of Persian Studies* 6 (1968).

Enayat, H. *Modern Islamic Political Thought* (Austin: University of Texas Press, 1982).

  "The Resurgence of Islam," *History Today* (February 1980), pp. 16–22.

Escobar, Arturo. *Encountering Development: The Making and Unmaking of the Third World* (Princeton: Princeton University Press, 1995).

Fabian, Johannes. *Time and the Other* (New York: Colombia University Press, 1983).

Fallaci, Oriana. "An Interview with Khomeini," *The New York Times Magazine* (October 7, 1979).

Farsoun, Samith K., ed. *Arab Society* (London: Croom Helm, 1983).

Feenberg, Andrew. *Alternative Modernity: The Technical Turn in Philosophy and Social Theory* (Berkeley, CA: University of California Press, 1995).

Ferguson, James. *The Anti-Politics Machine* (Minneapolis: University of Minnesota Press, 1990).

Fischer, M. *Iran: From Religious Dispute to Revolution* (Cambridge, MA: Harvard University Press, 1980).

Fisher, Michael, and Abedi, Mehdi. *Debating Muslims: Cultural Dialogues in Postmodernity and Tradition* (Madison, WI: University of Wisconsin Press, 1990).

Foster, Hal, ed. *The Anti-Aesthetic: Essays on Postmodern Culture* (Seattle: Bay Press, 1983).

Foucault, Michel. *Politics, Philosophy, Culture: Interviews and Other Writings*, ed. Lawrence D. Kritzman (New York: Routledge, 1988).

Friedman, Jonathon. "Cultural Logics of the Global System: A Sketch," *Theory, Culture and Society* 5: 2–3 (June 1988).

Furet, François. *Interpreting the French Revolution* (London: Cambridge University Press, 1981).

Furness, Raymond, and Humble, Malcolm. *A Companion to Twentieth-Century German Literature* (New York: Routledge, 1991).

Gellner, Ernest. "Forward," in Arjomand, Said A., ed. *From Nationalism to Revolutionary Islam* (Albany: State University Press of New York Press, 1984).

Muslim Society (New York: Cambridge University Press, 1981).

Postmodernism, Reason and Religion (New York: Routledge, 1992).

Giddens, Anthony. *The Consequences of Modernity* (Stanford, CA: Stanford University Press, 1990).

Social Theory and Modern Sociology (Stanford, CA: Stanford University Press, 1987).

Gide, André. *Return from the Soviet Union* (Tehran: Akhtar Shoma Publishing, 1954).

Gilbert, Felix, and Large, David Clay. *The End of the European Era: 1890 to the Present* (New York: W.W. Norton and Co., 1991).

Green, J. *Revolution in Iran: The Politics of Countermobilization* (New York: Praeger, 1982).

Guignon, Charles, ed. *The Cambridge Companion to Heidegger* (New York: Cambridge University Press, 1993).

Habermas, Jurgen. "Modernity – An Incomplete Project," in Hal Foster, ed. *The Anti-Aesthetic: Essays on Postmodern Culture* (Seattle: Bay Press, 1983).

The Philosophical Discourse of Modernity (Cambridge: MIT Press, 1987).

The Theory of Communicative Action (Boston: Beacon, 1984).

Hairi, A. *Shi'ism and Constitutionalism in Iran* [in Farsi] (Tehran: Amir Kabir Publishing, 1985).

Halliday, F. *Iran: Dictatorship and Development* (Harmondsworth: Penguin, 1979).

Halliday, F., and Alavi, H. *State and Ideology in the Middle East and Pakistan* (New York: Monthly Review Press, 1989).

Hamed, Raouf Abas. "Factors Behind the Political Islamic Movement in Egypt" (MESA Conference, Texas, 1990).

Hegel, Georg W. F. *The Philosophy of History* (New York: Dover Publications Inc., 1956).

Heidegger, Martin. *Being and Time* (San Francisco: Harper and Row, 1962).
   Introduction to Metaphysics (New Haven, CT: Yale University Press, 1986).
   Poetry, Language and Thought, new edn. (New York: HarperCollins, 1985).
   "The Self Assertion of the German University," in Wolin, Richard, ed. *The Hiedegger Controversy* (Boston: MIT Press, 1992).

Hentsch, Thierry. *Imagining the Middle East* (Montreal: Black Rose Books, 1992).

Herf, Jeffrey. *Reactionary Modernism: Technology, Culture and Politics in Weimar and the Third Reich* (New York: Cambridge University Press, 1984).

Hidayat, Mahdi Quli Khan. *Khatirat va Khatarat*, Memories and Dangers (Tehran, 1950).

Hillmann, Michael. *Iranian Culture: A Persianist View* (New York: University Press of America, 1990).

Hoogland, E. *Land and Revolution in Iran* (Austin: University of Texas Press, 1982).

Howard, Richard. *The Conquest of America: the Question of the Other* (New York: Harper, 1984).

Hoy, David. "Heidegger and the Hermeneutic Turn," in Guignon, Charles, ed. *The Cambridge Companion to Heidegger* (New York: Cambridge University Press, 1993).

Hulme, Peter. *Colonial Encounters: Europe and the Native Caribbean 1492–1797* (New York: Routledge, 1992).

Hulme, Peter, and Jordanova, Ludmilla, eds. *The Enlightenment and its Shadows* (New York: Routledge, 1994).

Hunt, L. *Politics, Culture and Class in the French Revolution* (Berkeley, CA: University of California Press, 1984).

Huntington, Samuel P. "The Clash of Civilizations?," *Foreign Affairs*, vol. 72 no. 3 (Summer 1993), pp. 22–49.

Ibrahim, I., ed. *Arab Resources* (London: Croom Helm, 1983).

Jacoby, Russell. "Marginal Returns: The Trouble with Post-Colonial Theory," *Lingua Franca* (September/October 1995).

Jami. *Gozashteh Cheraghe Rahe Ayandeh Ast*, The Past is the Light of the Future (Tehran: Ghoghnous, 1978).

Junger, Ernst. *Obour As Khat*, trans. Al-e Ahmad and Mahamud Human (Tehran: Kharazmi Publisher, 1965).
   Total Mobilization, in Wolin, Richard, ed. *The Heidegger Controversy* (Boston: MIT Press, 1992).

Katouzian, Homa. *The Political Economy of Modern Iran* (New York: New York University Press, 1981).

Kazemi, F. *Poverty and Revolution in Iran* (New York: New York University Press, 1980).

Keddie, N. "Islamic Revival in the Middle East: A Comparison of Iran and Egypt," in Farsoun, Samih K., ed. *Arab Society* (London: Croom Helm, 1983).

Keddie, N., ed. *Religion and Politics in Iran: Shi'ism From Quietism to Revolution* (New Haven: Yale University Press, 1983).
   Roots of Revolution (New Haven: Yale University Press, 1981).

Kedouri, E., and Haim, Sylvana, eds., *Towards a Modern Iran* (London: Frank Cass, 1980).

Khamenh'i, A. *Forsate Bozork-e Az Dast Rafteh*, The Big Chance that Was Lost (Tehran: Hafte Publisher, 1983).

Khomeini, R. *Velayat-e Faghih: hokumat-e Islami*, Islamic Government (Tehran: no publisher, 1977).

Khoury, Philip S. "Islamic Revivalism and the Crisis of the Secular State in the Arab World," in Ibrahim, I., ed. *Arab Resources* (London: Croom Helm, 1983).

Ladjevardi, H. *Labor Unions and Autocracy in Iran* (Syracuse: Syracuse University Press, 1985).

Lambton, A. K. S. *Theory and Practice in Medieval Persian Government* (London: Variorum Reprints, 1980).

Lash, Scott, and Friedman, Jonathon, eds. *Modernity and Identity* (Oxford: Blackwell, 1992).

Lee, Robert. "Authenticity in the Political Thought of Shari'ati," paper presented at the Middle East Studies Association, North Carolina (November 1993).

    Overcoming Tradition and Modernity: The Search for Islamic Authenticity (Boulder, CO: Westview Press, 1997).

Lewis, Bernard. *Islam and the West* (New York: Oxford University Press, 1993).

    "The Roots of Muslim Rage," *The Atlantic Monthly* 266 (September 1990).

Magee, Bryan. *The Great Philosophers* (London: BBC Books, 1987).

Maktabe Tashayo (Qum: Elmiye Publisher, 1959, 1960, 1965).

Martin, Vanessa. *Islam and Modernism* (Syracuse: Syracuse University Press, 1989).

Marx, Karl. "The British Rule in India," in Marx and Engels, *On Colonialism* (New York: International Publisher, 1972).

    Contribution to the Critique of Hegel's Philosophy of Right (New York: International Publishers, 1979).

Mernisi, Fatima. *Islam and Democracy* (New York: Addison-Wesley, 1992).

Milani, M. *The Making of Iran's Islamic Revolution* (Boulder, CO: Westview Press, 1988).

Mirsepassi, Ali. "The Crisis of Secular Politics and the Rise of Political Islam in Iran," *Social Text* (Spring 1994, no. 38).

Mirsepassi, Ali, and Moghadam, Val. "The Left and Political Islam in Iran," *Radical History Review* 51 (Fall 1991).

Mitchell, Timothy. *Colonizing Egypt* (Berkeley, CA: University of California Press, 1991).

Montesquieu. *Persian Letters* (Harmondsworth: Penguin Books, 1973).

Mosse, George. *Fallen Soldiers: Reshaping the Memory of the World Wars* (New York: Oxford University Press, 1990).

Motahhari, M. "Ijtihad dar Islam," in *Bahsi Dar Bare-e Rowhaniyat va Marja'yyat* (Tehran: Enteshar Publisher, 1962).

    "Moshkele Asasi Dar Sazemane Rowhaniyat," in *Bahsi Dar Bare-e Rowhaniyat va Marja'yyat* (Tehran: Enteshar Publisher, 1962).

Mottahedeh, Roy. *The Mantle of the Prophet: Religion and Politics in Iran* (New York: Simon and Schuster, 1985).

Narahgi, E. *Ghorbat-e Gharb*, The Alienation of the West (Tehran: Amir Kabir Publisher, 1975).

Nasr, H., Dabashi, H., and Nasr, M., eds. *Expectation of the Millennium: Shi'ism in History* (New York: State University of New York Press, 1989).

Nia, Mostafa Zammani, ed. *Fahang-e Jalal Al-e Ahmad*, The Encyclopedia of Jalal Al-e Ahmad (Tehran: Pasargad Publisher, 1984).

Nietzsche, Friedrich. *Beyond Good and Evil*, trans. Walter Kaufmann (New York: Vintage Press, 1989).

The Portable Nietzsche, ed. Walter Kaufmann (New York: Penguin, 1982).

Parsons, A. *The Pride and the Fall* (London: Jonathan Cape, 1984).

Ravandi, Morteza. *Social History of Iran* (Tehran: Amir Kabir Publisher, 1975).

Richard, Yann. "Ali Shari'ati," in Keddie, N., ed. *Roots of Revolution* (New Haven: Yale University Press, 1981).

Rodinson, Maxime. "Marxism and Socialism," in Adams, Michael, ed. *Marxism and Socialism in the Middle East* (New York: Fact on Files, 1988).

Said, Edward. *Culture and Imperialism* (New York: Vintage, 1994).

"Orientalism Revisited: An Interview with Edward Said," *Middle East Report* (January/February 1988).

Orientalism (New York: Pantheon Books, 1978).

Scaff, Lawrence. *Fleeing the Iron Cage* (Berkeley, CA: University of California Press, 1991).

Schrader, Barbel, and Schebera, Jurgen. *The Golden Twenties: Art and Literature in the Weimar Republic* (New Haven: Yale University Press, 1990).

Seidman, Steven. *Contested Knowledge: Social Theory in the Postmodern Era* (Malden, MA: Blackwell, 1998).

Sharabi, H. *Neopatriarchy: A Theory of Change in Arab Society* (New York: Oxford University Press, 1988).

Shari'ati, Ali. *Kavir* (Mashhad: Ashtiani Publisher, 1970).

Marxism and Other Western Fallacies: An Islamic Critique (Berkeley, CA: Mizan Press, 1980).

On the Sociology of Islam (Berkeley, CA: Mizan Press, 1979).

Sheehan, Thomas. "Reading a Life: Heidegger and Hard Times," in Guignon, Charles, ed. *The Cambridge Companion to Heidegger* (New York: Cambridge University Press, 1993).

Singer, Peter. *Hegel* (Oxford: Oxford University Press, 1983).

Sirnon, Reeva S. *The Middle East in Crime Fiction: Mysteries, Novels and Thrillers from 1916 to the 1980s* (New York: Lillian Barber Press, 1989).

Skocpol, T. "Rentier State and Shi'a Islam in the Iranian Revolution," *Theory and Society* 11 (1982), pp. 265–83.

State and Social Revolution (London: Cambridge University Press, 1979).

Solomon, Robert C. *In the Spirit of Hegel* (New York: Oxford University Press, 1983).

Stauth, George. "Revolution in Spiritless Times: An Essay on Michel Foucault's Enquiries into the Iranian Revolution," *International Sociology*, vol. 6 no. 3 (September 1991), pp. 259–80.

Tabataba'i, Javad. *The Decline of Political Thought in Iran* (Tehran: Kavir, 1993).

Ebn Khaldun and the Social Sciences (Tehran: Tarhe No, 1995).

A Philosophical Preface to the History of Political Thought in Iran (Tehran: Kavir, 1993).

Tabataba'i, M. *Maktabe Tashayo* (Qum: Elmiye Publisher, 1959, 1969, 1965).

"Valayat Va Za'amat," in *Bahsi Dar Bare-e Rowhaniyat va Marja'yyat* (Tehran: Enteshar Publisher, 1962).

Tbrizi, Hamid. *Jalal Al-e Ahmad: Mardi da kesh Keshe Tarikh-e Moaser* (Tabriz: Nashr-e Kave, 1978).

Todorov, Tzvetan. *The Conquest of America: the Question of the Other*, trans. Richard Howard (New York: Harper, 1984).

Tomilson, John. *Cultural Imperialism* (Baltimore: Johns Hopkins University Press, 1991).

Tully, James. *An Approach to Political Philosophy: Locke in Contexts* (Cambridge: Cambridge University Press, 1993).

Turner, Bryan. *Marx and the End of Orientalism* (London: George Allen & Unwin, 1978).

Weber and Islam: A Critical Study (London: Routledge & Kegan Paul, 1984).

Ulam, Adam. *The Unfinished Revolution* (Boulder, CO: Westview Press, 1979).

Vijenameye Ayatollah Morteza Motahhari, The Sixth Anniversary of the Martyrdom of Ayatollah M. Motahhari (Tehran: Islamic Republican Party, 1985).

Watt, W. Montgomery, "The Significance of the Early Stages of Imami Shi'ism," in Keddie, N., ed. *Religion and Politics in Iran: Shi'ism From Quietism to Revolution* (New Haven: Yale University Press, 1983).

Weber, Max. *From Max Weber*, ed. H. H. Gerth and C. Wright Mills (New York: Oxford University Press, 1981).

Wilson, Rob, and Dissanayake, Wimal, eds. *Global/Local* (Durham: Duke University Press, 1996).

Wolin, Richard. *The Heidegger Controversy* (Boston: MIT Press, 1992).

Zabih, Sepehr. *The Communist Movement in Iran* (Berkeley, CA: University of California Press, 1966).

The Left in Contemporary Iran (London: Croom Helm, 1986).

Zadeh, Mehdi M. *History of the Constitutional Revolution in Iran* (Tehran: Elmi Publisher, 1984).

Index

Abadi, Yahya Dowlat 59
Abrahamian, Evrand 190
Adami'yat, Fereydoun 57–8, 60, 62
Africa 33–5
Akhbarism 85
Al Afghani, Jamal al-Din 186
Al-e Ahmad, Jalal 76, 77–8, 96, 97–114, 155
Arian Poor, Yahya 60
Asre Bidari (Period of Awakening) 56
authentic knowing 124
authenticity 109–10, 121–2, 126, 148, 157,
    178–9
  discourse of 97, 187–8
    German discourse 132, 134–5, 137–46
  politics of 127
Azerbaijan 100

Bani-Sadr, Abolhassan 169, 170, 178
Bayat, M. 66
Bayat, Mongol 190
Bazargan, Mehdi 85, 178
Beheshti, Muhammad 85, 89, 90, 91, 169
Being and Time (Heidegger) 146, 147, 150
Bendix, Reinhard 78
Benjamin 129
Berman, Marshall 2–3, 4
Beumelburg, Werner 136
Bolshevik Revolution, Russia 161
Britain 60
  role in India 38–9
Buroujerdi, Ayatollah 82, 84, 107

Case of Sergeant Grischa, The (Zweig) 136
Central Council of Federated Trade
    Unions of Iranian Workers and Toilers
    (CCFTU) 67
China 30, 31
Christianity 138
civilizations 47–8
  clash of 13, 43–4, 47–9
class struggle 120
colonialism 4–5, 7, 12, 45
  Marx's views 36–9
  romanticization of 16–17

communist movement *see* Iranian Left
Community and Leadership (Shari'ati)
    126–7
Confederation of Iranian Students 165
constitutionalist movement, Iran 55–64,
    70, 81, 161
Corbon, Henri 89
culture 6, 8–9, 51, 148, 178–9
  local cultures 11–12, 186, 189
  of modernity 2
  survival of, modernization and 186–9
  Western culture 1–2, 33

Daneshvar, Simin 101, 103
Dar Khedmat va Khianate Rowshanfekran
    (Al-e Ahmad) 105
death of God 138
Decline of the West (Spengler) 135
democracy 68–70
Democratic Party of Azarbaijan 68, 100
Democratic Party of Iran 68
Democratic party of Kurdestan 68
development 27
  discourse 5–10
  Germany 132
  historical development 29–30
Dilthey, Wilhelm 140

East/West divide 8, 12, 29, 33, 158
Egypt 31
elemental time 151–2
Encountering Development (Escobar) 7
England *see* Britain
Enlightenment 3, 19, 60
Escobar, Arturo 7
Eternal Recurrence principle 139
Eurocentrism 1, 4–5
  development discourse and 7–8
expatriate movement 72

Fanon, Frantz 121
Fedayee Organization 163, 167–70
  revolution and 164–5
Fire and Blood (Junger) 141